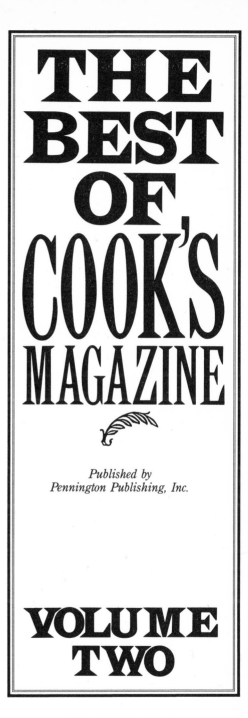

THE BEST OF COOK'S MAGAZINE

Published by
Pennington Publishing, Inc.

VOLUME TWO

Edited by Olga Rigsby

Published by Pennington Publishing, Inc.
2710 North Avenue
Bridgeport, Connecticut 06604

ISBN: 0-936599-09-X

Library of Congress Catalog Card Number
89-92006

ACKNOWLEDGEMENTS

COOK'S extends its warmest thanks to the cooks who contribute to the pages of the magazine and therefore to this book. It is their energy and love of food, that brings excitement and pleasure to our pages. Our thanks also go to Olga Rigsby who edited this volume and to Vicki Shearer and Julia Sharpe who assisted her.

We are grateful to COOK'S art director, Leith Harbold, who designed the recipe style for this book, and to Steven Doyle of Drenttel Doyle Partners in New York City, who designed the cover. Mimi Laaksonen, Cara Formisano, and Tracy Alia also contributed to the design and production of this book.

Thanks also to the editors and culinary staff of COOK'S who have made this book possible.

Christopher Kimball
Publisher & Editorial Director

INTRODUCTION

The staff of COOK'S, from the editor to an assistant in the circulation department, all cook from our magazine. We try the quick soups, the more elaborate menus, the ethnic main courses, the summer desserts, and the occasional sandwich. In fact, my wife and I prepare about one-third of the recipes in each issue, and we keep a file of our favorites, going back to the first charter issue in 1980. It was one of the easier editorial tasks, therefore, to compile the second volume of *The Best of COOK'S Magazine.* One evening with my dog-eared "home" copies quickly brought to mind more than a few great dinners, simple lunches, and even terrific breakfasts, my favorite meal of the day.

The strength of any food magazine, and COOK'S in particular, is the contributors. In one volume, you can have some of the best recipes from the top cooks and chefs in America today. America is a hodgepodge of different cuisines and *The Best of COOK'S Magazine, Volume Two* gives you a whirlwind tour from Spain to Brazil, from Seattle to Miami. Here is the best of cooking in America from 1987 through the present.

I used only one criterion in choosing these recipes. They could be easy or hard, inexpensive or dear, plain or spectacular. But they all share one simple rule. Each recipe is worth the time and expense of preparing it. Time and money are precious, and a recipe that takes more than 45 minutes to prepare had better be good.

Enjoy our second volume of *The Best of COOK'S Magazine.* It's really the best of America.

Christopher Kimball
Publisher & Editoral Director

CONTENTS

APPETIZERS

GRILLED SMOKED CHEESE WITH TOMATOES
SCAMORZA ALLA GRIGLIA

Makes 6 appetizer servings

The beauty of this dish is its simplicity. A good artisan-produced cheese and the best vine-ripened tomatoes are essential. Smoked mozzarella can be substituted for smoked *scamorza*.

2 medium tomatoes (about ¹/₂ pound)
1 teaspoon dried oregano
¹/₄ teaspoon extra-virgin olive oil
Salt and ground black pepper
1 pound *scamorza affumicata* **or smoked mozzarella**

PREPARATION: Core and cut tomatoes into ¹/₂-inch dice (1¹/₂ cups). Put the tomatoes, oregano, olive oil, ¹/₂ teaspoon salt and ¹/₄ teaspoon pepper in a small bowl and set aside at room temperature for at least one hour. (Can cover and set aside up to 4 hours.)

COOKING: Adjust oven rack to high position and heat broiler. Cut the cheese into ¹/₄-inch thick slices and put, slightly overlapping, on a heatproof plate. Broil 3 inches from element until cheese bubbles and begins to turn golden brown, about 2 minutes.

SERVING: Spoon the tomato mixture over the hot cheese. Serve immediately.

Evan Kleiman
Chef
Trattoria Angeli
Los Angeles, CA

MOZZARELLA "CHERRIES" WITH PROSCIUTTO
"CILIEGINE" CON PROSCIUTTO

Makes 30 Pieces

Like lovely edible flowers, the tiny mozzarella balls wrapped with prosciutto petals are a playful allusion to the term *fior di latte* (flower of the milk). Small, cherry-size balls of cow's milk mozzarella, packed in sealed plastic containers, are available in the dairy section of many supermarkets.

$^{1}/_{2}$ **medium lemon**
1 medium garlic clove
2 tablespoons snipped fresh chives
$^{1}/_{4}$ **cup olive oil**
$^{1}/_{4}$ **teaspoon hot red-pepper flakes**
9 ounces fresh mozzarella "cherries" *or* fresh mozarella
15 thin prosciutto slices (6 ounces)
1 medium bunch dill

PREPARATION: Squeeze lemon juice into a medium bowl. Peel and crush garlic and put it into the bowl along with the chives, olive oil, and red-pepper flakes. Drain and add cheese "cherries" or cut mozzarella into $^{3}/_{4}$-inch cubes and add to the mixture. Marinate at room temperature at least two hours. (Can cover and refrigerate overnight.)

SERVING: Cut prosciutto slices in half lengthwise. Wrap 1 slice of prosciutto around each piece of cheese and 1 small sprig of dill. Secure with a toothpick and serve immediately.

Anna Teresa Callen
Cookbook author and teacher
New York, NY

MOZZARELLA AND SUN-DRIED TOMATO CROSTINI
CROSTINI ROSATI

Makes 6 pieces

Sun-dried tomatoes under a melted mozzarella blanket are a rosy combination for *crostini*, slices of warm, toasted bread which can be rubbed with garlic and drizzled with extra-virgin olive oil. Possibilities include sautéed mushrooms and melted Fontina cheese. The most luxurious of all *crostini* are buttered with truffle paste.

1 jar marinated sun-dried tomatoes (8^1/$_2$ ounces)
1 medium shallot
^{1}/$_2$ cup heavy cream
6 slices crusty Italian bread (^{1}/$_2$ inch thick)
6 slices mozzarella (8 ounces)
6 stemmed basil leaves

PREPARATION: Drain tomatoes and reserve the oil. Thinly slice the shallot. Heat 4 tablespoons of the oil in a medium skillet. Add the shallot and cook over low heat until softened, about 5 minutes. Add the tomatoes and cook until softened, about 5 minutes. Stir in the cream, bring to a boil, reduce heat to low, and simmer until cream is absorbed and mixture is thickened, about 5 minutes. Transfer mixture to the workbowl of a food processor fitted with the metal blade and pulse until tomatoes are chopped but not pureed. (Can cover and refrigerate tomato mixture overnight.)

COOKING: Adjust oven rack to the middle position and heat oven to 400°F. Put bread on a baking sheet and bake until golden brown, about 5 minutes. Reduce oven temperature to 375°F. Put one slice of mozzarella on each slice of bread and top with tomato mixture. Bake until cheese is melted and tomato mixture is bubbly, about 10 minutes.

SERVING: Garnish each *crostino* with a basil leaf and serve immediately.

Anna Teresa Callen
Cookbook author and teacher
New York, NY

EGGPLANT CAPONATA

Makes 4 first-course servings

Prepare this Sicilian spread one or two days in advance to allow the sharpness of the vinegar and capers to flavor the eggplant.

1 tablespoon capers
1 small eggplant (about 10 ounces)
3 green olives
1 small onion
1 rib celery
¼ cup olive oil
2 teaspoons tomato paste
2 teaspoons red-wine vinegar
Salt
Pinch cayenne pepper
4 slices crusty, country-style bread

PREPARATION: Drain and chop the capers. Peel and cut the eggplant into ¼-inch dice. Pit and chop the olives. Cut the onion and celery into fine dice.

Heat 2 tablespoons of the oil in a large frying pan over medium heat and sauté the eggplant until soft, about 10 minutes. Transfer eggplant to a bowl. Add 1 tablespoon oil to the pan and sauté the onion over low heat until caramelized, about 15 minutes. Transfer onion to same bowl. Add the remaining tablespoon of oil to the pan and sauté the celery just until it begins to soften, 2 to 3 minutes. Transfer celery to bowl. Stir tomato paste, capers, olives, and vinegar into vegetables. Season to taste with salt and cayenne pepper.

Recipe can be completed several days in advance and stored, covered, in refrigerator.

SERVING: Toast the bread and cut into quarters. Spread the toast with the Caponata and serve.

Alice Waters
Owner Chez Panisse and Cafe Fanny
Berkeley, CA
Patricia Curtan
Cookbook author
Berkeley, CA

HUMMUS

Makes 4 servings

This popular Middle Eastern dip features chick-peas and tahini, a paste made from roasted sesame seeds.

1 clove garlic
2 tablespoons chopped parsley
2 lemons
2 cups canned chick-peas
1 tablespoon olive oil
$^1/_2$ cup tahini
$^1/_2$ teaspoon cumin
$^1/_8$ teaspoon cayenne
Salt and pepper
4 pitas

PREPARATION: Mince the garlic. Chop the parsley. Squeeze $^1/_3$ cup lemon juice. In a food processor, combine all the ingredients except the pitas and 1 tablespoon of the parsley and process until smooth. Season to taste.

Hummus can be made a day ahead.

SERVING: Warm the pitas if desired. Put Hummus in a bowl and sprinkle with the remaining parsley. Cut pitas into 8 wedges and pass with Hummus.

Stephanie Lyness
Free-lance writer
New York, NY

STEAK TARTARE

Makes 4 servings

You can grind the meat for Steak Tartare in a food processor, but be careful not to overprocess, or it will become mushy.

1 thin loaf French bread
   (baguette)
$1/2$ cup olive oil
$1/4$ cup capers
1 lemon
$1/4$ cup chopped parsley
1 scallion
1 pound lean, top-round beef
1 tablespoon Dijon mustard
Salt and pepper
1 egg yolk

PREPARATION: Cut bread on an angle into $1/4$-inch-thick slices. Brush both sides with olive oil, using about $1/4$ cup. Set aside.

Drain capers. Squeeze 2 tablespoons lemon juice. Chop parsley and scallion.

Recipe can be made to this point several hours ahead.

SERVING: Heat oven to 450°F. Toast bread in preheated oven until lightly browned, about 10 minutes.

Trim beef and cut into 1-inch cubes. Put the meat in a food processor and pulse several times until coarse ground. Transfer meat to a bowl and stir in the lemon juice, mustard, 2 tablespoons of the parsley, 2 tablespoons of the capers, $1/2$ the scallion, and the remaining oil. Season to taste with salt and pepper. Lightly mix the egg yolk into the meat mixture.

Mound beef on plates and garnish with remaining parsley, scallion, and capers. Pass the toasted bread separately.

Stephanie Lyness
Free-lance writer
New York, NY

OYSTERS WITH TWO MIGNONETTES

Makes 6 to 8 appetizer servings

This duet of mignonettes is bound to please any oyster fan. The first is a lively combination of Southwest flavors from Stephan Pyles, owner of the Routh Street Café in Dallas, and Goodfellows and Tejas restaurants in Minneapolis. The second is a more traditional combination of red-wine vinegar, garlic, freshly ground black pepper and a touch of lemon zest. Try them both, separately, on freshly-shucked oysters.

Southwest Mignonette
1 small shallot
1 small serrano chile
$1/2$ small red bell pepper
$1/2$ small green bell pepper
$1/2$ small yellow bell pepper
1 medium lime
2 teaspoons minced cilantro
$1/4$ cup white-wine vinegar
$1/4$ cup dry white wine
2 teaspoons tequila
Salt

Red-Wine Mignonette
1 small lemon
1 small garlic clove
$1/2$ cup red-wine vinegar
Ground black pepper

Crushed ice
5 dozen oysters

PREPARATION: *For the southwest mignonette*, peel and mince the shallot. Stem, seed, and mince the chile. Stem, seed, and cut bell peppers into $1/8$-inch dice (2 teaspoons each); wrap and refrigerate remainder for another use.

Put shallot, chile, and bell peppers in a small mixing bowl. Squeeze in 1 tablespoon lime juice. Add cilantro, white-wine vinegar, white wine, tequila, and $1/2$ teaspoon salt; set aside. (Can cover and refrigerate up to 3 hours.)

For the red-wine mignonette, remove and mince zest from $1/2$ the lemon (1 teaspoon). Peel and mince the garlic, and put it with the minced zest in a small bowl. Add the red-wine vinegar and $1/2$ teaspoon pepper. (Can cover and refrigerate overnight.)

SERVING: Cover the surface of a large platter with crushed ice. Scrub and shuck the oysters. Remove and discard the flat top shells. Arrange oysters, on the half shell, on the bed of crushed ice. Transfer mignonettes to 2 serving dishes or drizzle over oysters. Serve immediately.

Susan Hermann Loomis
Cookbook author
Seattle, WA

GARLIC AND MINT-MARINATED ZUCCHINI
ZUCCHINE A SCAPECE

Makes about 40 pieces

Named for Apicius, the Roman gastronome, these tender sautéed zucchini spirals, suffused with garlic, balsamic vinegar and mint, celebrate a legion of spiced and marinated dishes that have existed since ancient times.

6 small zucchini (about 1³/₄ pounds)
3 medium garlic cloves
1 cup vegetable oil
24 stemmed mint leaves
¹/₄ cup balsamic vinegar
1 medium head radicchio

PREPARATION AND COOKING: Cut the zucchini lengthwise into thin slices. Mince and set the garlic aside. Pat zucchini slices dry with paper towels. Heat oil in a medium skillet. Fry zucchini in batches until golden, about 1¹/₂ minutes on each side. Drain on paper towels. Layer zucchini, alternating with garlic and mint leaves in an 8- by 4-inch nonreactive baking dish. Pour vinegar over the layered zucchini, cover and refrigerate at least 1 hour. (Can cover and refrigerate overnight.)

SERVING: Rinse and pat the radicchio dry. Drain the zucchini; discard the liquid. Roll up each zucchini slice and secure with a toothpick. Put radicchio leaves on a serving platter and arrange zucchini over the leaves.

Anna Teresa Callen
Cookbook author and teacher
New York, NY

BACON AND EGG SALAD SANDWICHES WITH CHERRY TOMATOES

Makes 16 sandwiches

These tasy, bite-size sandwiches go well with cocktails as well as afternoon tea.

2 eggs
2 slices bacon
2 tablespoons minced chives
1/4 cup mayonnaise
Salt and pepper
4 thin slices bread
4 cherry tomatoes

PREPARATION: Put eggs in a saucepan, cover with water, and bring to a simmer. Cover, remove from heat, let sit at least 12 minutes, and drain. Peel and chop. Cook the bacon until crisp. Drain, cool, and crumble. Mince the chives.

Combine eggs, bacon, 1 tablespoon chives, and mayonnaise and season with salt and pepper. Trim crusts from bread. Spread each slice of bread with 1/4 of the egg salad and cut into 4 triangles. Sandwiches can be made to this point, covered, and refrigerated several hours ahead.

SERVING: Slice the tomatoes. Garnish each sandwich with a tomato slice and sprinkle with remaining chives.

Angela Hynes
Cookbook author
Los Angeles, CA

TOMATO AND BRIOCHE SANDWICHES

Makes 32 finger sandwiches

The simplicity of these sandwiches does not detract from their universal appeal. First-rate tomatoes are a must.

Mayonnaise
1 egg yolk
1 tablespoon Dijon mustard
1 tablespoon red-wine vinegar
1 teaspoon lemon juice
Salt
³/₄ cup olive oil
Pepper

1-pound brioche loaf or a
**   firm-textured white bread**
4 ripe tomatoes (about ³/₄ pound)

PREPARATION: *For the mayonnaise,* in a small bowl or in the workbowl of a food processor fitted with the metal blade, whisk or process the egg yolk with the mustard, vinegar, lemon juice, and ¹/₄ teaspoon salt until smooth. Whisk or process in the oil, drop by drop at first. As the mayonnaise begins to thicken, add the remaining oil in a slow, thin stream. Season mayonnaise to taste with salt and pepper.

Mayonnaise can be made several days ahead and refrigerated in an airtight container.

Cut the bread into sixteen ¹/₄-inch-thick slices. If using white bread, remove the crusts. Core the tomatoes and slice them thinly. Spread each slice of bread with mayonnaise. Cover half of the bread slices with a single layer of tomatoes. Top with the remaining bread slices. Quarter each sandwich diagonally. Arrange sandwiches on a serving platter, cover with plastic wrap, and keep cool (do not refrigerate) until ready to serve.

Sandwiches can be made several hours ahead.

SERVING: Pass sandwiches as an appetizer.

Florence Fabricant
Food columnist
New York Times
New York, NY

SOUPS

BLACK-EYED PEA SOUP

Makes 4 servings

This hearty and hospitable soup is especially good served with homemade cornbread.

1¼ cups dried peas, such as
   black-eyed, pink-eyed,
   purplehull cow *or* crowder
2 cloves garlic
1 onion
2 ribs celery
⅔ cup dry white wine
½ cup olive oil
3 sprigs fresh thyme *or*
   ½ teaspoon dried
¾ pound rabbit *or* chicken parts
Salt and pepper
1 ounce pancetta *or* slab bacon
Bouquet garni of parsley stems
   and bay leaf
1 tablespoon butter
2 quarts water

PREPARATION: Soak peas overnight in water to cover by 2 inches. Or put peas in a saucepan with cold water to cover, and bring to boil, covered, for 1 minute. Remove from heat and let sit 1 hour. Drain and set aside.

Mince the garlic. Chop the onion and celery. Put ⅓ cup of wine and 5 tablespoons olive oil in a baking dish just large enough to hold the rabbit. Add thyme sprigs, 1 tablespoon minced garlic, ¼ cup onions, half the chopped celery, and the rabbit pieces. Season with salt and pepper. Marinate at room temperature for 2 hours or refrigerate overnight. Dice pancetta. Tie together parsley and bay leaf.

Drain the rabbit and pat dry. Heat 1 tablespoon of the olive oil and 1 tablespoon of butter in a large frying pan. Add the rabbit pieces and cook over medium-high heat until browned, about 10 minutes. Pour off fat. Add remaining ⅓ cup of wine and stir with a wooden spoon to deglaze bottom of pan. Add 2 cups of water to cover and simmer until rabbit is tender, 45 minutes to 1 hour. Remove rabbit from pan, reserving broth. When cool enough to handle, remove rabbit meat from bones.

Heat remaining oil in a stockpot. Add remaining onions, celery, garlic, and pancetta to the stockpot and sauté over low heat until onions are soft, about 5 minutes.

Add peas and *bouquet garni* and season with ½ teaspoon salt and ½ teaspoon pepper. Add 1½ quarts water to cover and bring to boil. Reduce heat and simmer, uncovered, for 30 minutes. Add reserved rabbit broth and simmer until peas are tender, about 30 minutes. Remove parsley and bay leaf. Add the rabbit and simmer until rabbit is heated through, about 3 minutes. Season to taste with salt and pepper. Soup can be made a few days ahead.

SERVING: Reheat soup if necessary and pour into bowls.

Susan Spicer
Chef
The Bistro at Hotel Maison de Ville
New Orleans, LA

CHEESE AND ASPARAGUS SOUP

Makes 4 servings

Asparagus and fontina cheese are a natural match in this delicious soup which is enhanced by crisp croutons.

2 tablespoons butter
2 slices bread
1 1/2 ounces fontina cheese
   (about 1/2 cup grated)
2 leeks
2 shallots
1 clove garlic
1/2 pound asparagus
1 small potato
3 cups chicken stock
1/4 cup heavy cream
Salt and pepper

PREPARATION: Heat oven to 425°F. Melt 1 tablespoon of the butter. Remove crusts from bread and cut each slice in half diagonally and then in half again. Brush bread with melted butter and toast in the upper half of preheated oven until golden brown, about 5 minutes. Grate the cheese.

Chop the leeks and shallots. Mince the garlic. Trim the asparagus, cut off and reserve tips, and chop stalks into approximately 1-inch pieces. Peel the potato and cut into thin slices.

Melt the remaining 1 tablespoon butter in a frying pan and sauté the leeks, shallots, garlic, potato, and asparagus stalks until tender, about 20 minutes. Stir in chicken stock, cover, and gently bring to a boil. Lower heat and simmer until asparagus is cooked through, about 30 minutes.

Working in batches, if necessary, puree the soup in a food processor until smooth. Strain puree into a large saucepan and add heavy cream and 6 tablespoons of the cheese. Stir to combine and season to taste. Recipe can be made to this point a day ahead.

COOKING AND SERVING: Heat the broiler. Sprinkle the remaining 2 tablespoons cheese over the croutons and cook under preheated broiler until cheese melts, about 2 minutes.

Cook the reserved asparagus tips in a small saucepan of boiling, salted water until tender, about 3 minutes. Meanwhile, bring soup to a simmer. Put soup into individual bowls and garnish with cheese croutons and asparagus tips.

John Braun
Chef
Le Coq Hardi
Ridgefield, CT

QUICK GAZPACHO

Makes 4 servings

This chilled soup, a Spanish classic, may be garnished with chopped hard-boiled egg, garbanzo beans, slivered ham, sliced scallions, sour cream, crumbled bacon, or croutons.

7 medium tomatoes (about
   1³/₄ pounds)
3 slices (³/₄-inch-thick) Italian
   bread
1 medium garlic clove
3 tablespoons red wine vinegar
¹/₃ cup olive oil
4 cups tomato juice, chilled
2 cups canned beef broth, chilled
2 tablespoons minced fresh basil
   leaves *or* 2 teaspoons
   dried basil
1 large green bell pepper
1 medium onion
1 medium cucumber
2 teaspoons Worcestershire
   sauce
¹/₂ teaspoon hot red-pepper
   sauce
Salt and ground black pepper

PREPARATION AND SERVING: Core and seed the tomatoes. Tear the bread into small pieces. Peel the garlic and put into the workbowl of a food processor along with the tomatoes and bread. Pulse 3 times until blended. With the motor running, pour the vinegar and oil through the feed tube and process until smoothly pureed. Mix the tomato puree, tomato juice, beef broth, and basil together in a large bowl and refrigerate until chilled. Stem, quarter, and seed the pepper. Peel and quarter the onion. Peel and halve cucumber lengthwise, remove the seeds with a spoon, and cut pieces in half. Place all the vegetables in the food processor and pulse until coarsely chopped. Stir vegetables, Worcestershire sauce, hot red-pepper sauce, ¹/₄ teaspoon salt, and ¹/₄ teaspoon pepper into the soup. Serve chilled.

Brooke Dojny and Melanie Barnard
Nationally syndicated food writers and cookbook authors
Fairfield County, CT

MUSHROOM SOUP WITH SWEET VERMOUTH AND TOMATO

Makes 6 servings

This vermouth-flavored soup is embellished with domestic or Italian brown field mushrooms, or with a combination of chanterelles and domestic mushrooms. Wild mushrooms give the soup a stronger, earthier flavor, but less exotic domestic mushrooms will not disappoint.

2 medium onions
1 pound mushrooms
3 tablespoons butter
6 tablespoons tomato puree *or* 3 tablespoons tomato paste
2 cups beef stock *or* canned beef broth
2 cups chicken stock *or* canned chicken broth
6 tablespoons sweet vermouth
Salt and ground black pepper
3 tablespoons grated Parmesan cheese
3 tablespoons minced parsley

PREPARATION: Peel and thinly slice the onions. Thinly slice the mushrooms.

COOKING: Heat the butter in a large, heavy saucepan. Add the onions and sauté over low heat until softened, about 10 minutes. Add the mushrooms and sauté until the onions have softened, about 5 minutes longer. Add the tomato puree and the beef and chicken stocks; bring the mixture to a boil. Add the vermouth and season with salt, if necessary, and 1/2 teaspoon pepper. Adjust seasoning to taste. Simmer 2 to 3 minutes over low heat.

SERVING: Transfer soup to warm soup bowls, and sprinkle with freshly grated Parmesan cheese and minced parsley. Serve immediately.

Joyce Goldstein
Chef/owner
Square One
San Francisco, CA

WILD MUSHROOM SOUP
MINESTRA DE FUNGHI SELVATICI

Makes 8 to 10 servings

In Italy, wild porcini mushrooms are gathered and used to make intensely flavored soups. Here, a variety of fresh or dried mushrooms — porcini, chanterelles, shiitake, and morels — can be used. However, a single type of fresh mushroom (wild or cultivated), or a combination of dried and cultivated mushrooms, also will produce an excellent soup. Dried porcini and other dried mushrooms can be purchased in Italian and other specialty food stores.

$1/4$ **ounce dried porcini mushrooms (8 large pieces)**
3 medium potatoes
2 small carrots
1 medium onion
1 small shallot
2 pounds wild *or* cultivated fresh mushrooms
2 bacon slices (2 ounces)
10 tablespoons olive oil
$2^{1}/_{2}$ **quarts homemade *or* canned chicken broth**
Salt
$1/4$ **cup minced flat-leaf parsley**
Ground black pepper

PREPARATION: Put dried porcini mushrooms in a small bowl with $1/2$ cup hot water. Let stand until mushrooms soften, about 20 minutes. Remove mushrooms and strain liquid through a fine sieve. Return mushrooms and liquid to the bowl; discard the sediment. Peel and coarsely shred the potatoes and carrots. Peel and coarsely chop the onion. Peel and mince the shallot. Thinly slice the fresh mushrooms. Mince the bacon.

COOKING: Heat 5 tablespoons of the oil in a 6-quart soup kettle. Add the bacon and onions and sauté over medium heat until onions soften and bacon is translucent, about 2 minutes. Bring broth to a boil in a large saucepan. Add the boiling broth to the soup kettle along with the potatoes, carrots, dried mushrooms, and reserved mushroom liquid. Return to a boil and simmer until vegetables are tender, about 10 minutes. Heat the remaining oil in a large skillet. Add the fresh mushrooms and 1 teaspoon salt and sauté over medium heat until mushroom liquid has evaporated, about 10 minutes. Add mushrooms to the soup kettle and simmer for 30 minutes. Season with salt, if necessary.

SERVING: Ladle soup into warm bowls. Sprinkle with parsley and ground black pepper. Serve immediately.

Lidia Bastianich
Executive chef and co-owner
Felidia
New York, NY

POTATO AND RICE SOUP
PATATE E RISI

Makes 8 to 10 servings

This soup is a minestrina, but the carrots, celery, and tomatoes give it a richer and decidedly more acidic flavor than most.

3 medium carrots
2 medium boiling potatoes
¹/₄ pound Parmesan cheese
6 tablespoons olive oil
2 tablespoons tomato paste
2 medium celery stalks
3 quarts homemade or canned
  chicken broth
2 bay leaves
1 cup Arborio *or* long-grain rice
  (7 ounces)
Salt and ground black pepper

PREPARATION: Peel and coarsely shred the carrots. Peel and cut the potatoes into ¹/₂-inch dice. Grate the cheese (1 cup).

COOKING: Heat the oil in a 6-quart soup kettle. Add potatoes and sauté until lightly browned, about 5 minutes. Add carrots and tomato paste and cook until carrots soften, about 3 minutes. Cut celery stalks in half and add to kettle along with the broth and bay leaves. Bring to a boil, cover, and simmer for 45 minutes, skimming occasionally. Add rice and simmer until tender, 18 to 20 minutes longer. Discard celery and bay leaves. Season with salt, if necessary.

SERVING: Ladle soup into warm bowls. Sprinkle with black pepper and cheese.

Lidia Bastianich
Executive chef and co-owner
Felidia
New York, NY

RICE AND SPINACH SOUP

Makes 8 to 10 servings

Because of its high starch content, short-grain Italian (Arborio) rice will give this soup a slightly creamy consistency. A *minestrina* such as this often serves as a prelude to a substantial entree.

1 pound spinach
2 medium onions
2 medium garlic cloves
¹/₄ pound Parmesan cheese
6 tablespoons olive oil
2 tablespoons butter
**2¹/₂ quarts homemade *or* canned
  chicken broth**
**³/₄ cup Arborio *or* long-grain rice
  (5 ounces)**
Salt and ground black pepper

PREPARATION AND COOKING: Rinse, drain, and stem the spinach. Bring 4 quarts of water to boil in a large soup kettle. Add the spinach and blanch until bright green and tender, about 1 minute. Drain, refresh under cold, running water, and coarsely chop. Peel and coarsely chop the onion peel and crush the garlic. Grate the cheese (1 cup).

Heat oil and butter in a 6-quart soup kettle. Add the garlic and onion and sauté over medium heat until softened, about 5 minutes. Add the spinach and sauté 3 minutes longer. Add the broth and bring to a boil. Add the rice and simmer until tender, 18 to 20 minutes. Season with salt, if necessary.

SERVING: Ladle soup into warm bowls; sprinkle with pepper and cheese. Serve immediately.

Lidia Bastianich
Executive chef and co-owner
Felidia
New York, NY

TOASTED GOLDEN GARLIC SOUP
BRODO BROSTULA

Makes 6 to 8 servings

Fortified with garlic and filaments of lightly poached egg, it becomes an earthy, full-bodied peasant soup for the lustiest appetites

Croutons
3 slices white bread
4 tablespoons butter

4 medium garlic cloves
$^1/_2$ cup olive oil
1 cup all-purpose flour
2$^1/_2$ quarts homemade or canned chicken broth
4 eggs
Salt and ground black pepper

PREPARATION AND COOKING: *For the croutons*, remove and discard the bread crusts and cut crumb into $^1/_2$-inch cubes. Heat butter in a medium skillet. Add bread cubes and sauté over medium heat until crisp and golden, about 2 minutes. Transfer to a plate lined with paper towels; set aside.

For the soup, peel and mince the garlic. Heat oil in a 4-quart saucepan. Add garlic and flour and cook, over low heat, stirring constantly, until mixture turns nut-brown, 8 to 10 minutes. Gradually whisk in the broth and bring to a boil. Simmer soup for 20 minutes. Strain soup through a fine sieve, return it to the saucepan, and bring to a simmer. Beat the eggs and slowly whisk them into the soup. When soup returns to a simmer, remove it from the heat. Season with salt, if necessary.

SERVING: Ladle soup into warm bowls. Sprinkle with black pepper and croutons.

Lidia Bastianich
Executive chef and co-owner
Felidia
New York, NY

POTAGE PRINTANIERE
SPRING VEGETABLE SOUP

Makes 8 servings

This green vegetable soup recipe can be varied by adding diced green beans, zucchini, or shredded greens of any kind. Coarser vegetables such as cabbage benefit from a sprinkling of cheese.

$2/3$ **pound green peas (about 1 cup**
  or $1/4$ pound shelled)
3 leeks
3 ribs celery plus leaves for
  garnish
$1/2$ **head romaine lettuce (about**
  $1/2$ pound or 4 cups)
$1^1/2$ **quarts chicken stock**
Pinch of sugar
Salt and pepper

Croutons
4 tablespoons butter
6 slices firm white bread

PREPARATION: Shell the peas. Trim the leeks, leaving about 3 inches of green. Quarter lengthwise to just above the root end and rinse under cold water, fanning the layers. Cut leeks and celery into thin slices, reserving the celery leaves for garnish. Cut the lettuce leaves crosswise into strips. Bring stock to a simmer in a large saucepan over medium heat. Add the peas, leeks, celery, lettuce, and sugar and season to taste with salt and pepper. Reduce heat to low and cook, uncovered, until the vegetables are tender, about 15 minutes.

For the croutons, melt the butter. Remove crusts and toast the bread. Brush both sides of bread with the butter, cut into $1/2$-inch cubes, and wrap in foil.

Recipe can be prepared to this point a day ahead.

COOKING AND SERVING: Heat oven to 300°F. Bake croutons in foil in preheated oven until crisp and warm, about 10 minutes. Reheat soup if necessary, pour into bowls, and garnish with celery leaves. Pass croutons separately.

Anne Willan
Founder
La Varenne Ecole de Cuisine
Paris, France

TURNIP SOUP WITH THYME

Makes 2 quarts

This unusual autumnal soup combines turnips and turnip greens. This version of the soup is pureed, but it is equally good if the onions, diced turnips, and potatoes are left intact in the flavorful broth.

Croutons
2 slices white bread (¹/₂ inch thick)
3 tablespoons butter

Soup
1 small red onion
2 small garlic cloves
9 medium turnips (about 2¹/₂ pounds)
1 medium red potato (about ¹/₂ pound)
³/₄ pound turnip greens *or* 1 package frozen turnip greens (10 ounces)
5 cups chicken stock *or* canned chicken broth
2 tablespoons butter
1 teaspoon fresh thyme leaves
Salt and ground black pepper
1 thin slice prosciutto (optional)
Olive oil

PREPARATION: *For the croutons*, remove and discard the bread crusts and cut the bread into ¹/₂-inch cubes. Heat the butter in a medium skillet. Add the bread cubes and sauté over medium heat until they become crisp and golden brown, about 2 minutes. Transfer croutons to a plate lined with paper toweling. (Can cover and set aside overnight at room temperature.)

For the soup, peel and thinly slice the onion and garlic. Peel and cut the turnips and potato into ¹/₂-inch cubes. Rinse fresh turnip greens (thaw frozen greens); drain and set aside.

COOKING: Bring chicken stock to a boil and set aside. Heat butter in a soup kettle or Dutch oven. Add onions and garlic and sauté over medium heat until softened, about 5 minutes. Add the turnips, potato, thyme, 1 teaspoon salt, and ¹/₂ teaspoon pepper. Cover and stew over low heat until turnips and potatoes have softened slightly, 10 to 15 minutes. Add 3 cups warm chicken stock, cover and simmer until vegetables are tender about 10 minutes. Add turnip greens and simmer 5 minutes longer. Cool slightly and puree in batches in a food processor fitted with the metal blade. Return soup to the kettle, stir in remaining chicken stock, and adjust seasoning to taste. (Can cover and refrigerate up to 2 days.)

SERVING: Mince prosciutto (optional). Bring soup to a boil. Ladle soup into bowls. Dribble each serving with 1 teaspoon olive oil, and top with croutons and prosciutto.

Alice Waters
Owner Chez Panisse and Cafe Fanny
Berkeley, CA
Patricia Curtan
Cookbook author
Berkeley, CA

TWO SOUPS IN ONE BOWL

Makes 8 servings

Two different soups of contrasting colors and compatible flavors are stunningly presented in one bowl. Oniony Fennel-Leek Soup offsets the sweetness of Butternut-Squash Soup, and each has sufficient body to maintain its own space if the soups are simultaneously poured into bowls.

Fennel-Leek Soup
1 small bunch celery (1 pound)
1 bulb fennel (1 pound)
2 medium leeks
1 medium garlic clove
1 large potato
4 tablespoons butter
1 quart chicken stock
³/₄ cup half-and-half
1 lemon
¹/₄ teaspoon hot red-pepper sauce
Salt and ground white pepper

Butternut-Squash Soup
1 medium garlic clove
1 medium onion
1 large leek
2 medium butternut squash (4 pounds)
4 tablespoons butter
1 quart chicken stock
¹/₂ cup half-and-half
Salt and ground white pepper

PREPARATION AND COOKING: *For the Fennel-Leek Soup*, trim and slice celery into ¹/₂-inch pieces. Core, trim, and cut fennel into ¹/₂-inch dice. Rinse and coarsely chop the white part of the leeks. (Reserve greens for use in stock). Peel garlic clove. Peel and thinly slice potato.

Melt butter in a 4- to 6-quart soup kettle. Sauté celery, fennel, leeks, and garlic over medium heat until vegetables soften and release juices, about 15 minutes. Add potato and stock. Bring to boil, reduce heat, cover, and simmer until vegetables are very soft, about 40 minutes. Puree soup in 2-cup batches in food processor fitted with metal blade until smooth, about 30 seconds. Return puree to kettle; stir in half-and-half, 1 teaspoon lemon juice, red-pepper sauce, 1 teaspoon salt, and ¹/₄ teaspoon white pepper. Set aside until. (Can cover and refrigerate overnight.)

For the Butternut-Squash Soup, peel and mince garlic and onion. Rinse and coarsely chop white part of the leek. Peel, seed, and cut squash into 1-inch cubes.

Heat butter in a 4- to 6-quart soup kettle. Sauté garlic, onion, and leek over medium heat until softened, about 5 minutes. Add squash and stock. Bring to a boil, reduce heat, cover, and simmer until vegetables are softened, about 40 minutes. Puree mixture in 2-cup batches in a food processor fitted with the metal blade until smooth, about 30 seconds. Return puree to kettle; stir in half-and-half, 1 teaspoon salt, and ¹/₄ teaspoon white pepper. Set aside until serving time. (Can refrigerate overnight.)

SERVING: (Warm over low heat.) Use two measuring cups to simultaneously pour ¹/₂ cup of each into bowls. Do not mix soups together. Serve immediately.

Jane Freiman
Food columnist and cookbook author
New York, NY

HAM BONE SOUP WITH WHITE BEANS, ESCAROLE, AND SAGE BUTTER

Makes 8 servings

A ham bone from a 12- to 13-pound ham is sufficient to flavor about 4 quarts of ham stock. This recipe will use about 2 quarts; freeze the remainder for a second batch of soup.

1 ham bone (from a 12- to 13-pound smoked ham)
1/4 pound softened butter
3 tablespoons minced fresh sage leaves
10 ounces dry white beans, such as great northern (1 1/2 cups)
1 small head escarole (about 1 pound)
2 ounces Parmesan *or* Romano cheese
4 ounces smoked ham (optional)
2 medium onions
2 medium carrots
2 medium celery stalks
3 medium garlic cloves
1/4 cup olive oil
2 bay leaves
Salt and ground black pepper

PREPARATION: Put ham bone in a soup kettle with cold water to cover. Bring to boil and simmer for 2 hours, skimming frequently. Discard bone and strain stock. (Can cool, cover, and refrigerate up to 3 days, or freeze up to 1 month.) Cream butter and beat in sage. Shape herb butter into a 1-inch thick log. Wrap in plastic and refrigerate. (Can refrigerate up to 3 days or freeze up to 1 month.)

Pick through beans, put them in a large bowl with cold water to cover by 3 inches, and let stand 24 hours. Or, put beans in a soup kettle with water to cover, bring to a boil, cover, and let stand 1 hour. Drain. Trim, rinse, and drain escarole; set aside. Grate and set cheese aside (1/2 cup). (Chop smoked ham — 3/4 cup.) Peel and coarsely chop onions and carrots. Chop celery. Peel and mince garlic.

COOKING: Heat the olive oil in a 6-quart soup kettle. (Add the ham and sauté over medium heat until golden brown, about 5 minutes.) Add the onions, carrots, celery, and garlic. Cover and simmer until vegetables soften, about 15 minutes. Add beans, 2 quarts stock, and bay leaves. Bring to a boil, partially cover, and simmer until the beans are tender, about 50 minutes.

Strain the liquid and return to kettle. Discard bay leaves, and puree solids in the workbowl of a food processor fitted with the metal blade. Return puree to soup kettle. Bring to a simmer. Coarsely chop 8 cups of escarole, add to the soup, and simmer until the escarole wilts, about 10 minutes. Season with salt, if necessary, and 1/2 teaspoon pepper. (Can cool, cover, and refrigerate up to 3 days.)

SERVING: Bring sage butter to room temperature. Ladle hot soup into bowls and top with 1 tablespoon cheese and 1 tablespoon butter. Serve immediately.

Michael McLaughlin
Free-lance writer
Brooklyn, NY

LAMB AND CHICK-PEA SOUP

Makes 4 servings

Here's a downhome-style soup that will make you hope for chilly weather.

$^2/_3$ **cup dried chick-peas**
Salt and pepper
$^2/_3$ **pound boneless lamb leg**
1 large onion
1 rib celery
6 tablespoons chopped parsley
6 tablespoons chopped coriander
2 cloves garlic
2 tablespoons olive oil
2 teaspoons paprika
2 tablespoons tomato paste
1$^1/_2$ quarts water
$^1/_3$ **cup orzo *or* other pasta**

PREPARATION: Soak the chick-peas overnight in water to cover by 2 inches. Or put chick-peas in a saucepan with cold water to cover, bring to a boil, and cook for 1 minute. Cover, remove from heat, and let sit for about 1 hour.

Drain water from the chick-peas (for both the overnight-soak and quick method). Add fresh cold water to cover and bring to a boil. Lower heat and simmer, partially covered, about 30 minutes. Stir in 1 teaspoon salt and continue to cook gently until peas are tender, about 30 more minutes. Drain.

Cut lamb into $^1/_2$-inch cubes. Chop the onion, celery, parsley, and coriander. Mince the garlic.

Heat the oil in a large stockpot and sauté lamb, in batches if necessary, over medium-high heat until browned, about 5 minutes. Remove from pot and set aside. Add the onion, celery and garlic and cook until the onion is softened, about 3 minutes. Add 2 tablespoons of water and stir to deglaze the pot.

Return the lamb to the pot. Add the paprika, tomato paste, parsley, coriander, chick-peas, and 1$^1/_2$ quarts of water and bring to a boil. Cook over low heat for 25 minutes. Add pasta and continue cooking until meat is tender, about 20 minutes more. Season to taste.

Soup can be made two days ahead.

SERVING: Reheat soup if necessary and ladle into individual bowls.

Ahmed Abida
Chef
Helen's
Washington, D.C.

TURKEY SOUP WITH BROCCOLI, LEMON, AND TARRAGON

Makes 4 servings

Turkey breast is a welcome change from chicken. Lemon and tarragon enliven the soup, and the addition of pasta makes it a complete meal in a bowl.

1¹/₄ pounds broccoli
1 pound boneless, skinless
    turkey breast
1 large can chicken broth
    (46 ounces)
²/₃ cup orzo *or* tubettini
    (4 ounces)
1 tablespoon minced fresh
    tarragon *or* 1 teaspoon dried
1 small lemon
Ground black pepper

PREPARATION: Cut the broccoli heads into florets; wrap and reserve stems for another use. Cut the turkey into ¹/₂-inch strips and set aside with the broccoli.

COOKING: Bring broth to a boil in a soup kettle. Add the pasta and simmer for 5 minutes. Add the broccoli florets and turkey strips and simmer until both are tender, about 5 minutes. Remove soup from heat, stir in tarragon, and squeeze in 2 tablespoons lemon juice. Season with ¹/₂ teaspoon pepper and serve immediately.

Pam Parseghian
Free-lance writer
New York, NY

SAUSAGE AND SEAFOOD SOUP

Makes 4 servings

Accompany this hearty, full-flavored soup with French bread and fennel butter — softened butter flavored with minced fennel tops and a generous grind of black pepper.

10 squid (about 1 pound)
**³/₄ pound fennel sausage *or*
   sweet Italian sausage**
1 onion
2 large cloves garlic
1 small bulb fennel
4 red bell peppers
**4 plum tomatoes *or* 2 cups
   canned**
24 shrimp (about 1¹/₂ pounds)
¹/₂ cup olive oil
**2 cups fish stock *or* 1 cup clam
   juice plus 1 cup water**
¹/₂ cup red wine
Salt and pepper
¹/₄ cup chopped flat-leaf parsley

PREPARATION: Clean squid. Remove heads and entrails. Cut bodies into 1-inch-wide slices. Cut tentacles into quarters and set aside.

Prick the sausage with a fork and sauté, covered, over low heat until cooked through, about 10 minutes. Remove the sausage from the pan. Drain and set aside.

Chop the onion. Mince the garlic. Set aside fennel tops for garnish and cut the bulb into dice. Core and seed the bell peppers and cut them into 3-inch squares. Peel, seed, and chop the tomatoes. Shell and devein the shrimp.

In a large frying pan, heat ¹/₄ cup of the olive oil over low heat. Add onion and cook until softened, about 4 minutes. Add the diced fennel, garlic, and red pepper, and cook for another 4 minutes. Cover the pan and continue cooking until vegetables are soft, about 5 minutes more. Remove the vegetables from the pan and puree. Set aside.

In a large frying pan, heat remaining ¹/₄ cup olive oil over medium heat and cook tomatoes for 3 minutes. Add the vegetable puree, fish stock, red wine, and sausage and simmer, covered, for 10 minutes. Add the squid and shrimp and simmer until just cooked through, about 2 minutes. Season to taste with salt and pepper.

Sausage and Seafood Soup can be made a day ahead. Chop the fennel tops and parsley up to several hours ahead.

SERVING: Reheat soup gently if necessary. Serve in large bowls and sprinkle with fennel and parsley.

Rick O'Connell
Chef
Rosalie's
San Francisco, CA

FISH BROTH
BRODO DI PESCE

Makes 2 quarts

A two-pound red snapper will yield bones for the *brodo* and fillets for the Red Snapper Soup (recipe, page 42).

2 medium onions
2 medium leeks
2 tablespoons olive oil
1 pound heads and bones from
    red snapper, rockfish, cod,
    flounder, porgy, *or* sea bass
Salt
1 tablespoon tomato paste
2 quarts boiling water
1 celery stalk
2 sprigs fresh thyme *or* 1
    teaspoon dried

PREPARATION: Peel and coarsely chop the onions. Rinse leeks, remove green tops, and reserve white parts for another use.

COOKING: Heat oil in a 6-quart soup kettle. Add onions and sauté over medium-high heat until softened, about 2 minutes. Add fish heads and bones and sauté until golden, about 5 minutes. Stir in salt and tomato paste. Add the boiling water to the soup kettle. Cut the celery stalk in half, and add it to the soup with the thyme and leek greens. Simmer 25 minutes. Strain broth through a fine sieve and return it to the soup kettle; set aside. (Can cool, cover and refrigerate up to 2 days or freeze up to 1 month.)

Lidia Bastianich
Executive chef and co-owner
Felidia
New York, NY

LOUISIANA CRAB, CORN, AND SHRIMP BISQUE

MAKES 4 SERVINGS

Here's a soup that doesn't take all day to make. Quick-cooking shellfish combine with corn in this Cafe Vermilionville favorite.

Shrimp Stock
2 pounds unshelled shrimp
1 small onion
$^1/_2$ lemon
6 black peppercorns
$^1/_4$ cup white wine
3 cups water

1 small onion
1 rib celery
3 scallions
3 tablespoons chopped parsley
3 cloves garlic
$^1/_4$ red bell pepper
$^1/_4$ green bell pepper
3 ears of corn *or* 1$^1/_2$ cups frozen corn kernels
$^1/_4$ cup oil
$^1/_4$ cup flour
4 tablespoons butter
$^1/_2$ cup dry white wine
1$^1/_2$ teaspoons fresh thyme *or* $^1/_2$ teaspoon dried
3$^1/_2$ cups heavy cream
1 teaspoon hot red-pepper sauce
Salt and pepper
$^1/_2$ pound fresh lump crabmeat
16 crab claws, cooked and shelled, for garnish (optional)

PREPARATION: *For the Shrimp Stock*, remove shells from shrimp and reserve shrimp and shells separately. Quarter the onion. Cut a slice from the lemon. Put the shrimp shells, onion, lemon slice, peppercorns, and white wine in a large pot with 3 cups water and simmer over low heat for 20 minutes. Strain.

Chop the onion, celery, scallions and parsley. Mince the garlic. Core, seed, and chop the red and green bell peppers. Cut corn kernels from the cobs.

To make a roux, heat the oil in a small saucepan over medium-low heat. Gradually whisk in the flour and cook until golden, about 4 minutes. Remove from heat.

Heat butter in a large saucepan. Add onion, red and green bell peppers, celery, and garlic and sauté until onion is softened, about 1 minute. Add 2$^1/_2$ cups shrimp stock, the white wine, and thyme. Bring to a boil and whisk in the roux. Reduce heat to a simmer and continue to cook, stirring frequently, until thickened, about 4 minutes. Add the cream, hot red-pepper sauce, and corn. Season to taste with salt and simmer for 3 to 4 minutes. Add reserved shrimp, crabmeat, crab claws, scallions, and parsley and simmer over low heat until shrimp turn pink, about 2 minutes.

Bisque can be made a day ahead.

SERVING: Reheat bisque if necessary and serve in large bowls.

Patrick Mould
Chef
Cafe Vermilionville
Lafayette, LA

LOBSTER AND CORN CHOWDER

Makes 4 servings

Lobster had a rather shaky start in the colonies. In 1662, Plymouth governor William Bradford apologized because there was nothing better to eat. Early American fishermen's wives prudently extended their seafood chowders by tossing in handfuls of corn.

1 lobster (about 1¹/₂ pounds)
2 medium potatoes
1 medium onion
4 ears fresh corn *or* 2 cups
  thawed frozen corn kernels
1 quart half-and-half
4 tablespoons butter
¹/₈ teaspoon cayenne pepper
Corn Crisps (recipe page 63)

PREPARATION: Bring 4 quarts of water to a boil in a 6 to 8-quart soup kettle. Add lobster, cover, and boil about 10 minutes. Remove and reserve the shells and carcass for stock. Cut lobster meat into 2-inch pieces. (Can wrap and refrigerate meat and shells overnight.) Peel and cut potatoes into ¹/₂-inch dice. Mince the onion (1 cup). Remove the corn kernels from the cobs (or drain and set aside thawed corn).

COOKING AND SERVING: Put the reserved lobster shells and carcass in a large saucepan with the half-and-half. Bring the half-and-half to a boil, lower heat, and simmer for 4 minutes. Remove from heat and set aside. Melt the butter in the soup kettle. Add the potatoes, onion, and corn kernels and sauté over medium-low heat until the onion is translucent, about 5 minutes. Strain the lobster cream over the vegetables, bring to a simmer and then simmer slowly until the potatoes are tender, 6 to 8 minutes. Stir in the lobster meat, cayenne pepper, ¹/₄ teaspoon salt, and ¹/₄ teaspoon pepper. Simmer just until lobster meat is hot, about 5 minutes. Ladle into bowls and serve with Corn Crisps.

Larry Forgione
Chef/owner
An American Place restaurant
New York, NY

MUSSEL SOUP WITH TOMATOES AND LEEKS

Makes 4 servings

For a more elegant soup, shell the mussels, puree the vegetable broth, and add a little heavy cream and a dash of Pernod.

1 leek
1 clove garlic
2 fresh tomatoes *or* 1 cup canned
   tomatoes
4 pounds mussels
1 small orange
1/2 cup white wine
1 tablespoon olive oil
1 cup fish stock *or* chicken broth
1 tablespoon butter
Salt and pepper
4 tablespoons chopped fresh
   parsley

PREPARATION: To trim the leek, remove the roots, then cut off the tough green leaves about two inches above the white part. Quarter the leek lengthwise and rinse it well in cold water. Chop the leek. Mince the garlic. If using fresh tomatoes, peel, seed, and coarsely chop them. Scrub the mussels, discarding any with opened or cracked shells, and pull out fibers that protrude from the straight sides of mussel shells. Remove one 2-inch strip of zest from the orange.

COOKING: In a 6- to 8-quart soup kettle, combine the mussels and wine. Cover, bring to a boil, and cook, stirring occasionally, until mussels just open, about 3 minutes. Remove mussels from pot with a slotted spoon and set aside. Strain liquid in kettle through a sieve lined with several layers of cheesecloth or a coffee filter. In the same kettle, heat the olive oil, add the leek and garlic and sauté over medium-low heat until soft, about 5 minutes Add the tomatoes, stock or broth, mussel juice, and orange zest and simmer over low heat, about 10 minutes. Recipe can be made to this point a few hours ahead. Cool and set aside; refrigerate mussels separately.

SERVING: Just before serving, add mussels to the pot and reheat. Stir in the butter; season to taste with salt and pepper. Sprinkle with parsley and serve.

Elizabeth Riely
Free-lance writer
Newton Centre, MA
Brooke Dojny
Free-lance writer
Westport, CT

OYSTER STEW

Makes 4 servings

A sublime combination of flavors, this stew is served at the Ark restaurant in Nahcotta, Washington. Use the freshest oysters possible; pick over the shucked oysters to remove any bits of sand or shell. Serve with a lightly chilled muscadet.

2 dozen extra-small oysters
4 medium shallots
5 cups half-and-half
4 tablespoons plus 4 teaspoons butter
1/2 teaspoon hot red-pepper sauce
Salt and ground black pepper
2 tablespoons dry sherry
2 tablespoons minced flat-leaf parsley

PREPARATION: Shuck oysters over a small bowl to catch the liquor. Put oysters in another bowl, discarding the shells; set aside. Peel and mince the shallots.

COOKING: Heat half-and-half in a large saucepan until hot; do not boil. Cover and remove from heat. Heat 4 tablespoons butter in large soup kettle. Add the shallots and hot red-pepper sauce and sauté over medium heat, stirring frequently, until shallots are lightly browned, 5 to 7 minutes. Season with 1 teaspoon salt and 1/2 teaspoon pepper. Add the oysters and sauté until the edges begin to curl, 2 to 3 minutes. Stir in the sherry and the half-and-half, and strain in the oyster liquor through damp cheesecloth or a coffee filter. Adjust seasoning and heat thoroughly.

SERVING: Ladle soup into 4 warm soup bowls. Garnish each bowl with 1 teaspoon butter and 1/2 tablespoon parsley and serve immediately.

Susan Hermann Loomis
Cookbook author
Seattle, WA

SCALLOP AND SHRIMP CHOWDER

Makes 4 servings

Two different types of potatoes lend their unique characters to this soup. The starchy Idahos are used as a thickener, while red potatoes (which hold their shapes) play a traditional role.

3 ounces salt pork *or* bacon
1 medium onion
¹/₂ pound Idaho potatoes (2 medium)
¹/₂ pound red potatoes (2 medium)
¹/₂ pound medium shelled deveined shrimp
²/₃ pound bay scallops
1 teaspoon dried thyme
1 bay leaf
¹/₄ cup dry white wine
2¹/₂ cups milk
1 cup half-and-half
¹/₄ teaspoon hot red-pepper sauce
Salt and ground black pepper

PREPARATION: Remove rind from salt pork and cut into ¹/₈-inch dice. Peel and thinly slice the onion and potatoes. Rinse and pat dry the shrimp and scallops.

COOKING: Sauté salt pork in a 4-quart soup kettle over medium-high heat until crisp, about 10 minutes. Transfer salt pork to a plate lined with paper towels; set aside. Pour off all but 2 tablespoons of the drippings. Add the onions, thyme, and bay leaf, and sauté until the onions soften, about 2 minutes. Add the potatoes and sauté over high heat until they soften, about 5 minutes. Add the white wine and simmer until the wine completely reduces, about 3 minutes. Add the milk and half-and-half. Simmer until potatoes are tender, about 15 minutes. Stir in the shrimp and scallops and simmer until seafood is just cooked, about 5 minutes. Season with hot red-pepper sauce, 1 teaspoon salt, and ¹/₄ teaspoon pepper.

SERVING: Ladle soup into 4 warm bowls, and garnish with salt pork or bacon. Serve immediately.

Betsy Schultz
Food consultant
New York, NY

SEAFOOD SOUP
TAPADO

Makes 4 to 6 servings

The Caribbean coast of Guatemala has a wealth of fresh fish and coconuts. This dish, which frequently contains a wide variety of seafood, including squid, crab, shrimp, red snapper, sea bass, or mako shark, is an expression of this natural bounty. Achiote, also known as annatto, is a red-orange vegetable dye used to color dishes throughout Latin America.

2 cups Coconut Milk (recipe page 281)
1 small onion
1 medium red bell pepper
2 pounds fish fillets (red snapper, sea bass, *or* tilefish)
1 pound medium shrimp
1 tablespoon corn oil
1 teaspoon dried oregano
$1/4$ teaspoon achiote (optional)
Salt and ground black pepper
1 medium banana
1 medium tomato
3 tablespoons minced cilantro leaves

PREPARATION: Make the Coconut Milk. Peel and thinly slice the onion ($1/2$ cup). Core, seed, and cut the bell pepper into $1/4$-inch strips. Cut the fish fillets into 2-inch pieces. Peel, rinse, and devein the shrimp.

COOKING: Heat the corn oil in a large skillet. Add the onion and red pepper and sauté over medium heat until softened, about 1 minute. Add the Coconut Milk, oregano, (achiote,) $1/2$ teaspoon salt, and $1/4$ teaspoon pepper. Bring liquid to a boil and then simmer over low heat until slightly thickened, about 5 minutes. Stir in the fish and the shrimp and simmer until seafood is just cooked through, about 10 minutes.

Peel and cut the banana into 1-inch slices. Cut the tomato into 1-inch dice ($3/4$ cup) and add it to the soup along with the banana. Simmer the soup until the banana and tomato are just cooked, 5 minutes. (Can cover and refrigerate up to 4 hours.)

SERVING: Reheat the soup if made in advance. Stir in the cilantro.

Copeland Marks
Cookbook author
Brooklyn, NY

RED SNAPPER SOUP
ZUPPA DI PESCE

Makes 8 to 10 servings

This recipe uses fillets in the finished soup. Since bones impart body and flavor, this soup is best made with Fish Broth (recipe page 35). Any fish from the snapper family, rockfish, seabass, porgy, flounder, or cod can be substituted for red snapper.

2 small potatoes
2 small carrots
1 pound red snapper fillets
4 teaspoons olive oil
2 cups boiling water
1 teaspoon white-wine vinegar
Salt
2 quarts Fish Broth (recipe page 35) *or* canned chicken broth
3/4 cup Arborio *or* long-grain rice (5 ounces)
2 tablespoons minced flat-leaf parsley
1/4 teaspoon dried red-pepper flakes
Ground black pepper

PREPARATION: Peel and cut the potatoes into 1/2-inch dice. Peel and coarsely shred the carrots. Cut the fish fillets into 1/2-inch pieces.

COOKING: Heat oil in a 6-quart soup kettle. Add the diced potatoes and sauté over high heat until lightly browned, about 5 minutes. Add the shredded carrots and sauté until slightly softened, about 2 minutes longer. Add the boiling water to the soup kettle, along with the vinegar and 1 1/2 teaspoons salt. Simmer until vegetables are tender, about 10 minutes. Add the broth and the rice and simmer 15 minutes. Add the fish and simmer until fish is cooked and rice is tender, about 5 minutes longer. Remove soup kettle from heat, stir in parsley and hot red-pepper flakes, and season with salt, if necessary.

SERVING: Ladle soup into warm bowls and sprinkle with ground black pepper. Serve immediately.

Lidia Bastianich
Executive chef and co-owner
Felidia
New York, NY

SALADS

AVOCADO VINAIGRETTE

Makes 4 servings

The sharpness of the mustard vinaigrette contrasts with the smooth richness of the avocado.

Mustard Vinaigrette
1 teaspoon chopped parsley
1 teaspoon chopped chives *or*
   scallion top
1 tablespoon Dijon mustard
1 tablespoon red-wine vinegar
1 tablespoon lemon juice
Salt and pepper
¹/₂ cup olive oil

2 ripe avocados

PREPARATION: *For the vinaigrette*, chop the parsley and chives. In a small bowl, combine the mustard, vinegar, lemon juice, ¹/₄ teaspoon salt, and pepper to taste. Whisk in the oil and add the herbs. Season to taste with salt and pepper.

Mustard Vinaigrette can be made several hours ahead.

SERVING: Halve and pit the avocados, leaving the skin on. Put each half in a bowl or on a plate and fill the hollow with vinaigrette. Pass remaining vinaigrette separately.

Stephanie Lyness
Free-lance writer
New York, NY

GREEN BEAN SALAD WITH FETA-WALNUT MIMOSA

Makes 4 servings

Concentric circles in contrasting colors make a strong visual statement in this salad. It is perfect for a party buffet or an elegant picnic.

Vinaigrette
1 scallion
4 teaspoons white-wine vinegar
$^1/_4$ cup walnut *or* vegetable oil
Salt and pepper
1$^1/_4$ ounces walnut halves (about $^1/_3$ cup)

1$^1/_2$ pounds green beans
2 eggs
2$^1/_2$ ounces feta cheese (about $^1/_2$ cup crumbled)

PREPARATION: *For the vinaigrette*, mince the scallion. In a small bowl, mix the vinegar, oil, and scallion. Season to taste with salt and pepper.

Heat oven to 350°F. Put walnuts in a cake pan and toast, stirring once or twice, until lightly browned, about 7 minutes. Cool and then chop finely.

Cook beans in a large pot of boiling, salted water until crisp-tender, about 4 minutes. Rinse under cold running water and drain thoroughly. Gently pat dry.

Put eggs in a saucepan, cover with water, and bring to a simmer. Cover, remove saucepan from heat, let stand for 20 minutes, drain. Cool eggs, separate whites from yolks, and chop separately into fine dice. Recipe can be made to this point several hours ahead.

SERVING: Arrange beans on a round serving platter in a circular fashion with the ends meeting in the center. Whisk vinaigrette and spoon it evenly over the beans. Crumble the feta cheese and sprinkle it in the center of the plate. Sprinkle chopped walnuts in a circle around the cheese. Sprinkle chopped egg yolks in a circle around walnuts; then sprinkle chopped egg whites in a circle around the yolks, covering all but the outer ends of the beans. Serve at room temperature.

Faye Levy
Cookbook author
Santa Monica, CA

SPICY BROCCOLI SALAD

Makes 12 servings

Although the broccoli for this salad can be cooked in advance, do not add the dressing until shortly before serving. The acid in the dressing can dull the bright green color of the vegetable.

3 pounds broccoli (about 3 bunches)
Salt and pepper

Dressing
$1/3$ cup sherry wine vinegar
$1^1/2$ tablespoons soy sauce
1 tablespoon Dijon mustard
$1/2$ cup olive oil
1 small, fresh hot green chile pepper

$1/4$ teaspoon red pepper flakes

PREPARATION: Trim and peel broccoli stems and cut into thin slices on an angle. Cut broccoli heads into small florets. Cook florets and stems in boiling, salted water until tender, about 4 minutes. Drain. Season with salt and pepper.

For the dressing, in a small bowl, stir together the vinegar, soy sauce, and mustard. Slowly whisk in the oil. Seed and mince chile pepper and add it to the dressing. Broccoli and dressing can be prepared a day ahead and stored separately in the refrigerator.

SERVING: Bring dressing and broccoli to room temperature. Toss the broccoli with the dressing and sprinkle with red pepper flakes.

Florence Fabricant
Food columnist
New York Times
New York, NY

RED CABBAGE SALAD WITH BACON AND GOAT CHEESE

Makes 6 servings

Crimson cabbage, crunchy bacon, and tangy goat cheese join forces to make an exceptional salad that is great as a first course or as a main course for lunch. A hot bacon dressing lightly wilts and softens the cabbage, and the goat cheese is sprinkled on the top right before serving so that it is not discolored by the vinegar.

$^1/_2$ **small head red cabbage (about 1 pound)**
1 pound sliced bacon

Dressing
2 medium garlic cloves
$^1/_2$ **cup vegetable oil**
$^1/_4$ **cup red-wine vinegar**
Salt and ground black pepper
5$^1/_2$ ounces fresh goat cheese, American or imported

PREPARATION: Remove and discard the tough outer leaves and core of the cabbage. Shred the cabbage finely using a large, sharp knife or the thin or medium slicing blade of a food processor. Transfer the shredded cabbage to a large bowl; set aside

COOKING: Sauté the bacon slices in a large skillet over low heat until crisp and browned, about 7 minutes; drain the slices on paper towels. Carefully transfer $^1/_4$ cup of the bacon fat to a small heatproof bowl or heatproof jar; set aside at room temperature to cool. Cool and discard the remaining fat.

For the dressing, peel and mince the garlic cloves. In a medium bowl whisk the minced garlic into the reserved bacon fat with the vegetable oil, red-wine vinegar, $^1/_2$ teaspoon salt, and $^1/_4$ teaspoon pepper. (Can cover and separately refrigerate cabbage, bacon, and dressing overnight. Can loosely cover bacon and store at room temperature.)

SERVING: Bring cabbage and bacon slices to room temperature, if refrigerated. Warm the dressing in a small saucepan over medium heat. Crumble the bacon over the cabbage, add the warm dressing, and toss well. Adjust seasoning to taste.

Transfer the tossed salad to six individual salad plates. Crumble the goat cheese evenly over each plate and serve immediately.

Marlene Sorosky
Cookbook author
Towson, MD

GOLDSBORO COLESLAW

Makes 8 servings

This unusual coleslaw is made without vinegar or sugar and has a simple, fresh taste that is a foil for the flavor of barbecued meat.

$^1/_2$ **medium cabbage (about
   1 pound)**
1 medium onion
1 cup mayonnaise
Salt and ground black pepper

PREPARATION: Remove the tough outer leaves from cabbage. Shred and mince the cabbage (4 cups) and transfer to a mixing bowl. Peel and mince the onion ($^2/_3$ cup). Put the onion and mayonnaise in a bowl and season to taste with salt and pepper. Stir well and adjust seasoning. (Can cover and refrigerate overnight.)

Craig Claiborne
Food critic and cookbook author
East Hampton, NY

GRILLED EGGPLANT SALAD

Makes 4 servings

Typically Mediterranean ingredients such as roasted red peppers, black olives, and fresh basil add great color to this salad. The recipe calls for Japanese eggplant, distinguished by their long, narrow shapes.

Vinaigrette
2 shallots
1 tablespoon balsamic vinegar
1 tablespoon red-wine vinegar
5 tablespoons extra-virgin olive oil
Salt and pepper

1 red pepper
2 pounds Japanese eggplant
4 slices crusty, country-style bread
¹/₂ cup olive oil
3 ounces black Niçoise olives (about 24)
¹/₄ cup shredded basil leaves
1 clove garlic

PREPARATION: *For the vinaigrette*, mince the shallots. In a bowl, combine the shallots and vinegars and let stand for 10 minutes. Gradually whisk in the olive oil and season to taste with salt and pepper. Set aside. Roast the red pepper over a gas flame, under the broiler, or on the grill until skin blackens and blisters. Cool, remove skin, seed, and coarsely chop pepper. Recipe can be made to this point several hours ahead.

COOKING AND SERVING: Cut the eggplant lengthwise into ¹/₄-inch-thick slices. Brush both sides of the sliced eggplant and the bread with olive oil; set bread aside. Grill the eggplant over a hot fire until browned on each side, about 7 minutes. Arrange the eggplant on a serving platter. Drizzle with the vinaigrette and garnish with the roasted red pepper, black olives, and basil. Grill the bread on both sides until crisp, about 4 minutes total. Remove from grill and immediately rub with the garlic. Serve the grilled bread with the salad.

Alice Waters
Owner
Chez Panisse and Cafe Fanny
Berkeley, CA
Therese Shere
Vegetable grower
Sonoma County, CA

FRENCH POTATO AND BEET SALAD

Makes 4 servings

Fresh beets and the sharp herbal vinaigrette enliven this colorful salad which is perfect for late spring or summer.

Vinaigrette
3 tablespoons herb vinegar *or* white-wine vinegar
Salt and pepper
$1/2$ cup mild olive *or* vegetable oil

4 medium beets (about $1/2$ pounds including leaves)
2 scallions
2 pounds small, red potatoes, as uniform in size as possible
2 tablespoons dry white wine
1 tablespoon herb vinegar *or* white-wine vinegar
1 tablespoon mild olive *or* vegetable oil
Salt and pepper
2 tablespoons chopped fresh parsley

PREPARATION: *For the vinaigrette*, in a small bowl, combine the vinegar with salt and pepper to taste. Gradually whisk in the oil; set aside.

Remove leaves from beets, leaving a $1/2$-inch stem. Mince the scallions. Put beets in a saucepan with enough water to cover and bring to a boil. Cover, reduce heat to low, and cook until just tender, about 35 minutes. Drain and cool. Peel and cut the beets into $3/8$-inch dice; set aside.

Put unpeeled potatoes in a large saucepan with cold, salted water to cover and bring to a boil. Cover and boil until potatoes are just tender, about 25 minutes. Do not overcook. Drain. While still hot, set potatoes on a cutting board and use a paring knife to peel. Cut the potatoes into $3/8$-inch dice and put in a large bowl.

In a small bowl whisk together the wine, vinegar, and oil, with salt and pepper to taste. Pour mixture over the potatoes; toss until thoroughly mixed. Add the scallions and parsley and cool to room temperature. Rewhisk the vinaigrette and add $1/2$ cup to potato mixture, tossing gently. Ingredients can be prepared to this point one day ahead, covered, and refrigerated.

SERVING: Bring vegetables to room temperature if made ahead. Adjust seasoning to taste. Add beets to the potato salad, with remaining vinaigrette. Serve at room temperature.

Faye Levy
Cookbook author
Santa Monica, CA

GOLDSBORO POTATO SALAD

Makes 8 servings

Craig Claiborne notes that many Southern restaurants use Hellman's mayonnaise for this salad, as well as for the Goldsboro Coleslaw (recipe page 48).

**5 medium potatoes (about
   1³/₄ pounds)**
3 eggs
1 small red onion
1 small dill pickle
1 cup mayonnaise

PREPARATION AND COOKING: Put the potatoes in a large saucepan with cold water to cover, bring to a boil and cook until just tender, about 20 minutes. Drain and cool. Put eggs in a small saucepan, cover with water, and bring to a simmer. Remove from heat, cover, and set aside 15 minutes. Drain and cool. Peel and chop onion (¹/₂ cup) and pickle (¹/₄ cup). Peel and cut potatoes into ¹/₂-inch cubes. Peel and coarsely chop eggs. Put potatoes, eggs, onion, and pickle in a bowl. Add the mayonnaise and toss until combined. (Can cover and refrigerate overnight)

Craig Claiborne
Food critic and cookbook author
East Hampton, NY

SOUTHWEST VEGETABLE SALAD

Makes 8 servings

Cucumber can be substituted for chayote, and sliced water chestnuts can replace the jicama.

Salad

3 ounces shelled pine nuts (¹/₃ cup)

4 blue or yellow corn tortillas (6-inch diameter)

3 cups peanut oil *or* vegetable oil

1 cup packed lettuce leaves such as oak leaf or bibb (optional)

2 medium carrots

1 medium yellow bell pepper

1 medium red bell pepper

1 small jicama (about 7 ounces)

1 medium chayote squash (about 9 ounces)

1 medium zucchini

Herb Vinaigrette

³/₄ teaspoon minced winter savory or ¹/₄ teaspoon dried

³/₄ teaspoon minced tarragon or ¹/₄ teaspoon dried

1 tablespoon minced cilantro *or* basil, *or* 1 teaspoon dried basil

1 teaspoon dry mustard

¹/₃ cup red-wine vinegar

²/₃ cup safflower oil

Salt and ground white pepper

PREPARATION AND COOKING: *For the salad*, adjust oven rack to middle position and heat oven to 300°F. Spread pine nuts in a pan and toast, stirring once or twice, until golden, 8 to 10 minutes; set aside. Cut the tortillas into ¹/₄-inch julienne strips and set aside for 1 hour or as long as 8 hours to dry. Heat oil in a saucepan to 350°F. Fry tortillas until golden, 1 to 2 minutes. Drain and set aside. (Can cover and set aside overnight.) (Rinse and spin lettuce dry; reserve.) Bring 2 cups water to boil in a saucepan. Peel and cut carrots into ¹/₄-inch julienne strips. Simmer carrots until just tender, about 2 minutes. Drain and refresh under cold water; drain. Stem, seed, and cut bell peppers into ¹/₄-inch julienne strips. Peel and cut jicama, chayote, and zucchini into ¹/₄-inch julienne strips.

For the vinaigrette, whisk the first 5 ingredients in a bowl. Gradually whisk in oil. Season with salt and pepper.

SERVING: Toss vegetables with dressing. Top with tortillas. Sprinkle with pine nuts and garnish with lettuce.

Anne Lindsay Greer
Cookbook author
Dallas, TX

WINTER GREENS WITH BLUE-CHÈVRE DRESSING

Makes 8 servings

Blue-veined versions of this most popular of cheeses are showing up in stores around the country. The best of them have ordinary chèvres' tangy flavor, along with a moister texture and a spectacular blue-veined taste — splendid after-dinner cheeses. The creamy dressing used in the recipe below employs a generous amount of blue chèvre, served over a gutsy salad of winter greens. If you can't find blue chèvre, try combining three ounces of ordinary goat cheese pureed into the dressing and three ounces of good blue cheese crumbled in at the end.

1 bunch watercress
1 head escarole
1 large fennel bulb
$^1/_4$ head red cabbage
1 red onion

Blue-Chèvre Dressing
$^1/_4$ cup red-wine vinegar
1$^1/_2$ tablespoons Dijon mustard
2 egg yolks
Salt and pepper
6 ounces blue-veined chèvre
$^3/_4$ cup olive oil
$^3/_4$ cup vegetable oil

PREPARATION: Trim, wash, and gently dry the watercress and escarole. Trim the fennel bulb. Cut the fennel bulb and the cabbage into thin julienne strips. Cut the onion into thin slices and separate into rings.

For the dressing, in a food processor, combine the vinegar, mustard, egg yolks, 1 teaspoon pepper, and $^1/_2$ the chèvre and process until smooth. With the machine running, slowly add the oils in a thin, steady stream. Season to taste with salt and pepper and transfer to a bowl. Crumble the remaining chèvre and stir into the dressing. Cover and refrigerate.

Recipe can be made to this point seven hours ahead.

SERVING: Toss the greens with dressing and garnish with slices of red onion separated into rings.

Michael McLaughlin
Free-lance writer
Brooklyn, NY

SAUTEED LAMB AND MUSHROOM SALAD
WITH WARM BALSAMIC VINAIGRETTE

Makes 4 servings

To give the salad a more formal presentation than the recipe directs, set the sautéed lamb medallions aside while preparing the dressing. Dip medallions briefly in the dressing, then transfer dressed greens to dinner plates. Slice and arrange lamb on top of the salad.

**6 cups mixed salad greens
(arugula or watercress,
radicchio or red-leaf lettuce,
and curly endive)**
**4 loin lamb chops (about
1³/₄ pounds)**
¹/₂ pounds mushrooms
2 medium shallots
7 tablespoons olive oil
Salt and ground black pepper
1 tablespoon butter
3 tablespoons balsamic vinegar
**2 tablespoons minced fresh
chives or scallions**
1 tablespoon capers

PREPARATION: Rinse and thoroughly dry the salad greens, tear them into bite-size pieces, and put them in a salad bowl. Trim and bone the lamb chops. Split the boneless medallions horizontally, and pound them slightly. Trim and thinly slice the mushrooms. Slice the shallots.

COOKING AND SERVING: Heat 1 tablespoon of oil in a large skillet until hot but not smoking. Sprinkle lamb medallions with salt and pepper to taste. Sauté about 3 minutes. Turn and cook 2 minutes longer. Lamb should be browned and medium-rare in center. Transfer lamb to the salad bowl. Immediately add the butter, mushrooms, and shallots to the skillet. Sauté until mushrooms have released their liquid, about 4 minutes. Add 2 tablespoons vinegar to the skillet and remove from heat. Stir in the remaining 6 tablespoons oil. Toss warm mushroom mixture with greens, lamb, chives, capers, and remaining tablespoon of vinegar. Season to taste with salt and pepper, and serve immediately.

Pam Parseghian
Free-lance writer
New York, NY

PORK TENDERLOIN SALAD

Makes 4 servings

Oriental seasonings lend their sprightly flavors to this warm, main-dish salad.

Honey-Ginger Dressing
1 teaspoon minced ginger
3 tablespoons balsamic *or* red
 wine vinegar
1 teaspoon Dijon mustard
¼ cup peanut *or* vegetable oil
2 teaspoons honey
Salt and pepper

1 pound pork tenderloin
1 clove garlic
2 teaspoons soy sauce
1 tablespoon Oriental
 sesame oil
Ground black pepper
1 small head iceberg lettuce
1 red bell pepper
5 scallions
1 rib celery

PREPARATION: *For the dressing*, whisk together the ginger, vinegar, mustard, oil, and honey in a bowl. Season to taste with salt and pepper. Dressing can be made 1 day ahead.

With a cleaver or side of a large chef's knife, pound the pork to ½-inch thickness. Mince the garlic. Rub the meat with the garlic, soy sauce, sesame oil, and ¼ teaspoon black pepper. Shred the lettuce. Seed and cut the pepper into thin strips. Slice the scallions into thin rings. Cut celery diagonally into thin slices. Recipe can be made to this point several hours ahead.

COOKING AND SERVING: Heat the broiler. Set the pork on a rack about 5 inches from heat source and cook, turning once, until browned and just cooked through, 6 to 8 minutes. Transfer meat to a plate and let rest for 5 minutes. Pour juices remaining in pan into the dressing. Arrange shredded lettuce on a serving platter. Cut pork across the grain into thin slices and arrange over the lettuce. Scatter the red pepper, scallions, and celery around the meat and drizzle with the dressing. Serve immediately.

Elizabeth Riely
Free-lance writer
Newton Centre, MA
Brooke Dojny
Free-lance writer
Westport, CT

BREAD, ROLLS, AND PIZZA

PAIN AUX NOIX
WHOLE-WHEAT WALNUT BREAD

Makes 1 large loaf

A round loaf somehow conveys an agreeable country air, though baking the bread in the usual brick shape makes slicing easier.

3 cups whole-wheat flour
1 cup all-purpose flour plus
   more if needed
2¹/₂ teaspoons salt
1³/₄ cups lukewarm water
1 tablespoon honey
2 tablespoons dry yeast
1¹/₄ cups walnuts
1 egg

PREPARATION: In a large bowl, combine the flours and 1¹/₂ teaspoons of the salt. Make a well in the center and pour in 1 cup of the lukewarm water. Add the honey and the yeast to the well and set bowl aside until the yeast is dissolved and starts to foam, about 5 minutes. Add the remaining ³/₄ cup water and gradually draw in the wall of flour with your fingers to make a smooth dough. If the dough is too soft and sticky, work in additional flour, 1 tablespoon at a time. Turn dough onto a floured work surface and knead until smooth and elastic, about 8 minutes, adding more flour if needed to prevent sticking.

Brush a large bowl with oil. Put dough in prepared bowl and turn to coat surface with oil. Cover with a damp cloth and let rise in a warm place until doubled in size, about 1¹/₂ hours. Meanwhile, break walnuts into pieces and butter a baking sheet.

Punch dough down and knead again, working in walnut pieces. Shape dough into a round loaf and put on prepared baking sheet. Cover loosely with damp cloth and allow to rise again until dough is doubled in size, about 40 minutes.

COOKING: Heat oven to 425°F. Beat egg with remaining teaspoon salt and brush over the dough. With a small, sharp knife, cut a lattice pattern about ¹/₄ inch deep on the top of the bread dough. Bake in preheated oven until well browned, about 15 minutes. Lower heat to 375°F and continue baking until the loaf sounds hollow when tapped on the bottom, about 40 minutes. Cool bread on a rack.

Bread can be made several hours ahead, or it can be frozen and freshened by heating in a 325°F oven for 10 minutes.

Anne Willan
Founder
La Varenne Ecole de Cuisine
Paris, France

PARMESAN AND BLACK-PEPPER BREAD

Makes 3 loaves

Parmesan cheese, oregano, and black pepper distinguish these loaves, and their special rustic look comes from wrapping a cigar-shaped core of dough with thin, narrow strips of dough. When baked, the central core swells around the strips and the cheese gives the crust a rich brown color.

1 package dry active yeast
1 teaspoon sugar
1^1/$_3$ cups warm (110°F) water
6 ounces Parmigiano-Reggiano (Parmesan) cheese (1^1/$_2$ cups, grated)
3^1/$_2$ to 3^3/$_4$ cups bread flour *or* unbleached all-purpose flour
^{3}/$_4$ teaspoon salt
2 tablespoons olive oil
Vegetable shortening
1^1/$_2$ teaspoons dried oregano
^{3}/$_8$ teaspoon ground black pepper
1 egg white

PREPARATION: Mix yeast with sugar and ^{2}/$_3$ cup warm water in a cup and set aside for 10 minutes. Grate the cheese, measure ^{1}/$_2$ cup, and set the remaining 1 cup aside. Put 3^1/$_2$ cups flour, ^{1}/$_2$ cup cheese, salt, and oil in the workbowl of a food processor fitted with the metal blade. Process, adding remaining ^{2}/$_3$ cup warm water in a thin stream. Stir yeast mixture well, add it to the machine, and process until the dough forms a soft, moist ball, adding flour by tablespoons if dough seems wet. Transfer dough to large, wet mixing bowl. Cover with plastic wrap and set aside until tripled in size, about 1^1/$_2$ to 2 hours. Or, rinse inside of a zipper-lock plastic bag, add dough, press out air, seal, and refrigerate overnight.

Generously coat a curved metal French bread pan or baking sheet with vegetable shortening; set aside. Remove dough from bowl (or bag) without kneading and cut it into three even pieces. Remove and reserve ^{1}/$_3$ dough from each piece.

To shape loaves, sprinkle 1 tablespoon cheese on work surface. Roll out 1 large piece of dough to a 12- by 8-inch rectangle, turning to coat both sides evenly with cheese. Sprinkle 1^1/$_2$ tablespoons cheese, ^{1}/$_2$ teaspoon oregano, and ^{1}/$_8$ teaspoon pepper evenly over top of dough. Fold into thirds lengthwise to make a long, thin rectangle. Pinch long edges together tightly to form a cigar-shaped loaf. For dough strips, sprinkle work surface with 1 tablespoon cheese. Roll out the small piece of dough to 12- by 3-inch rectangle and cut in half to form two strips. With cheese side facing down, attach one strip of dough at one end of the shaped loaf, then wrap it around the dough clockwise. Attach the second strip where the first ended and wrap it counterclockwise to form a crisscross or diamond pattern

PARMESAN AND BLACK-PEPPER BREAD

(continued)

around the shaped loaf. Pinch the dough strips at ends to fasten securely. Put each loaf, seam side down, in the pan or on baking sheet. Repeat steps to form second and third loaves. Cover all three loaves with a dry towel and set aside at room temperature until they double in size, about 1½ to 2 hours, or refrigerate up to 4 hours.

COOKING: Adjust oven rack to low position and heat oven to 425°F. Beat egg white until foamy. Use a soft, damp pastry brush to glaze tops of risen loaves with beaten egg white. Gently press 1 tablespoon cheese onto top of each loaf. Bake until golden brown, about 20 to 25 minutes. While still hot, loosen loaves from bread pan or baking sheet with a metal spatula. Cool to room temperature.

Jane Freiman
Food columnist and cookbook author
New York, NY

ROSEMARY BREADSTICKS

Makes about 3 dozen

These savory breadsticks, *grissini* in Italian, are quite unlike any you can find in a market.

Sponge

1/2 cup bread flour *or* unbleached all-purpose flour
3/4 teaspoon dry active yeast
1/3 cup warm water (about 110°F)

Dough

2/3 to 3/4 cup bread flour *or* unbleached all-purpose flour
1/2 cup plain cake flour
3/4 teaspoon salt
2 to 3 tablespoons warm water
2 tablespoons olive oil
1 tablespoon crushed, dried rosemary

PREPARATION: *For the sponge*, put flour in a mixing bowl. Add yeast and water and stir to form a smooth paste. Cover tightly with plastic wrap and set aside until mixture doubles, about 2 hours. (Can stir down, cover, and refrigerate overnight.)

For the dough, put 2/3 cup flour, cake flour, salt, 2 tablespoons warm water, oil, and rosemary into the workbowl of a food processor fitted with the metal blade. Process to thoroughly mix. Stir yeast mixture, add to machine, and process until mixture forms a soft ball. If ball does not form, add more water by tablespoons. Transfer dough to a large, wet bowl. Cover tightly with plastic wrap and let dough rise until tripled in volume, about 2 1/2 hours. Punch dough down and refrigerate in plastic wrap for 2 hours before cutting breadsticks. (Or, rinse the inside of a zipper-lock plastic bag, add dough, press out air, seal, and refrigerate up to 2 days.)

Without kneading, press air out of dough and divide into two pieces. On a lightly floured work surface, roll each piece of the dough into a 7- by 9-inch rectangle. Using the plain wheel of a ravioli cutter, cut dough lengthwise into 1/4-inch-wide strips. Roll strips between hands to round edges without twisting the dough. Transfer the strips to a baking sheet and repeat process.

COOKING: Adjust oven rack to middle position and heat oven to 400°F. Bake until breadsticks are crisp and brown, about 12 minutes. Cool to room temperature before serving.

Jane Freiman
Food columnist and cookbook author
New York, NY

COACH HOUSE CORN STICKS

Makes 28 corn sticks

The Coach House restaurant in New York City has been serving these popular corn sticks for over forty years.

**1 cup plus 2 tablespoons
  vegetable shortening**
4 cups yellow cornmeal
3 cups all-purpose flour
4 tablespoons sugar
2 tablespoons baking powder
1¼ teaspoons salt
4 large eggs
3 cups milk

PREPARATION: Heat 1 cup of shortening in a saucepan until softened but not fully melted. Mix cornmeal, flour, sugar, baking powder, and salt in a bowl. Stir in eggs, one at a time. Stir in milk, add the shortening, and mix well. Cover and refrigerate 1 hour. (Can refrigerate overnight.)

COOKING: Adjust oven rack to low position and heat oven to 500°F. Coat 2 corn stick pans (each with seven 5½- by 1½-inch molds) generously with shortening. Heat pans in oven until very hot, about 5 minutes. Using a pastry bag without a tip, quickly pipe batter into the hot molds. Bake until golden, about 10 minutes. Repeat with remaining batter.

Marion Cunningham
Cookbook author
San Francisco, CA

CORN CRISPS

Makes 20 crisps

These crackers are akin to thin, crisp cornbread. They become slightly sweet when brushed with butter. They are the perfect complement for a thick, hearty chowder.

5 tablespoons butter
$^1/_2$ cup white cornmeal
$^1/_2$ cup all-purpose flour
$^1/_4$ teaspoon salt
$1^1/_2$ teaspoons sugar
$1^1/_2$ teaspoons baking powder
1 egg
$^3/_4$ cup milk

PREPARATION: Melt the butter and lightly brush it over 2 sheets of parchment paper. Line 2 baking sheets with the paper, buttered side up. Set remaining butter aside. Adjust oven racks to middle position and heat oven to 425°F. Sift cornmeal with the flour, salt, sugar, and baking powder into a large bowl. Beat egg lightly with milk and stir into dry ingredients until batter is lump-free. Stir in $2^1/_2$ tablespoons melted butter.

COOKING AND SERVING: Drop tablespoons of the batter 5 inches apart onto the parchment paper. With the back of a spoon, spread batter into 4-inch disks, leaving a 1-inch margin between each crisp. Bake until browned, 10 to 12 minutes. Brush crisps with the remaining melted butter and cool on wire rack. (Can store 1 week in an airtight container.)

Larry Forgione
Chef/owner
An American Place restaurant
New York, NY

BAKING POWDER BISCUITS

Makes 12 biscuits

Unlike yeast doughs, biscuits require only very brief kneading. These biscuits have a tender crust; if you like them crustier, set them 1 inch apart in the pan.

$^1/_2$ **cup plus 1 tablespoon**
   vegetable shortening
2 cups all-purpose flour
$^1/_2$ **teaspoon salt**
4 teaspoons baking powder
$^1/_2$ **teaspoon cream of tartar**
1 tablespoon sugar
$^2/_3$ **cup milk**

PREPARATION AND COOKING: Adjust oven rack to low position and heat oven to 425°F. Use 1 tablespoon shortening to coat two 8-inch cake pans. Mix flour, salt, baking powder, cream of tartar, and sugar in a bowl. Work remaining shortening into flour with 2 knives or a pastry blender until mixture resembles coarse meal. Add milk; stir just until dough forms a ball. Turn dough onto a lightly floured surface and knead briefly until no longer sticky. Roll dough $^3/_4$ inch thick and cut into rounds with a 2-inch cookie cutter. Put biscuits in pans so they touch one another. Bake until golden and risen to twice their original height, 15-20 minutes.

Marion Cunningham
Cookbook author
San Francisco, CA

BAKING POWDER BISCUITS WITH ONIONS AND SHALLOTS

Makes 16 biscuits

The sautéed onion and shallot add a sweet and savory flavor to these biscuits, which are in constant demand at Rocco's restaurant in Boston.

1 medium onion
1 small shallot
11 tablespoons chilled butter
1 cup cold milk
2 cups all-purpose flour
1 cup plain cake flour
1 tablespoon baking powder
Salt

PREPARATION: Line a baking sheet with parchment or wax paper. Peel and mince onion and shallot. Heat 1 tablespoon butter in a skillet. Add onion and shallot, and sauté until softened, 5 minutes. Cool mixture and stir in milk; set aside. Mix flours, baking powder, and 1 teaspoon salt in a bowl, or in the workbowl of a food processor fitted with the metal blade. Cut 9 tablespoons butter into $1/2$-inch pieces and work butter into the dry ingredients with your fingertips, or pulse, until mixture resembles coarse meal. Stir or pulse in the milk mixture until the dough just holds together. Transfer dough to a lightly floured surface and knead 10 times.

COOKING: Adjust oven rack to middle position and heat oven to 400°F. Roll dough $3/4$ inch thick, cut into $1^1/2$-inch squares, and put 1 inch apart on baking sheet. Melt and brush remaining butter on top of the biscuits. Bake until golden brown, about 18 minutes. Serve warm.

Diane Boltz
Pastry chef
Rocco's
Boston, MA

BUTTER ROLLS

Makes 18 rolls

These tender rolls have a rich, buttery flavor. You can vary them by brushing the tops with egg glaze and sprinkling them with poppy or sesame seeds.

1¼ cups milk
6 tablespoons softened butter
1 teaspoon sugar
1 teaspoon dry active yeast
2 teaspoons salt
1 egg yolk plus 1 egg
3½ to 4 cups all-purpose flour

PREPARATION: Heat milk in a small saucepan until lukewarm; transfer it to a large bowl. Stir in 5 tablespoons of butter, the sugar, yeast, and salt. Stir egg yolk and 2 cups flour into the milk mixture, then stir in another cup of flour to form soft dough. Turn onto a lightly floured surface and knead for 2 minutes, adding flour by tablespoons if dough seems sticky. Let rest for 10 minutes. Resume kneading until dough is smooth and elastic, about 8 minutes. Put dough in a large bowl coated with ½ tablespoon butter. Cover the bowl with plastic wrap and let dough rise in a warm place until doubled in bulk, about 2 hours.

Use remaining butter to coat a large baking sheet. Punch down dough and cut it into 18 pieces about the size of golf balls. Roll each piece between your hands to form a smooth ball. Put dough balls about 1 inch apart on baking sheet. Loosely cover baking sheet with plastic wrap and let rise in a warm place until doubled in bulk, about 2 hours.

COOKING: Adjust oven rack to low position and heat oven to 350°F. Mix the egg with 1 tablespoon of water. Brush the tops of the risen rolls with the egg wash and bake until the tops of rolls are lightly browned, 20-30 minutes. Transfer to a wire rack and cool rolls slightly before serving.

Marion Cunningham
Cookbook author
San Francisco, CA

DINNER ROLL DOUGH

Makes enough dough for 2 dozen rolls

Slightly sweeter and fluffier than that used for Parker House Rolls, this dough is good for making at least eight different shapes (recipes follow.)

$1^{1}/_{4}$ **cups milk**
$^{1}/_{3}$ **cup sugar**
2 teaspoons salt
$4^{1}/_{2}$ **tablespoons softened butter**
1 teaspoon dry active yeast
1 egg
$3^{1}/_{2}$ **to** $4^{1}/_{2}$ **cups all-purpose flour**

PREPARATION: Heat milk in a saucepan until lukewarm and transfer it to a large bowl. Stir in sugar, salt, 4 tablespoons butter, and yeast. Let stand for 5 minutes. Stir in egg and gradually stir in $3^{1}/_{2}$ cups flour. Add up to 1 cup more flour as necessary until dough is no longer sticky. Turn dough onto lightly floured surface and knead until smooth, 6-8 minutes. Put dough in a large bowl coated with butter. Cover with plastic and let rise in a warm place until doubled in bulk, about $1^{1}/_{2}$ hours. Punch dough down and form into desired shapes.

BUTTERFLY ROLLS

Makes 20 rolls

Dinner Roll Dough (recipe above)
5 tablespoons softened butter

PREPARATION: Make Dinner Roll Dough and turn it onto a floured surface. Melt 4 tablespoons butter; use remaining butter to coat two baking sheets. Cut dough in half; cover and set one half aside. Roll dough into a 14- by 5-inch rectangle, $^{1}/_{4}$ inch thick. Brush with melted butter. Arrange rectangle with a long side facing you and roll up the dough tightly. Cut dough crosswise into ten $1^{1}/_{4}$- to $1^{1}/_{2}$-inch pieces. Press a chopstick or blunt edge of a knife blade across the center of each roll, making an indentation. Put rolls $1^{1}/_{2}$ inches apart on baking sheets and brush with melted butter. Loosely cover rolls with plastic wrap and let rise until doubled in bulk, about 2 hours.

COOKING: Adjust oven rack to low position and heat oven to 400°F. Bake until lightly browned, about 20 minutes. Transfer to a wire rack and cool slightly before serving.

CLOTHESPINS

Makes 28 rolls

Dinner Roll Dough (recipe page 67)
6 tablespoons softened butter

PREPARATION: Make Dinner Roll Dough and turn it onto a floured surface. Melt 5 tablespoons butter in a small saucepan; set aside. Brush 28 round wooden clothespins with melted butter; coat 2 large baking sheets with remaining softened butter. Cut dough in half; cover and set one half aside. Roll dough into a 14- by 5-inch rectangle, $1/4$ inch thick; cut into fourteen 2- by $2^1/2$-inch pieces. Roll each piece into a 10-inch long, $1/2$-inch thick rope. Starting at the knob end of the clothespin, spiral a rope around each with edges of dough overlapping. Tuck ends under to prevent unwrapping.

Repeat for remaining rolls. Put rolls $1^1/2$ inches apart on baking sheets; brush with melted butter. Cover with plastic wrap and let rise until doubled in bulk, about 2 hours.

COOKING: Adjust oven rack to low position and heat oven to 400°F. Bake until lightly browned, about 15 to 20 minutes. Transfer to a wire rack, cool slightly, and remove before serving.

CLOVER-LEAF ROLLS

Makes 2 dozen rolls

Dinner Roll Dough (recipe page 67)
6 tablespoons softened butter

PREPARATION: Make Dinner Roll Dough and turn onto a floured surface. Melt 4 tablespoons butter; set aside. Use remaining butter to coat twenty-four 2½-inch muffin cups. Cut dough into quarters. Roll each into a rope 14 by 1½ inches thick. Cut ropes into eighteen ¾-inch long pieces. Roll each between cupped hands to form a ball. Dip 3 balls in melted butter and put side by side in a muffin cup. Repeat with remaining dough. Loosely cover with plastic wrap and let rise until doubled in bulk, about 1½ hours.

COOKING: Adjust oven rack to low position and heat oven to 400°F. Bake until lightly browned, about 15 minutes. Transfer rolls to a wire rack and cool slightly before serving.

CRESCENTS

Makes 2 dozen rolls

Dinner Roll Dough (recipe page 67)
5 tablespoons softened butter

PREPARATION: Make Dinner Roll Dough; turn onto a floured surface. Melt 4 tablespoons butter; use remaining butter to coat 2 baking sheets. Cut dough in half; cover and set half aside. Roll dough into a 12-inch circle, ⅛ inch thick. Brush with melted butter. Cut circle into quarters; cut each quarter into 3 wedges. Arrange 1 wedge of dough with the wide end facing you; roll it up tightly. Tuck point of wedge underneath roll and curve ends toward one another to form a crescent shape. Put rolls about 1 inch apart on baking sheets and brush with melted butter. Cover with plastic wrap, and let rise until doubled in bulk, about 1½ hours.

COOKING: Adjust oven rack to low position and heat oven to 400°F. Bake until lightly browned, about 10-12 minutes. Transfer to a wire rack and cool slightly before serving.

CROOKED MILES

Makes 14 rolls

Dinner Roll Dough (recipe page 67)
5 tablespoons softened butter

PREPARATION: Make Dinner Roll Dough and turn it onto a floured surface. Melt 4 tablespoons butter in a small saucepan; set aside. Use remaining butter to coat two large baking sheets; set aside. Cut dough in half; cover and set one half aside. Roll dough into a 14- by 5-inch rectangle, $^{1}/_{4}$ inch thick. Cut into seven 5- by 2-inch pieces. Roll each piece into a 16-inch long and $^{1}/_{2}$-inch thick rope. Tie a loose knot at one end of rope to form a 2-inch circle; wrap remaining rope around the circle to form a wreath. Tuck loose end under the wreath. Repeat for remaining rolls. Put rolls $1^{1}/_{2}$ inches apart on baking sheets; brush with melted butter. Cover with plastic wrap and let rise until doubled in bulk, about 2 hours.

COOKING: Adjust oven rack to low position and heat oven to 400°F. Bake until lightly browned, about 20 minutes. Transfer to a wire rack and cool slightly before serving.

FAN-TANS

Makes 2 dozen rolls

Dinner Roll Dough (recipe page 67)
6 tablespoons softened butter

PREPARATION: Make Dinner Roll Dough and turn it onto a floured surface. Melt 4 tablespoons butter in a small saucepan; set aside. Use remaining butter to coat twenty-four $2^{1}/_{2}$-inch muffin cups. Cut dough in half. Roll one half into an 18- by 11-inch rectangle, $^{1}/_{8}$ inch thick. Brush with melted butter and cut into seven 18- by $1^{1}/_{2}$-inch strips. Stack strips and cut into twelve $1^{1}/_{2}$-inch squares. Put each stack, cut end up, into muffin cup. Cover with plastic wrap and let rise for 10 minutes.

COOKING: Adjust oven rack to low position and heat oven to 400°F. Bake until lightly browned, about 15-20 minutes. Transfer to a wire rack and cool slightly before serving.

KNOTS

Makes 28 rolls

Dinner Roll Dough (recipe page 67)
5 tablespoons softened butter

PREPARATION: Make Dinner Roll Dough and turn onto a floured surface. Melt 4 tablespoons butter; use remaining butter to coat two baking sheets. Cut dough in half; cover and set one half aside. Roll dough into a 14- by 5-inch rectangle, about $1/4$-inch thick. Cut rectangle into fourteen 2- by $2^1/2$-inch pieces. Roll each piece into a rope 10 inches long and $1/2$ inch thick. Tie each rope into a loose knot. Repeat for remaining Knots. Put rolls $1^1/2$ inches apart on baking sheets; brush with melted butter. Cover with plastic wrap and let rise until doubled in bulk, about 2 hours.

COOKING: Adjust oven rack to low position and heat oven to 400°F. Bake until rolls are lightly browned, about 20 minutes. Transfer to a wire rack and cool slightly before serving.

Marion Cunningham
Cookbook author
San Francisco, CA

WHOLE WHEAT SCONES

Makes 16 scones

Scones are closely related to biscuits, but they have more character and texture, especially when they are made with whole wheat flour. These scones must be served within minutes of baking to be at their best.

2 cups whole wheat flour
1 cup all-purpose flour
2 tablespoons sugar
$1/2$ teaspoon salt
$2^{1}/_{2}$ teaspoons baking soda
13 tablespoons butter
2 eggs
$3/4$ cup buttermilk

PREPARATION: Mix the whole wheat and all-purpose flours with the sugar, salt, and baking soda in a large bowl. Cut 12 tablespoons butter into $1/2$-inch pieces and work them into the dry ingredients with fingertips until mixture resembles a coarse meal. Beat the eggs with the buttermilk; set aside 2 tablespoons of the mixture for egg wash. Stir the egg mixture into the dry ingredients until the dough just holds together.

COOKING: Adjust oven rack to middle position and heat oven to 400°F. Use remaining butter to coat a large baking sheet. Turn dough onto a lightly floured surface and roll $3/4$ inch thick. Cut out 2-inch rounds of dough with a cookie cutter and put them $1^{1}/_{2}$ inches apart on baking sheet. Brush with reserved egg wash and bake until scones are golden brown, about 15 minutes.

James Villas
Cookbook author and food editor
Town & Country
New York, NY

PARKER HOUSE ROLLS

Makes 4 dozen rolls

The Parker House Roll originated in the old Parker House Hotel in Boston. The name has come to mean a dinner roll made by folding a small rectangle in half. The problem with most Parker House Roll recipes is that the rolls open during baking. This method of folding the unbaked dough helps to alleviate the problem.

1 package dry active yeast
2 cups milk
¹/₂ cup vegetable shortening
6 tablespoons sugar
1 tablespoon salt
2 eggs
7 to 8 cups all-purpose flour
5¹/₂ tablespoons softened butter

PREPARATION: Mix yeast and ¹/₂ cup lukewarm water in a large bowl and let stand 5 minutes. Bring milk to a simmer in a small saucepan, cool for 5 minutes, then stir in shortening, sugar, salt, and eggs. Add milk mixture to the bowl and stir in 4 cups of flour. Beat vigorously with a wooden spoon, adding more flour 1 cup at a time, until dough is no longer sticky. Turn dough onto a lightly floured surface, knead for 1 minute, then let dough rest for 10 minutes. Resume kneading until dough is smooth and elastic, about 5 minutes. Put dough in a large bowl coated with 1 tablespoon softened butter. Cover bowl with plastic wrap and let dough rise until doubled in bulk, about 2 hours. Melt 4 tablespoons butter in a small saucepan; set aside. Use remaining butter to coat two large baking sheets. Punch down dough and cut it into 4 equal pieces. Roll each piece into an 8- by 12-inch rectangle, about ¹/₄ inch thick. Cut each rectangle into four 2- by 12-inch strips. Cut each strip into three 2- by 4-inch rectangles. Brush each rectangle with melted butter and fold in half, so that the top half extends by ¹/₂ inch over the bottom. Put rolls slightly overlapping on a baking sheet, with the extended sides facing up. Repeat to shape remaining rolls. Cover with a sheet of plastic wrap and refrigerate 30 minutes. (Can refrigerate up to 2 hours.)

COOKING: Adjust oven rack to low position and heat oven to 350°F. Bake until tops of rolls are lightly browned, about 20 minutes. Transfer to a wire rack and cool slightly before serving.

Marion Cunningham
Cookbook author
San Francisco, CA

PIZZA DOUGH

Makes two 13-inch pizzas

The following recipe for pizza dough is one that Steve Connolly, pizza chef at New York's Mezzaluna restaurant, developed for use at home. He has only two words of advice about making great pizza crust: make it *thin* and *crisp*.

$^1/_2$ **package active dry yeast ($^1/_8$ ounce)** *or* $^1/_3$ **ounce compressed yeast**
$1^1/_4$ **cups lukewarm water**
2 tablespoons oil
$3^1/_2$ **cups all-purpose flour**
1 teaspoon salt

PREPARATION: In a large bowl, stir together yeast, water, and oil, then stir in flour and salt. With your hands, work together all the ingredients until the dough just holds its shape. Turn the dough out onto a floured work surface and knead until smooth and elastic, about 10 minutes. The dough should be very soft; add the absolute minimum of flour as you work. Or, using a food processor fitted with the metal blade, process yeast, water, and oil until just mixed. Add the flour and salt and continue processing until dough holds its shape, about 30 to 40 seconds. Turn dough into a clean, wet bowl, cover loosely with a towel or plastic wrap, and let rise in a warm place until dough has increased $1^1/_2$ times in bulk, about 1 hour. Divide the risen dough into two equal balls. Cover and let rest 20 minutes. Pizza dough can be made, wrapped, and refrigerated a few hours ahead, or it can be frozen for up to a week.

COOKING: Forty-five minutes before baking, put pizza stone or quarry tiles in the oven (if using) and heat oven to 450°F. Turn one ball of pizza dough in flour and set on a lightly floured work surface. Using your fingertips and working in a circular motion, flatten the ball of dough into a disk about 8 inches in diameter. Level the dough by giving it several pats with the palm of your hand.

To flip the dough, put one hand flat, palm-side up over one side of the dough disk and then, using your other hand, flip the disk over and onto your palm. Put dough on work surface. Flatten dough again with the palm of your hand. The dough should now be about $^3/_8$ inch thick.

Using the palms of your hands, enlarge the disk into a 13-inch round by giving it quick, sharp clockwise turns, and stretching the dough slightly between your hands with each turn. Use your fingertips to thin the edge of the dough. Supporting the dough with your palm, flip it onto a

(continued)

cookie sheet and cover with desired topping(s).

If using a pizza stone or quarry tiles, ease pizza off cookie sheet onto the stone or tiles. Or, put cookie sheet into the oven. Bake until edges of crust are golden brown and crisp, rotating as necessary for even cooking, about 10 minutes. Repeat method with second ball of pizza dough, or freeze for later use.

Steve Connolly
Pizza chef
Mezzaluna
New York, NY

FOUR SEASONS PIZZA

Makes one 13-inch pizza

This version of a Four Seasons pizza calls for artichokes, tomato, mushrooms, and prosciutto.

½ **Pizza Dough (recipe page 74)**

2 marinated artichoke hearts
1 tomato
¼ pound mushrooms
8 ounces fontina cheese (about
   2⅔ cups grated)
2 tablespoons butter
Salt and pepper
¼ pound thinly sliced prosciutto
2 tablespoons olive oil

PREPARATION: Make the Pizza Dough.

Cut the artichoke hearts, tomato, and mushrooms into thin slices. Cut the cheese into very thin slices or grate it. Heat butter in a medium frying pan and sauté mushrooms over medium heat until tender, about 5 minutes. Season with salt and pepper. Recipe can be made to this point several hours ahead.

Cover and set ingredients aside at room temperature; keep dough refrigerated.

COOKING AND SERVING: Heat oven to 450°F. Sprinkle cheese evenly over the flattened pizza dough, leaving a ½-inch border. Keeping the mushroom, tomato, prosciutto, and artichoke toppings separate, use one of each of them to cover a quarter of the pizza. Drizzle olive oil over the ham and tomato.

Bake pizza until crust is golden brown, about 10 minutes. Serve immediately.

Steve Connolly
Pizza chef
Mezzaluna
New York, NY

PESTO PIZZA

Makes one 13-inch pizza

For this pizza, the crust is baked unadorned and then garnished with pesto when it comes out of the oven. Be sure to pierce the dough to keep the crust flat as it cooks.

¹/₂ **Pizza Dough (recipe page 74)**

Pesto Sauce
1 clove garlic
1 cup fresh basil leaves
2 tablespoons pine nuts
¹/₄ cup olive oil
2 tablespoons grated Parmesan cheese
Salt and pepper

PREPARATION: Make the Pizza Dough.

For the sauce, chop the garlic. Puree the garlic, basil, pine nuts, and olive oil in a blender or food processor. Stir in the grated cheese and season to taste with salt and pepper. Recipe can be made to this point several hours ahead.

COOKING AND SERVING: Heat the oven to 450°F. Pierce pizza dough several times with a fork and bake in oven until crust is golden brown and crisp, about 8 minutes. Remove from oven and spread with pesto sauce, leaving a ¹/₂-inch border. Serve immediately.

Steve Connolly
Pizza chef
Mezzaluna
New York, NY

PIZZA WITH SAUSAGE AND PEPPERS

Makes one 13-inch pizza

Bell peppers and sausage add a sweet, rich flavor to this version of the classic tomato and cheese pizza.

¹/₂ **Pizza Dough (recipe page 74)**

Pepper and Tomato Sauce
2 cloves garlic
1 small onion
¹/₂ red pepper
¹/₂ yellow pepper
¹/₂ pound hot Italian sausage
1 tablespoon olive oil
1 35-ounce can of plum tomatoes
1 tablespoon tomato paste
1 tablespoon red-wine vinegar
1 tablespoon chopped fresh thyme *or* 1 teaspoon dried
1 tablespoon chopped fresh oregano *or* 1 teaspoon dried oregano
Salt and pepper
1 tablespoon chopped fresh parsley
6 ounces mozzarella cheese (about 2 cups grated)
1 tablespoon grated Parmesan cheese

PREPARATION: Make Pizza Dough.

For the sauce, mince the garlic and onion. Cut peppers into ¹/₂-inch-wide strips, discarding cores and seeds. Remove sausage meat from its casing. In a medium frying pan, cook sausage over medium-high heat until brown, about 5 minutes, breaking it up into small pieces with the side of a spoon. Add olive oil, garlic, and onion to pan, reduce heat to medium, and cook until vegetables soften, about 3 minutes. Add the peppers and cook until tender, about 3 minutes. Add the tomatoes with their juice, breaking them up into small pieces with the side of a spoon. Add the tomato paste, vinegar, thyme, and oregano, season to taste with salt and pepper, and cook, uncovered, over medium heat until reduced to 3 cups, about 30 minutes. Stir in parsley. Yield is enough for 2 pizzas. Sauce can be made one day ahead, then covered and refrigerated. Grate the mozzarella. Recipe can be made to this point several hours ahead.

COOKING AND SERVING: Heat oven to 450°F. Spread 1¹/₂ cups of the sauce evenly over the flattened pizza dough, leaving a ¹/₂-inch border. Sprinkle with mozzarella cheese.

Bake pizza until crust is golden brown and crisp, about 10 minutes. Remove from oven, sprinkle with Parmesan cheese, and serve immediately.

Steve Connolly
Pizza chef
Mezzaluna
New York, NY

THREE-CHEESE PIZZA

Makes one 13-inch pizza

Imported Italian cheeses will give this pizza the fullest favor. Six ounces of cheese yields 2 cups when grated.

¹/₂ Pizza Dough (recipe page 74)

6 ounces provolone cheese
6 ounces fontina cheese
1 ounce Gorgonzola (two 1-inch chunks)

PREPARATION: Make the Pizza Dough.

Cut the provolone and fontina cheeses into very thin slices or grate them. Cut the Gorgonzola into fine dice. Recipe can be made to this point a few hours ahead. Wrap and refrigerate cheeses and dough.

COOKING AND SERVING: Heat oven to 450°F. Put even layers of the provolone and fontina cheeses over the flattened pizza dough, leaving a ¹/₂-inch border. Sprinkle with the Gorgonzola and bake until crust is golden brown and crisp, about 10 minutes. Serve immediately.

Steve Connolly
Pizza chef
Mezzaluna
New York, NY

PROVOLONE AND PROSCIUTTO PIZZAS

Makes 4 servings

These Italian- or French-bread pizzas are utterly simple but surprisingly delicious.

1 loaf Italian *or* French bread
2 cups Rosemary-Marinated
  Tomatoes, drained (recipe
  page 291)
8 thin slices provolone cheese
  (1/4 pound)
1 1/4 ounces Parmesan cheese
  (1/3 cup grated)
8 paper-thin slices prosciutto
  (1/4 pound)
Ground black pepper

COOKING AND SERVING: Adjust oven rack to high position and heat broiler. Cut bread in half lengthwise and then in half crosswise. Evenly distribute the tomatoes over the four pieces of bread. Cover the tomatoes with provolone cheese. Grate the Parmesan and divide it evenly over the pizzas. Put the pizzas on a baking sheet and broil until the cheese turns golden brown, about 5 minutes. Top with prosciutto and season to taste with pepper. Serve immediately.

Pam Parseghian
Free-lance writer
New York, NY

GRAINS AND PASTA

GUATEMALAN FRIED RICE
SOPA DE ARROZ

Makes 8 servings

Rice was introduced to Guatemala by the Spaniards, who learned of it when the Moors planted it in Andalusia in the eighth century. The technique of lightly browning the rice to intensify its flavor probably originated in Asia.

2 cups long-grain rice
¼ small onion
1 small garlic clove
½ medium carrot
½ small tomato
2 tablespoons corn oil
3 cups chicken broth *or* water
Salt

PREPARATION: Rinse the rice under cold water; drain well. Peel and thinly slice the onion (2 tablespoons). Peel and mince the garlic (1 teaspoon). Grate the carrot (¼ cup). Cut the tomato into ¼-inch dice (3 tablespoons).

COOKING: Heat oil in a large saucepan. Add rice and sauté, stirring constantly, over medium heat until golden, about 1 minute. Add the onion, garlic, and carrot and sauté until vegetables are soft, about 2 minutes. Stir in the tomato, broth, and 1 teaspoon salt and bring to a boil. Reduce heat to low, cover, and simmer until rice is tender, about 15 minutes. If rice is still too firm, add 1 to 2 tablespoons water, cover, and steam until tender, about 2 minutes. Set rice aside, covered, for 10 minutes. Serve immediately.

Copeland Marks
Cookbook author
Brooklyn, NY

MIXED RICE AND ROASTED PEPPER SALAD

Makes 4 to 6 servings

Wild rice is often paired with long-grain rice in salads and here the two make a vivid contrast to strips of roasted peppers and minced parsley. Use a long-grain rice such as Basmati or Texmati for an extra helping of flavor. However, white "converted" rice is also a fine choice.

1 medium red bell pepper
1 medium yellow bell pepper
1/2 cup wild rice
1/2 cup long-grain white rice

Vinaigrette
1 lemon
6 tablespoons olive oil
Salt and ground black pepper

1 cup firmly packed, stemmed
    parsley leaves
1 tablespoon snipped chives
Salt and ground black pepper

PREPARATION: Roast peppers over a gas flame or under the broiler until the skin blisters. Peel, core, seed, and cut the peppers into 3/4-inch dice. Bring 2 cups of water to a boil in a medium saucepan. Stir in wild rice and simmer, covered, until rice is tender, about 45 minutes. Drain and cool to room temperature. In a separate saucepan, bring 1 1/2 cups water to a boil. Stir in long-grain rice and simmer, covered, until liquid is absorbed and rice is tender, about 20 minutes. Cool to room temperature.

For the vinaigrette, grate 1/2 teaspoon zest from lemon. Squeeze 1 1/2 tablespoons lemon juice. Combine zest and juice with the olive oil, 1 teaspoon salt, and 1/4 teaspoon pepper in the workbowl of a food processor fitted with the metal blade and process until smooth. In a large bowl, mix the two rices with the roasted peppers. Pour the vinaigrette over the salad and toss well. (Can make salad 4 hours in advance. Cover with plastic wrap and refrigerate, or set aside at room temperature.)

SERVING: Bring the salad to room temperature. Mince the parsley and stir into the salad. Add chives and season to taste with salt and pepper. Serve at room temperature.

Michele Urvater
Cookbook author
New York, NY

WILD-RICE CAKES WITH
MUSHROOMS, SCALLIONS, AND THYME

Makes 12 patties

At Printer's Row restaurant in Chicago, Michael Foley serves these cakes with roast turkey, venison, quail, or scallops. They can be varied with the addition of corn, diced red bell pepper, or leftover turkey scraps. He also sautés cooked wild rice with leftover turkey to make a wild rice hash.

1 small onion
1 small carrot
1 medium celery stalk
$^1/_4$ pound mushrooms (about 5 medium)
1 small scallion
1 slice white bread
$^1/_2$ cup plus 1 tablespoon wild rice
Salt
3 tablespoons butter plus 3 tablespoons (optional)
1 tablespoon vegetable oil
$^1/_4$ cup all-purpose flour
$^1/_8$ teaspoon hot red-pepper sauce
1 egg

PREPARATION: Peel and finely chop onion and carrot. Rinse and finely chop celery. Rinse, drain, and thinly slice mushrooms. Finely chop 1 tablespoon scallion green. Trim off bread crust and put crumb in the workbowl of a food processor; process to fine crumbs ($^1/_2$ cup).

COOKING: Bring 1 quart water to boil in a medium saucepan. Add rice and 1 tablespoon salt; cover and simmer until rice is tender but not mushy, about 35 minutes. Transfer rice to a colander, rinse under cold water, and drain well.

Heat 1 tablespoon butter with oil in a medium skillet. Add onion and sauté until softened, about 2 minutes. Add mushrooms and sauté until softened, about 2 minutes. Add carrots, celery, scallion, thyme, $^1/_4$ teaspoon salt, and $^1/_8$ teaspoon pepper, and sauté until softened, about 2 minutes. Stir in flour and cook 1 minute longer.

Stir vegetable mixture, bread crumbs, hot red-pepper sauce, 1 teaspoon salt, and $^1/_2$ teaspoon pepper into the bowl with the rice.

Adjust oven rack to middle position and heat oven to 200°F. Lightly beat egg and stir into rice mixture. Shape mixture into twelve $2^1/_2$-inch patties, each about $^3/_4$ inch thick. Heat 1 tablespoon butter in a large skillet. When foam subsides, sauté half the patties until browned on both sides, about 6 minutes. Transfer to a serving platter and keep warm in the oven. Sauté remaining patties in 1 tablespoon butter.

SERVING: Melt the remaining butter (optional) and drizzle over cakes. Serve immediately.

Michael Foley
Executive chef
Printer's Row
Chicago, IL

BARLEY SALAD WITH CUCUMBERS AND TARRAGON

Makes 6 servings

"Pearled" barley has been steamed and polished to reduce cooking time and in the process, the entire outer husk has been removed, leaving the center, or "pearl." Pearled barley is the practical choice for this delicate salad that also includes cucumber and summer squash.

¹/₂ cup pearled barley
2 medium cucumbers
1 medium yellow squash
1 medium zucchini

Dressing
¹/₄ cup mayonnaise
2 tablespoon tarragon vinegar
2 tablespoons minced fresh
   tarragon *or* dill
Salt and ground black pepper

1 medium bunch watercress

PREPARATION AND COOKING: Bring 2 cups of water to a boil in a medium saucepan. Stir in the barley and simmer, partially covered, until tender, about 20 minutes. Drain and cool to room temperature. (Can cover with plastic wrap and refrigerate overnight) Peel, seed, and cut cucumbers into ¹/₄-inch dice. Seed and cut the yellow squash and the zucchini into ¹/₄-inch dice. Bring 1 quart of water to a boil in a medium saucepan and cook the squash and the zucchini until slightly softened, about 30 seconds. Transfer the squash to a colander and refresh under cold running water; drain well.

For the dressing, in a small bowl, whisk the mayonnaise with the vinegar, tarragon, ³/₄ teaspoon salt, and ¹/₂ teaspoon pepper; adjust seasoning to taste. In a large bowl, toss the barley with the cooked vegetables and the dressing and season to taste with salt and pepper. (Can make salad 3 to 4 hours in advance. Cover with plastic wrap and refrigerate.)

SERVING: Arrange salad on a platter and garnish with watercress. Serve cool or at room temperature.

Michele Urvater
Cookbook author
New York, NY

BULGUR AND BASIL SALAD WITH PARMESAN CHEESE

Makes 4 servings

While there is nothing intrinsically Italian about this salad, the principal ingredients — extra-virgin olive oil, freshly grated Parmesan cheese, garlic, and fresh basil — are hallmarks of the Italian pantry. Bulgur, parboiled cracked wheat, hails from the opposite side of the Mediterranean but its nutty flavor and nubby, fibrous texture help it stand up beautifully here. Bulgur comes in three textures: fine, medium, and coarse, and requires no cooking.

1 pound green beans
¾ cup coarse bulgur

Dressing
½ small garlic clove
3 tablespoons minced fresh basil
6 tablespoons extra-virgin olive oil
Salt and ground black pepper

1 medium head Boston lettuce (about 6 ounces)
2 tablespoons grated Parmesan cheese

PREPARATION: Rinse, trim, and cut the green beans into ½-inch lengths. Bring 1½ quarts of water to a boil in a large saucepan. Blanch the beans until crisp-tender, about 3 minutes. Transfer beans to a colander and then refresh under cold running water. Drain well. Bring 1½ cups of water to a boil in the same saucepan. Remove pan from heat, stir in bulgur, cover, and set aside for 30 minutes. Strain bulgur, pressing with the back of a spoon to extract any excess liquid. Transfer bulgur to a large bowl and cool to room temperature. (Can cover and refrigerate beans and bulgur overnight.)

For the dressing, fit the workbowl of a food processor with the metal blade. Chop the garlic. Put the garlic, basil, olive oil, ¾ teaspoon salt, and ⅛ teaspoon pepper into the processor and process until smooth. (Can cover and set dressing aside for 4 hours.)

SERVING: At serving time, mix the bulgur with the green beans and the dressing; adjust seasoning. Arrange lettuce leaves on serving plate. Top lettuce with salad and sprinkle with Parmesan cheese.

Michele Urvater
Cookbook author
New York, NY

COUSCOUS SALAD WITH PLUM TOMATOES AND MINT

Makes 4 to 6 servings

Couscous has a grainlike appearance but it actually is a lesser-known form of pasta made from semolina flour. The primary ingredient of the national dish of Morocco, couscous cooks quickly and, together with ripe tomatoes and mint, is terrific with grilled lamb or shish kebabs.

1 cup couscous
$1/4$ cup olive oil
8 medium plum tomatoes (about $1^1/2$ pounds)
1 cup firmly packed, stemmed mint leaves
2 tablespoons white wine vinegar
Salt and ground white pepper
Mint sprigs for optional garnish

PREPARATION: Bring 2 cups water to a boil in a medium saucepan. Stir in the couscous and cover. Remove from heat and set aside until liquid is absorbed, about 15 minutes. Spread the couscous on a platter and use a fork to break up any lumps that may have formed. Set aside to cool. Toss the cool couscous gently with the olive oil. (Can cover loosely and set aside at room temperature for 4 hours.) Core, seed, and cut the tomatoes into $1/2$-inch dice (4 cups). Mince the mint leaves and combine with the couscous, tomatoes, vinegar, 1 teaspoon salt, and $1/4$ teaspoon pepper. Toss gently.

SERVING: Adjust seasoning to taste and serve salad at room temperature. Garnish with mint sprigs if desired.

Michele Urvater
Cookbook author
New York, NY

DAKOTA'S CREAMY JALAPENO GRITS WITH CHEESE

Makes 4 servings

The hot spiciness of this homey dish can be adjusted by adding all or none of the jalapeño seeds.

1 small onion
1 clove garlic
1 jalapeño pepper
$^1/_4$ cup grated hot-pepper cheese
1 teaspoon butter
$^1/_2$ cup quick-cooking grits
1 cup heavy cream
1 cup water
$1^1/_2$ teaspoons Worcestershire sauce
1 teaspoon salt
$^1/_2$ teaspoon pepper

PREPARATION: Chop the onion. Mince the garlic. Stem and mince $^1/_2$ teaspoon jalapeño pepper. Grate the cheese. Recipe can be prepared to this point seven hours ahead.

COOKING AND SERVING: Melt the butter in a frying pan over medium heat. Add the onion and jalapeño and cook until soft, about 2 minutes. Add the grits and cook, stirring, for 3 minutes. Add the cream, water, Worcestershire sauce, and salt and pepper. Raise heat to medium-high and simmer until grits begin to thicken, about $2^1/_2$ minutes. Stir in the grated cheese and adjust seasoning to taste.

Jim Severson
Chef
Dakotas's restaurant
Dallas, TX

MILLET SALAD MEXICANO

Makes 6 servings

You may recognize millet as birdseed, but do not turn up your nose. Nutritionally, millet is nearly perfect. It also cooks quickly and punctuates the Mexican favors in this salad — jalapeño, avocado, cilantro, and lime — with a distinctive crunch.

1 cup millet
6 ears corn *or* 8 ounces thawed
    frozen corn

Dressing
2 medium jalapeño peppers
2 scallions
2 limes
¼ cup extra-virgin olive oil
Salt
¼ cup firmly packed, stemmed
    cilantro *or* parsley leaves

4 medium tomatoes (about 1
    pound)
2 medium avocados
Salt and ground black pepper

PREPARATION AND COOKING: In a medium saucepan, bring 4 cups of water to a boil. Stir in the millet, lower heat, and simmer, covered, until the millet is tender, about 20 minutes. Drain and cool to room temperature. If fresh corn is being used, cut the corn kernels from the cob. In a medium saucepan, bring 1 quart of water to a boil. Blanch the corn until softened, about 1 minute. Transfer the corn to a colander and refresh under cold rnnning water; drain well. Mix the millet and corn together in a large bowl. (Can cover and set aside 3 to 4 hours at room temperature or refrigerate overnight.)

For the dressing, quarter, stem, seed, core, and rinse the jalapeños (2 tablespoons). Thinly slice the white parts of the scallions (2 tablespoons). Squeeze 6 tablespoons of lime juice. Put the jalapeños, scallions, lime juice, olive oil, ¼ teaspoon salt, and half the cilantro into a food processor fitted with the metal blade, or into a blender. Process or blend until pureed. (Can cover and set aside 3 to 4 hours at room temperature or refrigerate overnight.)

SERVING: Thinly slice the tomatoes and arrange around the edge of a serving platter. Peel and cut the avocados into ½-inch dice. Combine the millet mixture with the avocados and dressing. Toss well and adjust seasoning to taste with salt and pepper. Mound the salad in the center of the tomatoes. Mince and sprinkle the remaining cilantro over the salad.

Michele Urvater
Cookbook author
New York, NY

EGG PASTA DOUGH

Makes 14 ounces or 4 servings

You don't need any special ingredients for this basic, versatile pasta. The recipe simply calls for eggs and unbleached, all-purpose flour, in a ratio of 1 egg to 2/3 cup flour.

Approximately 2 cups unbleached, all-purpose flour plus more for kneading
3 eggs

PREPARATION: Sift flour onto a flat surface and make a well in the center. Beat the eggs and pour into the well. With fingertips or a fork, mix flour and eggs together until the dough is soft and begins to stick together, about 3 minutes. When the dough comes together in a mass, turn it out onto a lightly floured work surface, and knead until satiny and resilient, 10 to 15 minutes. If using a food processor, put flour and eggs in the workbowl and process until dough forms a ball. Wrap in plastic and set aside to rest at least 1 hour.

Pasta can be refrigerated for up to 1 day, or it can be frozen.

Pam Parseghian
Free-lance writer
New York, NY

BOW TIES WITH BUTTER AND CREAM

Makes 4 side-dish servings

The simple elegance of this pasta makes it the perfect accompaniment to any simply prepared fish, meat, or poultry. For a slightly more piquant dish, top the pasta with a sprinkling of Parmesan. If you use capellini (angel-hair pasta), watch the pot closely since these fine strands are done almost as soon as they are dropped into boiling water.

²/₃ **Egg Pasta Dough, using**
    2 eggs (recipe page 90)
    or ¹/₂ **pound dry farfalle**
    (bow ties) or capellini
    (angel-hair pasta)
2 tablespoons chopped fresh
    herbs, such as chives, basil,
    parsley, *and/or* oregano
1¹/₂ tablespoons butter
¹/₂ cup heavy cream
Salt and pepper
Grated Parmesan cheese
    (optional)

PREPARATION: Make the Egg Pasta Dough. Roll the dough as thin as possible. For farfalle, cut dough into ³/₄ to 1-inch-wide strips using a fluted pastry cutter. Then, cut each strip into 2-inch pieces. Pinch each piece in the center to form a bow tie. Or cut the sheet of dough into very fine strands, about ¹/₃₂- to ¹/₁₆-inch wide, for capellini. Chop the herbs.

Recipe can be made to this point several hours ahead.

COOKING AND SERVING: Cook the pasta in a large pot of boiling, salted water until tender, about 3 minutes if using farfalle, 1 minute for capellini. Drain the pasta and return to pot. Add the butter, heavy cream, and herbs and toss over low heat until well coated and warmed through. Season to taste with salt and pepper. (Sprinkle with grated Parmesan cheese.)

Pam Parseghian
Free-lance writer
New York, NY

CAVATELLI WITH SPICY TOMATO-SAUSAGE SAUCE

Makes 4 servings

The addition of hot Italian sausage and basil turns the basic Quick Tomato Sauce into a zesty pasta sauce.

Spicy Tomato-Sausage Sauce
2 cups Quick Tomato Sauce
   (recipe page 285)
12 ounces hot Italian sausage
1 tablespoon olive oil
$^1/_2$ cup reserved canned tomato
   juice from Quick Tomato
   Sauce, *or* water
2 tablespoons chopped fresh
   basil *or* 1$^1/_2$ teaspoons dried
$^3/_4$ pound cavatelli *or* penne
$^3/_4$ cup ricotta

PREPARATION: *For the sauce*, make the Quick Tomato Sauce (recipe page 285). Remove sausage from its casing. Heat the olive oil in a large frying pan over medium heat and sauté sausage, breaking it up into small pieces, until color turns pale and sausage is just cooked through, about 10 minutes. Add the Quick Tomato Sauce, basil, and tomato juice to the pan and simmer, uncovered, over low heat for 5 minutes. Sauce can be made 1 day ahead.

COOKING AND SERVING: Cook the pasta in 4 quarts of boiling, salted water until tender, about 8 minutes. Drain. Reheat the sauce. Toss the pasta with the sauce, garnish each serving with 3 tablespoons of ricotta.

Elizabeth Riely
Free-lance writer
Newton Centre, MA
Brooke Dojny
Free-lance writer
Westport, CT

FETTUCCINE ALL' ALFREDO

Makes 4 servings

This simple dish requires only the time it takes to cook the pasta. Serving it with abundant fresh-ground pepper has become traditional.

$1/4$ **pound Parmesan cheese**
   (about 1 cup grated)
1 pound fettuccine
1$1/2$ cups heavy cream
4 tablespoons butter
Salt and pepper

PREPARATION: Grate the cheese.

COOKING: Cook the fettuccine in a large pot of boiling, salted water until tender, about 10 minutes. Drain and return to pot. With pot set over the lowest heat, add the cream, butter, and $1/2$ cup of the Parmesan cheese to the pasta and toss until butter has melted. Season to taste with salt and pepper.

SERVING: Serve immediately and pass a peppermill and the remaining Parmesan cheese.

Stephanie Lyness
Free-lance writer
New York, NY

FETTUCCINE ALLA CARBONARA

Makes 4 servings

This carbonara sauce — featuring bacon, eggs, and Parmesan — has no cream and is thus a touch lighter than the classic sauce but just as tasty.

Egg Pasta Dough (recipe page 90) *or* **³/₄ pound dry fettuccine**
¹/₄ pound bacon (about 4 slices)
1 onion
2 ounces Parmesan cheese (about ¹/₂ cup grated)
3 eggs
Salt and pepper

PREPARATION: Make the Egg Pasta Dough. Roll the dough as thin as possible and cut into ¹/₈- to ¹/₄-inch-wide strips.

Cut the bacon into thin strips widthwise. Chop the onion. Grate the Parmesan cheese.

Recipe can be made to this point several hours ahead.

COOKING AND SERVING: Cook the bacon in a frying pan over medium heat until golden brown, about 10 minutes. Remove the bacon from frying pan and drain on a sheet of paper towel. Reduce the heat to medium-low and cook the onion in the bacon fat until soft, about 5 minutes. Remove frying pan from heat and set aside. Beat eggs together in a small bowl.

Cook the pasta in a large pot of boiling, salted water until tender, about 3 minutes if using fresh pasta. Drain the pasta and return it to the pot. Over low heat, toss the pasta with the bacon strips, onion, eggs, and cheese and heat until warm and the pasta is well coated. Season to taste with salt and pepper.

Pam Parseghian
Free-lance writer
New York, NY

FETTUCCINE ALLA GENOVESE

Makes 4 servings

The classic Genovese spinach sauté, *spinaci con pignoli e uvette*, is garnished with toasted pine nuts and raisins in the Arabian style. Goldstein adds a light cream sauce and a touch of fresh lemon juice.

$1/2$ **cup pine nuts**
$1/2$ **dark *or* light raisins**
8 ounces fresh spinach leaves (8 cups)
3 cups heavy cream
1 small lemon
Salt and ground black pepper
$3/4$ **pound fresh fettuccine *or* 8 to 10 ounces dried**

PREPARATION AND COOKING: Heat oven to 350°F. Spread the pine nuts in a small, shallow baking pan and toast until golden and fragrant, about 5 minutes; set aside. Put the raisins in a small bowl with warm water to cover and soak until softened, about 10 minutes; drain and set aside. Wash, drain, stem, and cut the spinach leaves into $1^{1}/_{2}$-inch strips. Heat the heavy cream to a simmer in a large nonreactive saucepan. Add the cut spinach and simmer until it begins to wilt, about 30 seconds. Grate 2 teaspoons of lemon zest into the saucepan and squeeze in 4 teaspoons lemon juice. Add the soaked raisins and half of the toasted pine nuts, and season with 1 teaspoon salt and $1/2$ teaspoon pepper. Cover and set sauce aside. Bring 4 quarts of water to a boil in a large soup kettle. Add 1 tablespoon of salt and all of the pasta. Cook pasta until tender, about 3 minutes for fresh or about 9 minutes for dried. Drain pasta well, return to soup kettle, and toss with sauce over very low heat. Adjust seasoning to taste.

SERVING: Transfer the pasta to 4 warm dinner plates and top with the pine nuts. Serve immediately.

Joyce Goldstein
Chef/owner
Square One
San Francisco, CA

FETTUCCINE WITH PROSCIUTTO AND PEAS

Makes 4 servings

Salty prosciutto and sweet peas combine for a simple classic pasta dish. Tear the prosciutto into pieces for a more graceful presentation.

Egg Pasta Dough (recipe page 90) *or* **$3/4$ pound dry fettuccine**
1 pound green peas (about $1^1/2$ cups *or* 7 ounces shelled)
$1/4$ pound thin-sliced prosciutto
3 ounces Parmesan cheese (about $3/4$ cup grated)
5 tablespoons butter
Pepper

PREPARATION: Make the Egg Pasta Dough. Roll the dough as thin as possible and cut into $1/8$- to $1/4$-inch-wide strips.

Shell peas and blanch in boiling, salted water until tender, about 5 minutes. Drain and refresh under cold water. Tear each slice of prosciutto into bite-size pieces. Grate the cheese.

Recipe can be made to this point several hours ahead.

COOKING AND SERVING: Cook the pasta in a large pot of boiling, salted water until tender, about 3 minutes if using fresh pasta. Drain.

Melt the butter in a large pot over low heat. Add the peas and pasta and cook until warmed through. Toss in the prosciutto and $1/2$ the cheese and season to taste with pepper.

Put pasta on plates and top each serving with a teaspoon of grated cheese. Pass the remaining cheese.

Pam Parseghian
Free-lance writer
New York, NY

FETTUCCINE WITH SAUSAGE, SUMMER SAVORY, AND SUN-DRIED TOMATOES

Makes 4 servings

If summer savory is not available, you can substitute fresh basil or chervil in this recipe.

Savory Butter
2 tablespoons stemmed summer savory leaves
6 tablespoons softened butter

Pasta and Sauce
8 sun-dried tomatoes
2 ounces goat cheese
1/2 pound sweet Italian sausage
2 medium garlic cloves
1/2 cup chicken stock
Salt
12 ounces dried fettuccine

PREPARATION AND COOKING: *For the Savory Butter*, mince the summer savory, then cream the butter and beat in the savory. Shape the herb butter into a 1-inch-thick cylinder, wrap in plastic, and refrigerate. (Can be refrigerated up to 3 days or frozen up to 1 month.)

For the pasta and sauce, chop and set the sun-dried tomatoes aside. Cut the goat cheese in 1/2-inch cubes and bring to room temperature. Remove the sausage from its casing. Peel and mince the garlic cloves. In a 12-inch skillet, sauté the sausage over medium-high heat until cooked through. Add the garlic and sauté 2 minutes. Add the chicken stock and sun-dried tomatoes and bring to a simmer. Stir in 3 tablespoons of the Savory Butter. Cover sauce and keep warm.

Bring 6 quarts of water to a boil in a large soup kettle. Add 2 tablespoons salt and then the pasta, all at once. Cook pasta until tender, about 9 minutes. Drain pasta well, and toss with sauce over very low heat.

SERVING: Transfer pasta to 4 warm dinner plates or a large pasta bowl. Top with goat cheese and serve immediately.

Brooke Dojny and Melanie Barnard
Nationally syndicated food writers and cookbook authors
Fairfield County, CT

FUSILLI WITH CHICKEN, OLIVES, AND ROSEMARY-MARINATED TOMATOES

Makes 4 servings

Green fusilli (corkscrew pasta) is the first choice for this dish from the standpoint of presentation. Penne (quills), conchiglie (shells), or radiatore (ruffles) can be substituted.

2 whole boneless, skinless chicken breasts, split (about 1½ pounds)
Salt and ground black pepper
2 tablespoons olive oil
½ cup loosely packed parsley leaves
5 ounces small black California pitted olives
1 cup Rosemary-Marinated Tomatoes and marinade (recipe page 291)
¾ pound dried spinach fusilli
2 ounces Parmesan cheese (½ cup grated)

PREPARATION: Pat chicken breasts dry with paper towels and sprinkle with salt and pepper. Heat oil in a large skillet until hot but not smoking. Sauté chicken 4 minutes. Turn and sauté until thoroughly cooked, about 4 minutes longer. Remove and cut chicken into bite-size pieces; set aside. Mince parsley (¼ cup). Drain the olives, then slice them into rings. Remove tomatoes from the marinade. Coarsely chop and return tomatoes to the marinade; set the mixture aside.

COOKING AND SERVING: Bring 3 quarts of water to a boil in a 6-quart soup kettle. Add 1 teaspoon salt and cook the fusilli until just tender, about 9 minutes. Drain and return the pasta to the kettle. Over low heat, stir in the tomatoes and the marinade, chicken, olives, and parsley. Sprinkle with the grated cheese, season to taste with salt and pepper and serve immediately.

Pam Parseghian
Free-lance writer
New York, NY

TRADITIONAL LASAGNA

Makes 4 servings

Traditional lasagna nooodles are cut either in wide strips or in squares. This classic northern Italian lasagna is layered with two delicious, rich sauces.

**2/3 Egg Pasta Dough, using
  2 eggs, (recipe page 90) *or*
  1/2 pound dry lasagna noodles**

Bolognese Sauce
1 onion
1/2 carrot
1/2 rib celery
1 clove garlic
2 tablespoons butter
1/2 pound ground pork
1/3 cup white wine
1/3 cup heavy cream
1/8 teaspoon grated nutmeg
**6 Italian plum tomatoes *or*
  1 cup canned**
Salt and pepper

Béchamel Sauce
3 tablespoons butter
1/4 cup flour
2 cups milk
Salt and pepper
**3 ounces Parmesan cheese
  (about 3/4 cup grated)**

PREPARATION: Make the Egg Pasta Dough. Roll the dough as thin as possible and cut into 2-inch-wide strips or approximately 4-inch squares.

For the Bolognese Sauce, dice onion, carrot, and celery. Mince the garlic. Melt butter over medium heat. Add pork and cook just until it loses its pink color, about 3 minutes. Add onion, carrot, and celery and cook until tender, about 5 minutes. Add garlic and cook 1 minute. Add wine, stirring with a wooden spoon to deglaze bottom of pan, and simmer until reduced by 1/2, about 15 minutes. Add cream and nutmeg and simmer until thickened, about 5 minutes. Stir in tomatoes, including juice, breaking them up with a spoon. Cover and simmer over low heat 2 hours, stirring occasionally. Season with salt and pepper.

For the Béchamel Sauce, melt butter in a saucepan over low heat. Whisk in the flour and cook for 1 minute. Gradually whisk in the milk and bring to a boil, stirring constantly. Reduce heat and season with salt and pepper. Simmer for 20 minutes. Grate the cheese.

Cook pasta in a large pot of boiling, salted water until tender, about 3 minutes if using fresh pasta. Drain and refresh under cold water.

Pour a thin layer of Bolognese Sauce into bottom of baking dish. Arrange a layer of pasta on top. Pour 1/3 of the Bolognese and then 1/3 of the Béchamel over pasta. Sprinkle 1/4 cup of Parmesan over all. Make 2 more layers. Lasagna can be made to this point a day ahead.

COOKING AND SERVING: Heat oven to 400°F. Loosely cover lasagna with foil and bake until warmed through, about 20 minutes. Remove foil and put lasagna under broiler until golden brown, about 5 minutes. Let sit 10 minutes before serving.

Pam Parseghian
Free-lance writer
New York, NY

SCALLION AND BLACK-PEPPER LASAGNA

Makes 6 servings

Tender scallion- and pepper-flecked noodles provide a delicious background for a colorful sauce. Serving one big noodle per person is a witty variation on the pasta theme

Black-Olive Pesto (recipe page 279)
4 large scallions
2 large eggs
1 large egg yolk
Salt and ground black pepper
$1^2/_3$ to $1^3/_4$ cups bread flour *or* all-purpose flour

PREPARATION: Make Black-Olive Pesto. Slice scallions into rings and put in the workbowl of a food processor fitted with the metal blade, with eggs, egg yolk, $^3/_4$ teaspoon salt, and $^1/_4$ teaspoon pepper. Process until pale and frothy, about 1 minute. Add $1^2/_3$ cups flour and pulse just until small beads form. If dough is wet and beads do not form, pulse in additional flour by tablespoons until dough forms small beads that hold together when pressed. Wrap dough in plastic, press into a flat disk, and set aside for 15 minutes. (Can refrigerate overnight.)

Unwrap and cut dough into 3 pieces. If dough sticks to wrap, sprinkle work surface with 2 to 3 tablespoons flour. Work on 1 piece of dough at a time; keep remaining dough wrapped. If using a manual pasta machine, roll dough through successive narrow openings to thinnest setting, dusting dough with flour to prevent it from sticking. Repeat process with remaining dough. If rolling dough by hand, roll each portion as thinly as possible, until you can see your hand through it. Cut dough into 5-inch squares and dust with flour. Put cut pasta squares in single layers on waxed paper. (Can put on a baking sheet, cover tightly with plastic wrap, and set aside at room temperature up to 6 hours, or refrigerate overnight.)

COOKING: Bring 4 quarts of water to a boil in a large soup kettle. Add 1 teaspoon salt. Cook 2 or 3 pasta squares at one time until tender, about 3 minutes. Drain well.

SERVING: Put one pasta square on each warm dinner plate and top with 3 to 4 tablespoons of the pesto. Garnish and serve immediately.

Jane Freiman
Food columnist and cookbook author
New York, NY

LINGUINE WITH CAULIFLOWER, GARLIC, AND HOT RED PEPPER

Makes 6 servings

This pasta dish is made in the Italian style, with sauce coating the noodles, but with little excess liquid. Up to $1/4$ cup of the pasta water may be added to the finished dish if it seems too dry.

2 medium cauliflower ($3^1/_2$ pounds)
4 medium garlic cloves
4 medium onions
6 plum tomatoes, fresh *or* canned
1 cup loosely packed parsley leaves
10 tablespoons olive oil
6 tablespoons butter
Salt and ground black pepper
1 teaspoon hot red-pepper flakes
1 ounce Romano cheese ($1/4$ cup grated)
1 pound fresh linguine *or* 12 ounces dried

PREPARATION: Trim and cut the cauliflower into florets. Peel and crush the garlic. Peel and thinly slice the onions. If using fresh tomatoes, peel, seed, and chop (seed and chop canned tomatoes). Mince the parsley ($1/2$ cup).

COOKING: Heat $1/2$ cup olive oil and 4 tablespoons butter in a large skillet. Add cauliflower and garlic and sauté over medium heat, stirring frequently, until cauliflower is lightly browned but not fully cooked, about 15 minutes. Transfer cauliflower to a large bowl; set aside. Add remaining olive oil and remaining butter to the skillet with the garlic. Add onions and sauté over medium heat until softened and lightly browned, about 10 minutes. Remove and discard garlic. Add tomatoes and return cauliflower to the skillet. Season with salt, $3/4$ teaspoon black pepper, and hot red-pepper flakes. Simmer 5 minutes. (Do not overcook the cauliflower.)

SERVING: Grate the cheese ($1/4$ cup). Bring 6 quarts water to a boil in a soup kettle. Add 1 tablespoon salt and cook pasta until tender, 1 to 2 minutes for fresh pasta, or 9 minutes for dried pasta. Drain, reserving $1/4$ cup of the pasta water. Transfer pasta to the skillet with the sauce, adding up to $1/4$ cup reserved pasta water if sauce is too dry. Toss over low heat; stir in parsley and cheese.

Pam Parseghian
Free-lance writer
New York, NY

PASTA WITH EASY TOMATO AND GARLIC SAUCE

Makes 4 servings

Fresh tomatoes make all the difference in this garlicky sauce. Good-quality plum tomatoes are now available year round. Choose either fettuccine or tagliatelle to go with this delicious sauce.

Egg Pasta Dough (recipe page 90) *or* **³/₄ pound dry fettuccine or tagliatelle**
16 Italian plum tomatoes
2 cloves garlic
2 tablespoons chopped parsley
2 tablespoons chopped fresh basil
¹/₃ cup olive oil
Salt and pepper
Grated Parmesan cheese, for serving (optional)

PREPARATION: Make the Egg Pasta Dough. Roll the dough as thin as possible and cut into ¹/₈- to ¹/₄-inch-wide strips.

Peel, seed, and chop the tomatoes. Mince the garlic.

Heat the olive oil in a nonreactive saucepan over low heat. Add the garlic and cook over medium heat until soft, about 3 minutes. Add the tomatoes, raise the heat to high, and cook until they give up some of their juice, about 5 minutes,

Recipe can be made to this point several hours ahead.

COOKING AND SERVING: Chop the parsley and basil. Cook the pasta in a large pot of boiling, salted water until tender, about 3 minutes if using fresh pasta. Drain pasta and return to pot. Add tomato sauce and fresh herbs. Toss over low heat until pasta is warmed through and lightly coated with sauce. Season to taste with salt and pepper. (Serve with grated Parmesan cheese.)

Pam Parseghian
Free-lance writer
New York, NY

PASTA WITH PESTO AND CHICKEN

Makes 4 servings

This is a wonderful dish to make in the summer when fresh basil is plentiful. Since pesto also freezes well, you can make a large batch and enjoy it year round.

Egg Pasta Dough (recipe page 90) *or* **$^3/_4$ pound dry farfalle (bow ties) or linguine**

Pesto
1$^1/_2$ ounces Parmesan cheese (about $^1/_3$ cup grated)
4 cloves garlic
Salt
1 quart loosely packed fresh basil leaves
$^1/_3$ cup pine nuts
$^3/_4$ cup olive oil

4 boneless, skinless chicken breasts (about 1$^1/_4$ pounds total)
1 tablespoon vegetable oil
Salt and pepper

PREPARATION: Make the Egg Pasta Dough. Roll the dough as thin as possible. For farfalle, cut dough into 1-inch-wide strips using a fluted pastry cutter. Then cut each strip into 2-inch pieces. Pinch the center of each piece to form a bow tie. Or cut dough into $^1/_8$-inch-wide strips for linguine.

For the Pesto, grate the cheese. Using a mortar and pestle or the side of a heavy knife, mash the garlic with 1 teaspoon of salt to form a smooth paste. In a food processor or blender, or with a mortar and pestle, combine the garlic paste, basil, pine nuts, and olive oil and puree until smooth. Stir in the cheese.

Recipe can be made to this point several hours ahead.

COOKING AND SERVING: Heat the grill or broiler. Toss the chicken with the vegetable oil and sprinkle with salt and pepper. Broil or grill the chicken, turning once, until just cooked through, about 10 minutes total. Cut the chicken into bite-size pieces.

Cook pasta in a large pot of boiling, salted water until tender, about 3 minutes if using fresh pasta. Drain. Return pasta to pot, toss with chicken and pesto sauce, and season with salt and pepper. Serve warm or at room temperature.

Pam Parseghian
Free-lance writer
New York, NY

PENNE WITH VEAL AND SPINACH MEATBALLS

Makes 12 servings

The only last-minute preparation here is cooking the pasta quills. Then *penne* are bathed in tomato sauce boosted by shiitake mushrooms, and garnished with garlic- and nutmeg-laced meatballs.

Tomato Sauce
2 medium onions (¹/₂ pound)
6 medium garlic cloves
²/₃ cup olive oil
4 teaspoons dried marjoram
2 bay leaves
1 large can Italian plum tomatoes (35 ounces)
1 medium can Italian plum tomatoes (28 ounces)
Salt
1 pound shiitake mushrooms
1 pound cultivated white mushrooms
Ground black pepper

Veal Meatballs
2 packages frozen, chopped spinach (10 ounces each)
3 pounds ground veal
3 eggs
3 medium garlic cloves
1¹/₂ cups packed parsley leaves
¹/₂ cup dried bread crumbs
1 tablespoon dried marjoram
1 teaspoon grated nutmeg
Salt and ground black pepper
4 ounces Parmesan cheese (1 cup grated)

2 pounds dried *penne* or *fusilli*

PREPARATION AND COOKING: *For the tomato sauce*, peel and chop the onions. Peel and mince the garlic (2 tablespoons). Heat ¹/₃ cup oil in a 5 quart, nonreactive saucepan. Add the onions, garlic, marjoram, and bay leaves; cover and cook over medium-low heat, stirring occasionally, until the vegetables are softened, about 15 minutes. Add the tomatoes with their juice and 1 tablespoon salt. Bring the liquid to a boil, and simmer, stirring occasionally, until the sauce reduces to 7 cups, about 50 minutes. Cool slightly and puree.

Detach and discard stems from the shiitake mushrooms. Trim the cultivated mushrooms. Slice all of the mushrooms ¹/₄-inch thick. Heat remaining olive oil in a large skillet until hot but not smoking. Add the mushrooms and 2 teaspoons salt and sauté until lightly browned, about 7 minutes. Stir them into the tomato sauce with 2 teaspoons pepper. Adjust seasoning to taste and set the sauce aside. (Can cover and refrigerate up to 3 days.)

For the meatballs, adjust oven rack to high position and heat oven to 400°F. Thaw the spinach, squeeze out all the moisture, and chop it finely. Put the spinach into a large bowl with the veal and the eggs. Peel and mince the garlic (1 tablespoon); add it to the bowl. Chop ¹/₂ cup of the parsley; wrap and refrigerate the remaining leaves. Add the chopped parsley to the bowl along with the bread crumbs, marjoram, nutmeg, 1 teaspoon salt, and 2 teaspoons pepper. Grate the Parmesan cheese. Stir ¹/₂ cup thoroughly into the veal mixture; set remaining cheese aside.

Shape the veal mixture into 1-inch balls and put them in a single layer on a jelly-roll pan. Bake, turning meatballs occasionally, until cooked through and well browned, 20 to

(continued)

25 minutes. Drain the fat from the pan and set meatballs aside. (Can cover and refrigerate overnight.)

ASSEMBLY AND SERVING: Adjust oven rack to high position and heat oven to 325° F. Chop the reserved 1 cup parsley leaves and set aside. Bring 12 quarts water to a boil in a large stockpot with 4 tablespoons salt. Add the pasta and cook until tender, about 10 minutes. Transfer to 2 colanders, drain, then return pasta to stockpot. Heat meatballs on the jelly-roll pan until warmed through, about 15 minutes. Bring tomato sauce to a boil in a heavy saucepan over low heat and toss with the pasta. Gently stir in the meatballs and ³/₄ cup parsley. Turn pasta into a large bowl and sprinkle with remaining parsley. Serve with remaining Parmesan cheese.

Michael McLaughlin
Free-lance writer
Brooklyn, NY

ROASTED RED ONION RAVIOLI

Makes 4 side-dish servings

The thyme in the roasted-onion filling is reinforced with a thyme-infused cream sauce.

$^2/_3$ **Egg Pasta Dough, using 2 eggs (recipe page 90)**

Roasted Red Onion Filling
3 small red onions
1 tablespoon minced fresh thyme *or* 1 teaspoon dried
1 tablespoon olive oil
Salt and pepper
1 tablespoon balsamic *or* red-wine vinegar

1 egg
1 ounce Parmesan cheese (about $^1/_4$ cup grated)

Cream Sauce
$^3/_4$ cup heavy cream
2 sprigs fresh thyme *or* $^1/_2$ teaspoon dried
1 tablespoon butter
Salt and pepper

PREPARATION: Make the Egg Pasta Dough and form into 2 balls.

For the filling, heat oven to 375°F. Trim and halve the unpeeled onions. Mince the thyme. In a shallow baking pan, toss the oil, onions, $^1/_2$ teaspoon salt, and fresh thyme, if using. Roast onions, cut side down, in oven until brown, about 40 minutes. Remove onions from pan and set aside to cool. Add the vinegar to the pan, stirring with a wooden spoon to deglaze the bottom.

When onions are cool enough to handle, peel and chop them. In a small bowl, combine the onions, pan juices, and dried thyme, if using. Season to taste with salt and pepper.

Whisk the egg in a small bowl. Roll both balls of dough as thin as possible into 2 rectangular sheets. Set aside 1 sheet and cover with a damp towel. Lightly brush the remaining sheet with beaten egg. Arrange 12 teaspoons of filling on top of the dough, spacing mounds about 2 inches apart. Cover with the second sheet of dough and press firmly around each mound. Cut between each mound with a fluted ravioli cutter or a knife. Put ravioli, well spaced, on lightly floured baking sheets or waxed paper. Refrigerate if not cooking immediately. Grate the cheese.

Recipe can be made to this point a few hours ahead.

COOKING AND SERVING: Cook ravioli in a large pot of boiling, salted water until tender, about 6 minutes. Drain.

Meanwhile, *for the sauce*, put the heavy cream and thyme in a small saucepan, bring to a simmer over medium heat, and cook until cream is reduced to $^1/_2$ cup, about 5 minutes. Stir in the butter. Strain sauce and season with salt and pepper.

Gently toss ravioli with the Cream Sauce and grated cheese until lightly coated. Serve with fresh-milled pepper.

Pam Parseghian
Free-lance writer
New York, NY

CHICKEN AND SPINACH TORTELLINI OR CAPPELLETTI

Makes 4 servings

The chicken and spinach filling used in this recipe is also extremely good in ravioli.

Egg Pasta Dough (recipe page 90)

Chicken and Spinach Filling
1 boneless, skinless chicken breast (about $1/4$ pound)
$2^1/2$ ounces fresh *or* frozen spinach (about $1/4$ cup cooked)
1 small shallot
1 tablespoon fresh thyme *or* 1 teaspoon dried
3 tablespoons butter
Salt and pepper
1 tablespoon white wine
$1/4$ cup heavy cream
1 egg yolk
Pinch of grated nutmeg

Cream Sauce (recipe page 106, in Roasted Red Onion Ravioli recipe)

PREPARATION: Make the Egg Pasta Dough. *For the filling*, cut chicken into 1-inch cubes. Wash and stem spinach. Chop shallot. Mince thyme. In a frying pan, melt butter over medium heat. Sprinkle chicken with salt and pepper and sauté until just cooked through, about 4 minutes. Add shallot and cook until shallot is soft, about 2 minutes. Add wine and cook until wine has thickened a bit, about 1 minute. Transfer to a food processor. Put spinach in same pan used for chicken and cook, covered, over medium-low heat until wilted. Drain well. Add spinach to food processor and pulse a few times until chicken is chopped. Transfer mixture to a bowl. Stir in cream and egg yolk. Season with nutmeg and salt and pepper. Recipe can be made to this point 1 day ahead. Roll pasta dough as thin as possible and cut into $2^1/2$-inch rounds for tortellini or squares for cappelletti. Put $1/4$ teaspoon filling in center of each piece of dough and brush edges with water.

To shape into tortellini, fold each filled round in half over filling and press edges together. Wrap semicircle around index finger, fold sealed edge upward, and seal ends.

To shape into cappelletti, fold each square over filling, making a triangle, and press edges together. Wrap triangle around index finger, fold pointed edge upward, and seal ends. The pasta can be filled several hours ahead.

COOKING AND SERVING: Cook the pasta in boiling, salted water until tender, about 6 minutes. Drain. Make Cream Sauce. Toss pasta in sauce until well coated. Serve immediately.

Pam Parseghian
Free-lance writer
New York, NY

SIDE DISHES

BLACK BEANS

Makes 8 servings

Ham hocks add a wonderful smoky flavor to the beans. If they are not available, substitute bacon.

1 pound black turtle beans (2 cups)
1 small red onion
2 medium garlic cloves
1 small carrot
2 serrano chiles or 1 jalapeño chile (optional)
2 tablespoons vegetable oil
1 pound smoked ham hocks (2 hocks) or ¼ pound bacon
2 bay leaves
1 tablespoon ground cumin
4¼ cups chicken stock *or* broth
Salt and ground black pepper
1 cup sour cream

PREPARATION: Rinse and soak beans overnight in 2 quarts of cold water. *Or,* put beans and 2 quarts of water in a 6-quart kettle, bring to a boil, cover, and let stand for 1 hour. Peel and coarsely chop onion. Peel and mince garlic. Peel and cut carrot into ¼-inch dice. (Stem, seed, and halve chiles.)

COOKING: Heat oil in a 6-quart soup kettle. Add onion, garlic, and ham hocks and sauté until vegetables soften, about 5 minutes. Drain and add beans to the kettle along with the carrot, (chiles), bay leaves, cumin, chicken stock, 1 tablespoon salt, and 1½ teaspoons black pepper. Cover and simmer until beans are almost tender, about 45 minutes. Uncover and simmer until tender when mashed with a spoon, about 15 minutes longer. Remove and discard ham hocks, bay leaves, (and chiles). (Can set aside for 6 hours or refrigerate 2 days.)

SERVING: Reheat beans, garnish with sour cream, and serve immediately.

Anne Lindsay Greer
Cookbook author
Dallas, TX

BLACK-EYED PEAS WITH ONIONS, GARLIC, AND TOMATO

Makes 6 servings

Black-eyed peas are bland on their own and greatly benefit from this preparation. Edna Lewis serves this dish with roast chicken or turkey, ham, or pork.

2 medium tomatoes *or* 1 can
**   whole tomatoes (16 ounces)**
1 medium onion
1 small garlic clove
1 cup dried black-eyed peas
$^{1}/_{2}$ cup olive oil
Salt and ground black pepper
2 tablespoons minced parsley

PREPARATION: Peel, seed, and chop tomatoes. Peel and chop onion. Peel and mince garlic.

COOKING AND SERVING: Rinse peas and put in a large soup kettle with 4 cups water. Bring to boil and simmer until tender, about 30 minutes. Transfer to a colander, rinse, and drain. Heat oil in a medium skillet. Add onion and garlic and sauté 1 minute. Add tomatoes and stew until softened, 10 minutes. Stir in peas, 1 teaspoon salt, and $^{1}/_{2}$ teaspoon pepper, and simmer 10 minutes longer. Stir in parsley, and adjust seasoning to taste.

Edna Lewis
Chef and cookbook author
New York, NY

BROCCOLI AND CARROTS IN CURRY OIL
HARE GOBHI AUR GAJJAR KARI

Makes 4 servings

This crisp sauté is a great accompaniment for any tandoori dish. It may be served hot, cold, or at room temperature.

1³/₄ **pounds broccoli (1 medium bunch)**
2 medium carrots
10 large garlic cloves
2 teaspoons curry powder (recipe page 282)
¹/₄ **cup vegetable oil**
¹/₂ **teaspoon sugar**
1 small lime

PREPARATION: Peel stems and cut broccoli into spears, leaving long stems attached to florets; peel the stems. Peel and slice carrots into ¹/₄-inch wide strips. Peel the garlic.

COOKING: Bring 3 quarts water to boil in a 6-quart soup kettle. Blanch broccoli and carrots until colors brighten and vegetables soften slightly, about 3 minutes. Drain, rinse under cold running water, and drain again. Shake off excess water and sprinkle with curry powder. Heat oil in a large skillet. Add the garlic cloves and sauté over medium heat until golden, about 6 minutes; set aside and keep warm. Add broccoli and carrots and sauté, stirring frequently, until vegetables soften, about 6 minutes. Sprinkle with sugar and sauté until vegetables are lightly browned, about 2 minutes longer.

SERVING: Arrange a bouquet of broccoli and carrots on a serving platter. Sprinkle with garlic and squeeze 1 teaspoon lime juice over the vegetables.

Julie Sahni
Cookbook author
New York, NY

SWEET AND SOUR RED CABBAGE

Makes 6 to 8 servings

The secret to this dish is very good red-wine vinegar to fix the bright red color of the cabbage, which requires very little salt, as the vinegar's acid intensifies saltiness. During the holidays, Barbara Kafka serves this dish with a turkey, goose, or duck; the rest of the year the cabbage goes well with simple dishes such as pot roast or boiled beef.

1 large red cabbage (2 to 2$\frac{1}{2}$
    pounds)
1 medium onion
2 tablespoons rendered chicken
    fat *or* butter
$\frac{3}{4}$ cup red-wine vinegar
4 teaspoons sugar
6 cloves
1 bay leaf
6 juniper berries
Salt and ground black pepper
2 to 3 tablespoons all-purpose
    flour
1 teaspoon butter
$\frac{1}{2}$ medium lemon
1 tablespoon light molasses

PREPARATION: Remove and discard tough outer leaves, and core the cabbage. Finely shred the cabbage; set aside. Peel and thinly slice the onion.

COOKING AND SERVING: Heat chicken fat in a large skillet or Dutch oven. Sauté onion until softened, about 3 minutes. Add vinegar, sugar, cloves, bay leaf, juniper berries, 1 teaspoon salt, $\frac{1}{2}$ teaspoon pepper, and 2 cups water, and bring to a boil. Stir in the cabbage and return mixture to a boil. Cover and simmer until cabbage is tender, about 45 minutes. Remove pan from heat and stir in flour, 1 tablespoon at a time, until liquid is thickened; cover and keep cabbage warm. Heat the butter in a small saucepan. Squeeze in $1\frac{1}{2}$ teaspoons lemon juice, and stir in the molasses to dissolve. Stir molasses mixture into cabbage, and serve very hot.

Barbara Kafka
Cookbook author and restaurant consultant
New York, NY

SAVOY CABBAGE WITH CARAWAY

Makes 4 servings

This braised cabbage dish is a great accompaniment for roast duck.

1 small onion
1 head savoy cabbage *or* other green cabbage
1 tablespoon caraway seeds
4 tablespoons butter *or* rendered duck fat
¼ cup Champagne vinegar *or* white-wine vinegar
Salt and pepper

PREPARATION: Slice the onion. Remove the tough ribs from cabbage leaves and slice the leaves into thin strips. Put caraway seeds in a frying pan and toast over low heat, stirring frequently, until seeds are fragrant, about 5 minutes.

Melt butter in a saucepan over low heat. Add onion and cabbage and cook, covered, until tender, about 12 minutes. Recipe can be made to this point a day ahead.

SERVING: Reheat cabbage if made ahead. Stir in the vinegar and caraway seeds and season with salt and pepper.

Tony Najiola
Chef
Village Green Restaurant
New York, NY

SAUTEED SAVOY CABBAGE WITH APPLES

Makes 4 servings

1 medium tart apple
1 small onion
1 medium savoy cabbage (about
   1^1/$_2$ pounds)
2 tablespoons olive oil
^{1}/$_4$ cup dry white wine
Salt and ground black pepper

PREPARATION: Core and thinly slice the apple. Peel and thinly slice the onion. Coarsely shred the cabbage.

COOKING: Heat olive oil in a large skillet. Add onions and apple slices and sauté until softened, about 4 minutes. Add cabbage and sauté, stirring constantly, until cabbage wilts, about 2 minutes. Add wine, ^{1}/$_2$ teaspoon salt, and ^{1}/$_4$ teaspoon pepper. Simmer, stirring occasionally, until cabbage is just tender, 6 to 8 minutes. Serve immediately.

Betsy Schultz
Food consultant
New York, NY

CARROTS SAUTEED WITH BACON

Makes 8 servings

This dish is easily made at the last minute, although it does not suffer if prepared a couple of hours in advance and finished in the microwave.

1¹/₂ pounds carrots
2 thin slices bacon (2 ounces)
**3¹/₂ tablespoons rendered duck
    or goose fat *or* butter**
Salt and ground black pepper
2 teaspoons minced parsley

PREPARATION: Trim, peel, and cut the carrots diagonally into thin slices. Cut the bacon into 1-inch pieces.

COOKING AND SERVING: Heat duck fat in a skillet over medium-high heat. Add carrots and bacon and sauté until bacon is crisp and carrots are tender, 8 to 10 minutes. Transfer carrots and bacon to a dish lined with paper toweling. Pour fat out of the skillet and discard. Raise heat to high, add ²/₃ cups water, bring to a boil, and swirl liquid in pan to emulsify.

SERVING: Transfer carrots and bacon to a serving plate; season with salt and pepper. Pour the contents of skillet over carrots and garnish with parsley.

Paula Wolfert
Cookbook author
New York, NY

GRATIN OF MELTING POTATOES

Makes 8 servings

The potatoes are simmered in light cream until swollen and then baked until tender.

4½ **pounds potatoes**
2 **small garlic cloves**
2 **medium scallions**
2 **teaspoons minced thyme**
½ **teaspoon grated nutmeg**
Salt and ground white pepper
3 **to 3½ cups half-and-half**
   or light cream
2 **tablespoons unsalted butter**

PREPARATION: Peel and cut potatoes into paper-thin slices. Rinse with cold water and drain. Peel and mince garlic. Trim and mince scallions. In a bowl, stir together garlic, scallions, thyme, nutmeg, 1¾ teaspoons salt and ½ teaspoon pepper.

COOKING: Heat oven to 300°F. Butter a 3- to 4-quart heatproof baking-serving dish. Put a layer of potatoes on the bottom of the dish and sprinkle with the scallion-garlic mixture. Repeat 4 times, finishing with a layer of potatoes. Pour in just enough half-and-half to cover the potatoes. Cover the dish and set over very low heat for 20 minutes. Remove cover, dot with butter, and bake until potatoes are tender, about 2 hours.

Paula Wolfert
Cookbook author
New York, NY

TURNIP AND POTATO GRATIN

Makes 4 servings

Turnips and potatoes are natural companions. This gratin is perfect with roasted meats.

1 small garlic clove
2 teaspoons softened butter
1 slice white bread ($^1/_2$ inch thick)
5 medium turnips (about $1^1/_2$ pounds)
1 medium red potato (about $^1/_2$ pound)
Salt and ground black pepper
$^1/_4$ pound turnip greens (optional)
$^2/_3$ to 1 cup whipping cream

PREPARATION: Peel, crush, and rub the inside of a 2-quart gratin dish with the garlic. Coat dish with butter. Remove and discard bread crust; process bread to crumbs in the workbowl of a food processor fitted with the metal blade; set aside. Peel and cut the turnips and potato into $^1/_8$-inch slices. Layer half the turnip and potato slices over bottom of gratin dish. Sprinkle with $^1/_2$ teaspoon of salt and $^1/_4$ teaspoon pepper. If using turnip greens, rinse, pat dry, and cut into thin shreds; distribute over potato and turnip slices. Finish with an even layer of remaining turnip and potato slices. Sprinkle with additional $^1/_2$ teaspoon salt and $^1/_4$ teaspoon pepper. Add enough cream to cover by half. Sprinkle top evenly with bread crumbs. Refrigerate.

COOKING: Adjust oven rack to low position and heat oven to 375°F. Bake gratin 30 minutes, then press vegetables down with a spatula to submerge them in the cream. Continue baking until top is golden brown, 50 to 60 minutes. (Can wrap and refrigerate up to 2 days.)

Alice Waters
Owner Chez Panisse and Cafe Fanny
Berkeley, CA
Patricia Curtan
Cookbook author
Berkeley, CA

RED POTATOES MASHED WITH GARLIC

Makes 4 to 6 servings

Potatoes are boiled, then baked briefly for a less starchy puree. Bradley Ogden serves this dish at his restaurant with roast turkey, chicken, or other poultry, or grilled steak. As an alternative, he suggests flavoring the potatoes with poached, pureed fennel as an accompaniment for fish.

$^1/_2$ **pounds red potatoes**
Salt
1 medium head of garlic
1 cup heavy cream
1 cup milk
$^1/_4$ **pound butter**
Ground black pepper

PREPARATION AND COOKING: Adjust oven rack to high position and heat oven to 350°F. Scrub and put potatoes in a large saucepan with 2 teaspoons salt and cold water to cover. Bring water to a boil, and simmer until potatoes are tender, about 20 minutes; drain. Transfer potatoes to a jellyroll pan and bake 10 minutes. Cool slightly and peel; set aside.

Peel and put garlic cloves in a medium saucepan with the cream, milk, and butter. Bring cream mixture to a boil, and simmer until garlic is tender, 12 to 14 minutes.

Force potatoes, garlic, and cream mixture through a food mill fitted with the fine disk into a large bowl. Stir in 1 teaspoon salt and 1 teaspoon pepper. Serve immediately.

Bradley Ogden
Chef
Campton Place
San Francisco, CA

SWEET POTATOES ANNA

Makes 6 servings

This variation on the traditional French potato cake is every bit as good if made a day in advance, particularly since raw sweet potatoes, unlike russets, will not discolor over time. The traditional copper pan for Potatoes Anna may be used, but a cake pan will work just as well.

$1/4$ **pound butter**
**4 medium sweet potatoes *or*
    yams ($2^{1}/4$ pounds)**
$1^{1}/4$ ounces Parmesan cheese
Salt and ground white pepper

PREPARATION: Melt the butter in a small saucepan. Peel and slice the potatoes into $1/8$-inch rounds with a large knife or the thin slicing disk of a food processor. Grate the cheese ($1/3$ cup). Line the bottom of a 9-inch cake pan with a circle of aluminum foil and coat with 1 tablespoon melted butter. Working in a spiral pattern, cover the bottom of the pan with a layer of closely overlapping sweet potato slices. Drizzle the potatoes with 1 tablespoon butter and lightly sprinkle with salt, pepper, and 1 tablespoon cheese. Continue layering all of the potato slices in the same manner using all of the melted butter and cheese. Cover the pan with foil, press down firmly with your hands to compress the potatoes, and cover tightly with aluminum foil. (Can refrigerate overnight.)

COOKING: Adjust oven rack to low position and heat oven to 425°F. Bake potatoes for 30 minutes. Remove foil and bake until potatoes are tender and the top of the cake is crisp and brown, about 35 to 40 minutes longer. (Can cool, cover, and refrigerate potato cake overnight.)

SERVING: If potato cake has been refrigerated, bake, uncovered, at 425°F, until sizzling around the edges, and a small, sharp knife inserted into the center of the cake for 10 seconds comes out hot, about 10 minutes. Cool 5 minutes in pan. Run a sharp knife around the edge of the pan to loosen the cake, and carefully invert onto a serving plate. Serve immediately.

Marlene Sorosky
Cookbook author
Towson, MD

BAKED SWEET POTATOES WITH HONEY-MINT BUTTER

Makes 4 servings

Serve this butter on sweet potatoes, squash, pumpkin, or roasted onions.

Honey-Mint Butter
1/4 pound softened butter
1 1/2 teaspoons honey
1/2 teaspoon minced mint or 1/4 teaspoon dried
Salt and ground black pepper

4 medium sweet potatoes (about 1 1/2 pounds)

PREPARATION: *For the butter*, cream butter, then beat in honey and mint. Season with salt and 1/8 teaspoon pepper; set aside. Scrub potatoes.

COOKING: Adjust oven rack to middle position and heat oven to 450°F. Bake sweet potatoes until tender, about 1 hour.

SERVING: Cut potatoes open and fill each with a dollop of the butter.

Danny Wisel
Chef
Rocco's
Boston, MA

SNOW-PEA AND BELL-PEPPER RIBBONS

Makes 8 servings

Fresh vegetables are given a buttery polish by a last-minute toss with softened butter.

$1/2$ **pound snow peas**
Salt
Ice water
2 medium red bell peppers ($3/4$ pound)
2 medium yellow bell peppers ($3/4$ pound)
2 tablespoons olive oil
Ground black pepper
1 tablespoon softened butter

PREPARATION: Remove stem ends and strings from snow peas. Bring 2 quarts water to a boil in a large saucepan with $1/2$ teaspoon salt. Add the peas and cook just until water returns to a boil. Drain and immediately immerse the pea pods in ice water. Drain and pat dry with paper toweling. (Can cover and refrigerate overnight.) Core and slice peppers lengthwise into $1/8$-inch julienne strips.

COOKING: Heat oil in a large skillet with $1/8$ teaspoon salt and $1/8$ teaspoon pepper. Add peppers and sauté over high heat, stirring constantly until slightly softened, about 1 minute. Add the snow peas in 2 batches, stirring constantly until vegetables are heated through, about 1 minute longer. Remove from heat and stir in the butter. Serve immediately.

Jane Freiman
Food columnist and cookbook author
New York, NY

RUTABAGA AND SWEET PEPPER GRATIN

Makes 4 to 6 servings

Rutabagas can be stored for several weeks in a dark, dry place. Evan and Judith Jones serve this earthy gratin with ham or roast turkey.

4 tablespoons butter
1 small rutabaga (1 pound)
1 medium onion
1 medium red bell pepper
1 medium green bell pepper
2 ounces Parmesan cheese
Salt and ground black pepper
1¼ cups heavy cream
½ teaspoon grated nutmeg

PREPARATION: Lightly coat a 1½-quart baking dish with 1 tablespoon butter. Peel, quarter, and slice rutabaga ¼ inch thick. Peel and coarsely chop onion. Slice two rounds of red, and three rounds of green pepper, ¼ inch thick. Grate cheese (½ cup). Evenly layer one-third of rutabaga in baking dish. Evenly distribute one-third of onion over rutabaga. Sprinkle with salt and pepper, and dot with 1 tablespoon butter. Repeat for 2 more layers. Pour cream over top, sprinkle with nutmeg, and decorate with pepper rounds. Sprinkle cheese over top.

COOKING AND SERVING: Heat oven to 350°F. Bake until rutabagas are tender and gratin is lightly browned, about 50 minutes. Serve immediately.

Evan Jones
Cookbook author
Judith Jones
Senior Editor and Vice President
Alfred A. Knopf Publishing
New York, NY

BEEF AND VEAL

THE BEST BURGER

Makes 4 servings

Serve this flavorful hamburger with a roasted garlic mayonnaise, which is a milder version of the traditional aioli that calls for raw garlic. Grill the hamburgers or sauté in a little butter for best-tasting results. Instead of the standard hamburger bun, serve these tasty burgers in warm pockets of pita along with lettuce and tomato if you like.

Roasted-Garlic Mayonnaise
15 cloves garlic
1 egg yolk
2 teaspoons white-wine vinegar
$1/2$ teaspoon mustard
Salt and pepper
$2/3$ cup peanut oil *and/or* olive oil

$1^1/2$ pounds ground beef
Salt and pepper
2 tablespoons butter if frying
4 pitas
Lettuce and tomato (optional)

PREPARATION: *For the Roasted-Garlic Mayonnaise*, heat the oven to 375°F. Put the unpeeled garlic in a small pan and roast in preheated oven until golden brown, about 20 minutes. Cool the garlic and then peel or squeeze out soft insides.

In a small bowl, whisk the egg yolk with the white-wine vinegar, mustard, and $1/2$ teaspoon salt. Whisk in the oil, drop by drop at first and then, when sauce has thickened, in a slow, thin stream. Add the roasted garlic and season to taste with salt, if needed, and pepper. The Roasted-Garlic Mayonnaise can be made a day ahead.

COOKING AND SERVING: Heat the grill if using. Shape the ground beef gently into patties. Sprinkle hamburger patties with salt and pepper and cook, turning once, about 10 minutes total for medium-rare. If frying burgers, heat a large frying pan over medium heat. Add the butter and when it melts add the patties and cook, turning once, about 10 minutes total for medium-rare. Cut pitas in half horizontally and warm pitas on the grill or in the oven.

Top each hamburger with Roasted-Garlic Mayonnaise and lettuce and tomato and serve in warm pita.

Pam Parseghian
Free-lance writer
New York, NY

BRAISED BRISKET IN ITS OWN BROTH

Makes 4 to 6 servings

Brisket is a savory, full-flavored cut of beef that's usually braised. You can use the "flat cut," which is the thinnest, leanest section of the brisket; but we recommend the pointed front cut for this dish. It's more economical and a bit richer in flavor.

1 tablespoon minced fresh
    thyme leaves *or* 1 teaspoon
    dried
1$^1\!/_2$ teaspoons minced fresh
    rosemary *or* $^1\!/_2$ teaspoon dried
4 cloves garlic
1 onion
7 whole plum tomatoes (about 2
    pounds)
1 tablespoon oil
2 to 2$^1\!/_2$ pounds beef brisket
Salt and pepper
2 carrots
1 rib celery
1 bay leaf
1 cup chicken stock

PREPARATION: Heat oven to 350°F. Mince the thyme, rosemary, and garlic. Halve the onion. Peel, seed, and chop the tomatoes. Heat the oil in a large ovenproof pot. Put the brisket in the pot, sprinkle with salt and pepper, and sear on both sides over high heat until well browned, about 6 minutes total. Lower heat to medium, add the garlic, thyme, and rosemary, and cook about 1 minute more. Add the tomatoes, onion halves, whole carrots, celery, bay leaf, and chicken stock, cover, and bring just to a simmer. Cook in preheated oven until beef is tender, about 2 hours. Remove and discard the celery, onion, and bay leaf. Recipe can be made to this point a couple of days ahead.

SERVING: Reheat the brisket if necessary. Remove the meat and carrots from the broth. Slice brisket against the grain into thin slices. Cut the carrots into chunks. Arrange meat and carrots on deep plates and pour some of the broth over each serving.

Pam Parseghian
Free-lance writer
New York, NY

BEEF FILLET WITH GORGONZOLA AND PISTACHIOS

Makes 4 servings

Sometimes invention is the result of chance and quick thinking. When Donato de Santis came to America, Piero Selvaggio (owner of Primi and Valentino in Los Angeles) took the chef to the kitchen and said "Do something." Says De Santis, "It was a trial. My eyes just fell on the Gorgonzola and the beef. The taste and texture worked; it melted in my mouth."

1 small shallot
4 2-inch-thick beef fillets
2 tablespoons oil
Salt and pepper
1 tablespoon butter
1 tablespoon pistachio nuts
$1/2$ cup red wine *or* 2 tablespoons red-wine vinegar
$1/4$ pound Gorgonzola cheese
$1/4$ cup veal *or* chicken stock

PREPARATION: Mince the shallot. Recipe can be prepared to this point several hours ahead. Bring the meat to room temperature.

COOKING AND SERVING: In a large frying pan, heat the oil over high heat and sauté the fillets until seared on both sides, about 3 minutes total. Season with salt and pepper. Reduce heat to low and cook, turning once, about 10 minutes total for medium-rare. Put fillets on a warm serving platter or individual plates and keep warm. Pour off fat. Melt the butter in the same pan and sauté the shallot until just golden brown and soft, about 3 minutes. Add the pistachios and wine and cook over medium-high heat, stirring with a wooden spoon to deglaze the bottom of the pan, until liquid is almost evaporated. Remove pan from heat and stir in the cheese with a wooden spoon until melted. Return pan to heat. Add the stock and cook, stirring, until sauce is thick and creamy, about 2 minutes. Top fillets with the sauce and serve.

Donato De Santis
Chef
Primi
Los Angeles, CA

COGNAC-MARINATED BEEF FILLET

Makes 8 servings

Juicy, rare, sliced tenderloin is a classic main course that has withstood the test of time and the vagaries of food trends.

3 pounds center-cut beef fillet, trimmed and tied
1 medium garlic clove
2 medium shallots
$1/2$ teaspoon dried thyme leaves
$1/2$ teaspoon dried summer savory leaves
Salt and ground black pepper
3 tablespoons Cognac *or* brandy
$1/3$ cup olive oil

PREPARATION: To age beef fillet before cooking, place in the coldest part of the refrigerator, unwrapped and uncovered, on a wire rack set over a baking sheet overnight, so air can circulate around meat. Peel and mince garlic and shallots. Combine garlic, shallots, thyme, summer savory, $1/4$ teaspoon salt, $1/8$ teaspoon pepper, Cognac, and $1/4$ cup olive oil in a large nonreactive baking dish. Turn meat in marinade, cover, and refrigerate 12 hours. (Can refrigerate up to 2 days.)

COOKING: Adjust oven rack to low position and heat oven to 450°F. Remove meat from marinade, pat dry with paper towels, and rub with remaining olive oil. Transfer meat to a heavy-duty roasting pan. Roast 15 minutes, turning to sear on all sides. Continue roasting 15 to 20 minutes longer for rare (125°F). Let stand 5 minutes, remove strings, slice, and serve immediately. Spoon any meat juices that result from slicing over the meat before serving.

Jane Freiman
Food columnist and cookbook author
New York, NY

BEEF AND BROCCOLI STIR-FRY

Makes 4 servings

This spicy stir-fry is an unusually quick dish to make from flank or top-round steak. The secret is in cutting the meat into thin pieces and searing it rapidly.

2 ounces rice noodles
1 bunch broccoli (about 1¼ pounds)
3 scallions
1½ tablespoons minced fresh ginger
1⅓ pounds flank *or* top-round steak
1½ teaspoons cornstarch
½ teaspoon sesame oil
1 tablespoon soy sauce plus more if necessary
¼ teaspoon red-pepper flakes
1 tablespoon rice-wine vinegar *or* white wine
1⅓ cups chicken stock
1 tablespoon vegetable or peanut oil
2 tablespoons fermented black beans (optional)

PREPARATION: Put the rice noodles in a bowl and cover with boiling water. Soak noodles until soft, about 5 minutes. Drain thoroughly. Trim and peel the broccoli stems and cut into thin slices on an angle. Cut broccoli heads into small florets. Blanch broccoli stems and heads in a large pot of boiling, salted water until almost tender, about 4 minutes. Drain and plunge into a bowl of cold water to stop cooking and drain again. Slice the scallions into thin rounds, keeping the green and white parts separate. Peel and mince the ginger. Cut the steak into thin slices against the grain and then into bite-size pieces. In a small bowl, combine the cornstarch, sesame oil, soy sauce, red-pepper flakes, vinegar, and chicken stock. Recipe can be made to this point a few hours ahead.

COOKING AND SERVING: Heat the vegetable oil in a wok or large frying pan over high heat until almost smoking. Sear the steak in batches, being careful not to overcrowd the pan, until well browned, about 2 minutes per batch. Remove meat from wok and set aside. Add the scallion bulbs, ginger, and fermented black beans to the pan and sauté, stirring, until scallions and ginger are soft, about 1 minute. Add the soy-sauce mixture and cook until heated through and slightly thickened, about 1 minute. Stir in softened noodles, steak, and broccoli, and cook until heated through, about 1 minute. Add scallion tops. Season to taste with soy sauce and serve.

Pam Parseghian
Free-lance writer
New York, NY

GRILLED FLANK STEAK WITH SUMMER VEGETABLES

Makes 4 servings

The grill makes quick work of cooking the meat, vegetables, and bread for this gorgeous main course that belies its ease of preparation.

1 medium lemon
1 medium garlic clove
6 tablespoons olive oil
1 pound flank steak
$^{1}/_{4}$ cup loosely packed, stemmed basil leaves
4 medium tomatoes (about 1 pound)
Salt and ground black pepper
4 medium zucchini (about 1 pound)
4 slices ($^{3}/_{4}$ inch-thick) Italian bread

PREPARATION: Squeeze $2^{1}/_{2}$ tablespoons lemon juice into a large, shallow dish. Peel and mince the garlic and add it to the lemon juice with 5 tablespoons of olive oil. Add the flank steak to the dish, turn once in the marinade, and set aside for 15 minutes. Mince the basil. Thinly slice the tomatoes and put them in a flat dish with the remaining olive oil. Sprinkle tomatoes with basil and salt and pepper; set aside. Trim and cut the zucchini lengthwise into $^{1}/_{4}$-inch-thick slices.

COOKING AND SERVING: Heat the grill. Season the meat with salt and pepper and place on the grill. Brush the zucchini and the bread with the remaining meat marinade and place on grill. Grill the meat, zucchini, and bread for 3 minutes. Turn, and grill 3 minutes more, until meat is medium-rare, zucchini is crisp and tender, and bread is toasted. Slice the meat thinly across the grain. Arrange the meat, zucchini, bread, and tomato slices on individual serving plates. Spoon any meat juices over the meat and bread. Serve immediately.

Brooke Dojny and Melanie Barnard
Nationally syndicated food writers and cookbook authors
Fairfield County, CT

PEPPERED ROAST BEEF

Makes 6 servings

This variation on *steak au poivre* has a more subtle favor since the peppery coating covers only the outside edge of each slice rather than both sides of individual steaks.

1 tablespoon salt
3 tablespoons cracked black
   peppercorns
1 2¹/₂-pound sirloin-tip roast
   beef
1 tablespoon oil

COOKING: Heat oven to 475°F. Combine the salt and black peppercorns. Rub the roast with oil and coat with the peppercorn mixture. Do not coat the ends. Put beef in a roasting pan and sear in preheated oven for 10 minutes. Lower heat to 350°F and continue roasting until internal temperature reaches 125°F, about 35 minutes more. Let the roast rest about 15 minutes before slicing.

SERVING: Cut the roast beef into thin slices against the grain.

Pam Parseghian
Free-lance writer
New York, NY

GINGER-MARINATED FLANK STEAK

Makes 4 servings

Boneless flank steak is a delicious lean cut of meat, especially when it is marinated in a highly seasoned liquid — such as the ginger-soy sauce marinade featured here — and then cut into thin slices against the grain.

1 clove garlic
3 tablespoons minced fresh
  ginger
1/2 cup dark soy sauce *or* tamari
1/4 cup oil
2 teaspoons cracked black
  peppercorns
1 1/2 pounds flank steak
Salt and pepper

PREPARATION: Mince the garlic. Peel and mince the fresh ginger. In a bowl, combine the garlic, ginger, soy sauce, oil, and the peppercorns. Put the flank steak in a pan, cover with the ginger-soy-sauce mixture, and marinate for 2 hours at room temperature, or refrigerate overnight.

COOKING AND SERVING: Heat the grill or broiler. Sear the flank steak on both sides, about 2 minutes total. Season the flank steak with salt and pepper and cook, turning once and basting with the ginger-soy sauce marinade every few minutes, about 6 additional minutes for medium-rare. Cut the flank steak against the grain into thin slices and serve.

Pam Parseghian
Free-lance writer
New York, NY

SEVEN-SPICE BROILED FLANK STEAK

Makes 4 servings

Coat steak with spices and refrigerate overnight for a more pronounced flavor.

$^1/_2$ **teaspoon dried thyme**
2 teaspoons dried basil
1$^1/_2$ teaspoons dried oregano
$^3/_4$ **teaspoon fennel seeds**
$^1/_4$ **teaspoon cayenne pepper**
$^1/_2$ **teaspoon pumpkin pie spice**
Salt and ground black pepper
1$^1/_2$ pounds flank *or* skirt steak

PREPARATION: Mix all the spices with $^1/_2$ teaspoon salt and $^1/_2$ teaspoon pepper. Cut the steak lengthwise into 2 equal pieces and rub with the spice mixture.

COOKING AND SERVING: Heat broiler. Broil steak about 3 minutes per side for medium-rare. Slice steaks thinly against the grain. Serve immediately.

Betsy Schultz
Food consultant
New York, NY

SPICY BEEF STEW

Makes 4 servings

This contemporary dish combines the robust flavor of a winter beef stew with that of a spicy Texas-style chili.

1 35-ounce can plum tomatoes
2 ears corn *or* 1 cup frozen corn
 kernels
1¹/₂ pounds beef chuck *or* stew
 meat
6 cloves garlic
1 onion
1 jalapeño *or* other hot pepper
1¹/₂ tablespoons oil
Salt
1 tablespoon cumin
1 tablespoon paprika
¹/₄ teaspoon cayenne
¹/₂ teaspoon oregano
³/₄ cup red wine
3 cups beef stock
4 scallions

PREPARATION: Drain the tomatoes. Cut corn kernels from cobs. Cut the beef into 1-inch cubes. Mince the garlic. Halve the onion and cut into thin slices. Core, seed, and mince the jalapeño, or leave seeds in, if desired, for a hotter stew. In a large, deep frying pan, heat 1 tablespoon of the oil. Add the onion and cook until soft, about 3 minutes. Add the garlic and jalapeño and cook until golden brown, about 1 minute. Remove the onion mixture from the pan and set aside. Sprinkle the beef with salt. In the same pan, sear the beef over medium-high heat, working in batches, until brown, about 5 minutes per batch. Return all beef to the pan. Stir in the cumin, paprika, cayenne, and oregano and cook for 30 seconds. Add the red wine and stir with a wooden spoon to deglaze the bottom of the pan. Add the onion mixture, tomatoes, and beef stock. Reduce heat, cover, and barely simmer until meat is tender, about 1 hour and 45 minutes, adding water if stew becomes too thick. Add the corn and cook until tender, about 10 minutes more. Season to taste with salt and more cayenne pepper if desired. Recipe can be made to this point a couple of days ahead.

SERVING: Cut scallions into thin slices. Reheat stew if made ahead, stir in scallions, and serve.

Pam Parseghian
Free-lance writer
New York, NY

TENDERLOIN WITH BROWN BUTTER AND SHALLOTS

Makes 4 servings

The beef tenderloin is the most tender cut of all. All that these prized steaks need is a simple yet delicious brown-butter sauce with shallots.

9 shallots
1 tablespoon oil
4 2-inch-thick fillet steaks
  (about 5 to 6 ounces each)
Salt and pepper
6 tablespoons butter

PREPARATION: Cut the shallots into thin slices.
Recipe can be made to this point several hours ahead.
COOKING AND SERVING: Heat the oil in a large frying pan. Sprinkle the fillets with salt and pepper and put them in the frying pan. Sear the steaks on both sides over high heat until well browned, about 3 minutes total. Lower the heat to medium, add the butter, and continue cooking, turning occasionally, about 6 minutes more. Add the shallots, arranging them around the fillets. Continue cooking, stirring the shallots occasionally, until the shallots and butter are golden brown, about 4 additional minutes for medium-rare fillets. Remove the steaks and shallots from the frying pan. Add $1/4$ cup of water to the pan, stirring to deglaze, and cook until the brown-butter sauce thickens. Put a fillet steak onto each serving plate and surround with the shallots. Top each steak with the brown-butter sauce and serve.

Pam Parseghian
Free-lance writer
New York, NY

VEAL CHOPS WITH DUXELLES AND HAM

Makes 4 servings

Duxelles is made by cooking finely chopped mushrooms with shallots and butter until all of the moisture given off by the mushrooms has evaporated and the butter is absorbed.

Duxelles
2 medium shallots
1 pound mushrooms
2 tablespoons butter
3 tablespoons minced parsley leaves
$^1/_4$ cup fresh bread crumbs
Salt and ground black pepper

Veal and Sauce
2 medium shallots
2 tablespoons vegetable oil
2 tablespoons butter
4 loin veal chops, $^3/_4$-inch-thick (about 2 pounds)
$^3/_4$ cup white wine
$^3/_4$ cup chicken stock
4 ounces thinly sliced cooked ham
1 teaspoon dried thyme

PREPARATION AND COOKING: *For the duxelles*, peel and mince the shallots and chop the mushrooms fine. In a large skillet heat the butter and sauté the shallots over medium heat until softened, 1 to 2 minutes. Add the mushrooms and sauté, stirring frequently, until all the liquid has evaporated, about 30 minutes. Stir in the parsley, bread crumbs, $^1/_4$ teaspoon salt, and $^1/_4$ teaspoon pepper. Transfer mixture to a bowl and set aside. (Can cover and refrigerate duxelles up to 2 days.)

For the veal and sauce, peel and mince the shallots. In a medium skillet, heat oil and butter until hot but not smoking. Sear the veal chops 1 minute on each side and transfer chops to a plate. Reduce heat to medium, add shallots and sauté until softened, about 30 seconds. Add wine and simmer until reduced to 6 tablespoons, about 5 minutes. Add chicken stock and reduce cooking liquid to $^1/_2$ cup, about 8 minutes. Set skillet aside.

ASSEMBLY: Julienne the ham slices (1 cup). Cut 4 parchment or foil pouches. Center 2 rounded tablespoons of *duxelles* on one side of each pouch, cover with a veal chop, and sprinkle with $^1/_4$ teaspoon thyme. Spoon 2 tablespoons reduced cooking liquid over each chop; top with 2 more tablespoons *duxelles* and $^1/_4$ cup ham. Seal pouches. (Can refrigerate parchment pouches up to 4 hours; foil pouches overnight.)

SERVING: Adjust oven rack to middle position and heat oven to 400°F. Put pouches on a baking sheet and bake until veal is medium rare, about 12 minutes (18 minutes if assembled pouches are refrigerated before cooking). Transfer pouches to plates and carefully pierce each to permit steam to escape. Serve immediately.

Peter Kump
President
Peter Kump's New York Cooking School
  and James Beard Foundation
New York, NY

SAUTEED VEAL CHOPS WITH MUSHROOMS, SHALLOTS, AND WHITE WINE

Makes 4 servings

Veal chops feature a rich sauce of shallots and mushrooms, accented with minced parsley. If loin chops are not available veal rib chops may be substituted.

2 medium shallots
$1/4$ pound mushrooms
1 tablespoon butter
4 veal loin chops, $3/4$ inch thick
Salt and ground black pepper
$1/2$ cup dry white wine
3 tablespoons minced parsley

PREPARATION: Peel and mince shallots. Rinse and slice mushrooms.

COOKING: Heat butter in a skillet. Sprinkle chops with salt and pepper and sauté until browned and medium rare, 6 to 8 minutes. Transfer to a serving platter and cover with aluminum foil. Add shallots to the skillet and sauté 1 minute. Add the mushrooms and sauté until softened, about 2 minutes. Add wine and simmer until liquid reduces and thickens slightly, about 2 minutes.

SERVING: Remove from heat, stir in parsley, and season with salt and pepper. Spoon sauce over chops and serve with egg noodles tossed with butter and black pepper.

Pam Parseghian
Free-lance writer
New York, NY

BRAISED VEAL SHANKS
WITH GARLIC, LEMON, AND PARSLEY
OSSOBUCO ALLA MILANESE

Makes 6 servings

Ossobuco (Italian for "bone with a hole") refers to the hollow shank bone filled with marrow, a delicacy which some consider to be the best part of the veal. Because they are more meaty and tender, cuts from the hind shanks are preferable to those from foreshanks. Serve Ossobuco with Milanese-style risotto (Arborio rice simmered in stock and flavored with saffron). During the final few minutes of braising, stir in the *gremolada*, a seasoning paste made of lemon rind, garlic, and parsley.

1 medium onion
2 medium carrots
1 celery stalk
1 can plum tomatoes (8 ounces)
6 large veal shanks (about 12 ounces each), tied
Salt and ground black pepper
$^1/_3$ cup all-purpose flour
6 tablespoons vegetable oil
4 tablespoons butter
1 cup dry white wine
1 cup chicken stock *or* canned chicken broth
$^1/_2$ teaspoon dried thyme

Gremolada
1 large garlic clove
1 tablespoon grated lemon zest
$^3/_4$ cup firmly packed parsley leaves

PREPARATION: Peel and cut onions and carrots into $^1/_2$-inch dice. Cut celery into $^1/_2$-inch dice. Chop tomatoes.

COOKING AND SERVING: Adjust oven rack to middle position and heat oven to 350°F. Pat veal shanks dry with paper towels, sprinkle with $^1/_2$ teaspoon salt and $^1/_4$ teaspoon pepper. Dredge shanks in flour. Heat oil in a 5-quart nonreactive Dutch oven. Sauté shanks over high heat, turning to sear on both sides, about 4 minutes. Transfer to a plate. Discard oil and heat butter. Add onion, carrots, and celery, and sauté, stirring occasionally, until vegetables soften and color slightly, about 10 minutes. Return shanks to the Dutch oven, placing on top of the vegetables. Add wine, stock, tomatoes, and thyme; bring liquid to boil. Cover and transfer pan to oven. Braise, basting every 30 minutes, until meat is tender, $1^1/_2$ to 2 hours. (Can cool, cover, and set aside for several hours, or refrigerate in sauce up to 3 days.)

For the gremolada, peel and mince garlic. Mince parsley. Mix garlic, zest, and parsley; set aside. (Warm shanks over low heat.) Transfer shanks to a platter. Skim the cooling liquid and puree vegetables and liquid in the workbowl of a food processor fitted with the metal blade. Adjust seasoning. Return meat and sauce to Dutch oven. Sprinkle *gremolada* over meat; simmer 5 minutes, until shanks are warmed through. Spoon sauce onto 6 warm plates. Put shanks over sauce and serve immediately.

Peter Kump
President
Peter Kump's New York Cooking School
  and James Beard Foundation
New York, NY

SALTIMBOCCA
VEAL WITH PROSCIUTTO AND SAGE

Makes 4 servings

The classic Italian dish *saltimbocca* means "jump in the mouth." Its three main ingredients — veal, sage, and prosciutto — make a great flavor combination.

8 veal scallops (about 1 pound total)
8 fresh sage leaves *or* 1/2 teaspoon dried
8 thin slices prosciutto
4 tablespoons butter plus more if needed
1 cup chicken stock
Pepper

PREPARATION: Pound veal scallops to flatten. Top each scallop with a sage leaf, or sprinkle with a pinch of sage, and top with a slice of prosciutto, trimming as needed.

Recipe can be made to this point several hours ahead.

COOKING AND SERVING: In a large frying pan, melt 2 tablespoons of the butter over medium heat until foamy. Working in batches and adding more butter if necessary, sauté veal scallops, turning once, until lightly browned, about 4 minutes total. Transfer veal scallops to a warm serving platter. Add the stock to the pan and stir with a wooden spoon to deglaze the bottom of the pan. Cook over high heat until reduced to about 1/4 cup, about 5 minutes. Remove pan from heat and stir in the remaining 2 tablespoons butter. Season to taste with pepper. Pour sauce over the veal scallops and serve.

Elizabeth Riely
Free-lance writer
Newton Centre, MA

PORK AND VEAL PATTIES WITH SAUTEED APPLES

Makes 4 servings

These patties, seasoned with Dijon mustard, are topped with sautéed apples.

1 pound ground pork
1 pound ground veal
1 tablespoon Dijon mustard
Salt and pepper
2 tart apples
2 tablespoons sugar
4 slices sourdough *or* other
    bread

PREPARATION: In a bowl, combine the pork, veal, and mustard and season with 1 teaspoon salt and $1/4$ teaspoon pepper. Shape gently into four patties. Recipe can be prepared to this point several hours ahead.

COOKING AND SERVING: Peel apples and cut into thin slices. In a large frying pan, sauté the patties over high heat until seared on both sides, about 1 minute per side. Lower heat to medium and cook, turning once, until patties are just cooked through, about 10 more minutes. Remove patties from pan, drain on paper towels, and keep warm. Pour off all but 1 tablespoon of fat from the pan. Add apples and sauté over medium-high heat until they soften, about 3 minutes. Stir in the sugar, scraping any loose bits from pan. Continue cooking until sugar has dissolved and apples are tender, about 2 minutes. Toast and butter the bread. Serve each patty on a slice of toast topped with a spoonful of sautéed apples.

Anne Byrn
Food editor
The Atlanta Journal and *The Atlanta Constitution*

LAMB AND PORK

MOROCCAN LAMB BROCHETTES
WITH CUMIN AND CILANTRO

Makes 4 servings

Serve spicy grilled lamb skewers on a bed of steamed couscous with broiled eggplant and peppers that have been brushed with the lamb marinade. Accompany with *harissa*, a fiery Moroccan condiment that is made from red bell peppers, dried hot red peppers, garlic, and olive oil and is available from Middle Eastern food stores.

1 small onion
4 large garlic cloves
1 tablespoon ground cumin
1 tablespoon paprika
$1/2$ teaspoon ground ginger
$1/2$ teaspoon cayenne pepper
Ground black pepper
1 small lemon
$2/3$ cup olive oil
2 tablespoons minced cilantro
2 pounds leg of lamb
Salt

PREPARATION: Peel and quarter the onion. Peel the garlic and put it with the onion, cumin, paprika, ginger, cayenne pepper, and 1 teaspoon black pepper in the workbowl of a food processor fitted with the metal blade; puree. Squeeze in 3 tablespoons of fresh lemon juice. Add the olive oil and minced cilantro, and pulse to mix. Trim and cut the lamb into 1-inch cubes. Put lamb cubes in a large, shallow nonreactive baking dish. Pour the marinade over the meat and toss well. Marinate lamb at room temperature for 4 hours. (Can cool, cover, and refrigerate overnight.)

COOKING: Heat grill or broiler. If using wooden skewers, soak at least 15 minutes in warm water. Thread 3 to 4 cubes of lamb onto each of 8 wooden or metal skewers. Sprinkle with salt. Grill or broil on all sides until medium-rare, about 10 minutes.

SERVING: Transfer the brochettes to 4 warmed serving plates and serve immediately.

Joyce Goldstein
Chef/owner
Square One
San Francisco, CA

CLASSIC LAMB CURRY
MASALA GOSHT

Makes 6 servings

Lamb curry, which originated in the royal kitchen of the Moghuls, remains the most popular dish in many Indian households. In this version, the fresh coriander and the acidity of the tomatoes form a graceful counterpoint to the classic base of sweet, caramelized onions.

2 pounds onions (6 medium)
6 medium garlic cloves
1¾ pounds tomatoes *or* 1 can
    crushed (28 ounces)
3 pounds lean boneless lamb
    shoulder *or* leg, trimmed
7 tablespoons vegetable oil
3 tablespoons grated ginger
4 tablespoons ground coriander
    seeds
1 teaspoon cayenne pepper
2 teaspoons turmeric
4 teaspoons *garam masala*
    (recipe page 282)
Salt
4 mild *or* hot chiles, such as
    serranos *or* jalapeños
1 cup loosely packed coriander
    leaves
½ cup half-and-half

PREPARATION: Peel and cut the onions in ¼-inch dice (4 cups). Peel and mince the garlic (2 tablespoons.) Quarter the tomatoes and put them in the workbowl of a food processor fitted with the metal blade; puree and set aside. Cut lamb into 1-inch cubes and pat meat dry with paper toweling.

COOKING: Heat 2 tablespoons oil in a 4-quart soup kettle. Working in batches, sear the lamb over medium-high heat until well browned; set aside. Heat the remaining 5 tablespoons oil in the kettle. Add the onions and sauté over low heat, stirring occasionally, until softened and lightly colored, about 20 minutes. Add the ginger and garlic and sauté until fragrant, 1 to 2 minutes longer. Add the ground coriander, the cayenne pepper, turmeric, *garam masala*, tomato puree, lamb, 2½ teaspoons salt, and 2 cups water. Bring to a boil, cover, and simmer slowly for 1 hour. Set cover ajar and simmer until the lamb is tender and the liquid thickens and reduces to a saucelike consistency, 30 to 45 minutes longer. (Can cool, cover, and set aside for 4 to 5 hours or refrigerate up to 3 days.)

SERVING: Reheat curry if it has been set aside or refrigerated. Stem, seed, and cut chiles into ⅛-inch julienne strips. Mince the coriander. Stir the half-and-half, coriander, and chiles into the curry. Simmer until hot, then serve immediately over rice.

Julie Sahni
Cookbook author
New York, NY

LEG OF LAMB ROASTED WITH SHALLOTS

Makes 8 to 10 servings

When buying the leg for this roast, ask the butcher to remove the fell or tough membrane, and cut the shank bone just above the break joint. The butcher should "french" the shank — free the tendons of the shank from the bone so that when the leg is cooked, a short section (about 2 inches) of the bone will be clean and accommodate a *manche à gigot* — an elegant instrument that screws onto the shank bone and provides the carver with a handle. Or, the end of the bone can be wrapped with a napkin and used as a "handle" while carving.

2 medium garlic cloves
¹/₂ teaspoon dried thyme
1 leg of lamb (7-8 pounds), trimmed
1 pound large shallots
Salt and ground black pepper
2 tablespoons oil
1¹/₂ cups lamb or beef stock *or* canned beef broth
¹/₃ cup dry red wine
1 tablespoon sherry-wine vinegar
2 tablespoons butter

PREPARATION: Peel and thinly slice the garlic, and toss it with the thyme in a small bowl. With a small, sharp knife, cut around the aitch bone, remove bone at the joint, and truss top of the leg to restore its shape. Cut shallow, evenly spaced incisions on both sides of the leg and slip a sliver of thyme-coated garlic into each incision. Transfer leg to a shallow baking dish and set aside at room temperature for at least one hour. (Can cover and refrigerate overnight.) Peel and trim the shallots and break into separate bulbs and set aside.

COOKING: (Bring lamb to room temperature.) Sprinkle with salt and pepper and rub with oil. Adjust oven rack to low position and heat oven to 450°F. Sear lamb 15 minutes, then lower heat to 350°F. Scatter shallots around lamb in baking dish and roast, stirring shallots occasionally, until internal temperature of the lamb at the thickest point reaches 130°F, about 1 hour. Transfer roast to a carving board or large platter and cover with a tent of foil. Transfer shallots with pan juices to a medium saucepan. Add beef stock, red wine, and vinegar; bring to simmer and skim. Simmer over medium-high heat, mashing shallots with a wooden spoon, until stock is reduced to 2 cups, 10 to 15 minutes. Puree shallot mixture in the workbowl of a food processor fitted with metal blade. Return puree to saucepan, season with salt and pepper, and whisk in butter over low heat. Remove from heat, cover, and keep warm.

SERVING: Carve slices from the lamb and pass the sauce at the table.

Michael McLaughlin
Free-lance writer
Brooklyn, NY

LAMB AND WHITE BEAN RAGOUT
WITH OLIVES, TOMATOES, GARLIC, AND HERBS

Makes 8 servings

The shoulder of lamb is a very good cut for stew. Ask the butcher to bone the shoulder and trim it completely of fat. If available, boned, trimmed neck meat is also delicious in this dish. As with many stews, this will improve with age, but reserve the beans, olives and parsley to add to the stew just before serving.

1¹/₂ cups dried Great Northern
   beans (about 10 ounces)
Salt
1 lamb shoulder (6-7 pounds),
   trimmed and boned
8 garlic cloves
1 cup red wine
¹/₃ cup red-wine vinegar
¹/₂ cup olive oil
1 teaspoon dried thyme
1 teaspoon dried marjoram
1 teaspoon dried basil
2 bay leaves
2 medium onions
5 carrots
1 can plum tomatoes (35 ounces)
¹/₄ cup all-purpose flour
2 cups beef stock *or* canned beef
   broth
¹/₂ cup Niçoise olives
¹/₂ cup firmly packed stemmed
   parsley leaves
Ground black pepper

PREPARATION: Rinse, pick over beans, and put them in bowl with cold water to cover by 3 inches. Let stand for 24 hours; drain. Or, put beans in a 5-quart soup kettle or Dutch oven with water to cover, bring to a boil, cover, remove from heat, and let stand 1 hour; drain. Return drained beans to soup kettle, and add cold water to cover by 3 inches. Bring to a boil, turn heat to low and simmer, partially covered, until the beans are almost tender, about 1 hour. Stir in 1 teaspoon of salt and continue cooking until the beans are tender, 15 to 20 minutes. Drain and set aside. Cut lamb into 1¹/₂-inch cubes. Peel and crush the garlic and put it in a nonreactive bowl with the wine, vinegar, 3 tablespoons oil, thyme, majoram, basil, and bay leaves. Add the lamb and marinate for at least two hours. (Can cover and refrigerate the beans and meat separately overnight.) Peel and chop the onions (2 cups). Peel and cut carrots into ¹/₂-inch slices. Drain the tomatoes and set vegetables aside separately.

COOKING: Adjust oven rack to low position and heat oven to 350°F. Remove the lamb from the marinade and pat dry on paper toweling. Heat 3 tablespoons of the oil in the Dutch oven or soup kettle until hot but not smoking. Working in batches, sear the lamb over high heat until well browned, adding additional oil as needed, and removing lamb to a bowl with a slotted spoon or tongs. Add 1 tablespoon oil, lower heat, add the onions and cook, covered, stirring occasionally until tender about 10 minutes. Stir in the flour and cook 3 minutes. Whisk in the reserved marinade and beef stock. Stir in the tomatoes and

LAMB AND WHITE BEAN RAGOUT
WITH OLIVES, TOMATOES, GARLIC, AND HERBS

(continued)

2 teaspoons salt, and bring to a boil. Return meat to the kettle with any accumulated juices, cover with foil and the lid, and bake 1 hour. Skim, stir in the carrots, and bake, uncovered, for 30 minutes. Stir in the beans and bake until stew thickens slightly, about 15 minutes. Rinse and drain the olives. Mince the parsley. Stir in olives and parsley and season with $1/2$ teaspoon pepper and salt to taste.

Michael McLaughlin
Free-lance writer
Brooklyn, NY

MARINATED GRILLED LAMB WITH LIME AND CUMIN

Makes 8 to 10 servings

This dish was inspired by a recipe from Madhur Jeffrey's *An Introduction to Indian Cooking*. Ask the butcher to bone and butterfly the leg to produce a fat piece of meat that is easy to carve. The finished leg furnishes meat ranging from medium rare to well done, and the crusty, spicy exterior is a wonderful foil for the juicy meat. The leg can be served fajitas-style, sliced thin across the grain and folded, along with salsa and guacamole, into warmed flour tortillas or served with potatoes and vegetables.

2 medium onions
6 medium garlic clove
$1/2$ cup olive oil
$3^1/2$ tablespoons chili powder
$1^1/2$ tablespoons cumin
$1^1/2$ tablespoons dried oregano
Salt
3 medium limes
3 medium jalapeños
1 leg of lamb (about $7^1/2$ pounds),
   boned and butterflied

PREPARATION: Peel and cube the onions and put them into the workbowl of a food processor fitted with the metal blade. Peel the garlic and add it to the processor along with the olive oil, chili powder, cumin, oregano, and $2^1/2$ teaspoons salt. Squeeze in $1/4$ cup lime juice. Stem the jalapeños, add them to the processor, and process to a smooth paste. Put the lamb and the paste in a large, nonreactive bowl or baking dish and turn the meat once or twice to coat it completely. Cover and refrigerate, turning occasionally, for 24 hours.

COOKING: Remove the meat from the refrigerator and bring it to room temperature. Heat the grill and adjust the rack to about 6 inches from the coals. Or, adjust oven rack to high position and heat the oven to 400°F. Grill or roast the lamb, turning occasionally and basting frequently with the paste, until the internal temperature of the lamb at the thickest point registers 130°F, 45 to 50 minutes.

SERVING: Transfer lamb to a cutting board, cover loosely with foil, and let rest 10 minutes. Thinly slice the lamb across the grain.

Michael McLaughlin
Free-lance writer
Brooklyn, NY

SAUTEED LAMB MEDALLIONS
WITH RED WINE AND FRESH MINT

Makes 4 servings

Medallions, or "noisettes" of lamb are boneless slices cut from the loin. Ask the butcher to bone and split the double saddle for this purpose, which will yield two loin strips, to be trimmed, tied, and cut crosswise into medallions.

1 whole saddle of lamb, boned, split, with loins wrapped and tied (1¹/₂ to 2 pounds), and aprons reserved
1 medium onion
1 medium carrot
2 garlic cloves
1 leek
3 tablespoons vegetable oil
¹/₂ cup loosely packed stemmed mint leaves
¹/₂ teaspoon dried thyme
1 bay leaf
2 cups lamb or beef stock *or* canned beef broth
1¹/₂ cups red Bordeaux wine, such as Merlot or Cabernet Sauvignon
2 tablespoons chilled butter
Salt and ground black pepper

PREPARATION: Trim apron meat of fat and set aside. Peel onion, carrot, and garlic. Coarsely chop onion and carrot; set aside with garlic in a bowl. Trim, clean, and coarsely chop leek (using all of white and about 2 inches of green), and add to the bowl. In a heavy nonreactive skillet, heat 1 tablespoon oil. Quarter each apron and sauté over medium heat, until very brown, about 7 minutes. Measure 2 tablespoons mint leaves; add to skillet along with chopped vegetables, thyme, and bay leaf. Cover skillet, lower heat, and cook, stirring occasionally, until vegetables are lightly colored and tender, about 20 minutes. Stir in stock and red wine and bring to boil. Lower heat and simmer, partially covered, skimming frequently, until liquid reduces to 1¹/₄ cups, 50-60 minutes. Discard solids and set liquid aside.

COOKING: Mince remaining mint leaves. Cut butter into small pieces; set aside. Slice loins into six to eight 1¹/₄-inch thick medallions and sprinkle with salt and pepper. In a large nonreactive skillet, heat remaining oil until very hot, but not smoking. Sauté medallions 2 minutes on each side until medium rare. Transfer to a plate and cover with foil. Increase heat to high, pour stock into skillet, and bring to boil, scraping bottom with a wooden spoon to deglaze. Reduce stock to 1 cup, 2-3 minutes. Remove from heat and whisk in butter, 1 piece at a time. Stir in mint; season with salt and pepper. Cover and keep warm.

SERVING: Transfer meat to a cutting board and stir accumulated juices into sauce. Remove string and transfer medallions to warm plates. Spoon sauce around medallions; serve immediately.

Michael McLaughlin
Free-lance writer
Brooklyn, NY

SPICY MOUSSAKA WITH POTATOES AND PARMESAN

Makes 12 servings

Made over the course of a few days, this *moussaka* is best finished the day before serving in order to allow its flavors to develop fully and mellow. Sautéed eggplant, spicy lamb sauce under creamy *béchamel*, and layers of potatoes make this particularly substantial.

Lamb Sauce
3 medium onions (³/₄ pound)
8 medium garlic cloves
¹/₄ cup olive oil
1¹/₂ pounds lean ground lamb
4 teaspoons dried oregano
4 teaspoons dried thyme
1¹/₂ teaspoons ground cinnamon
1¹/₂ teaspoons dried cumin
1¹/₂ teaspoons hot red-pepper flakes
1 teaspoon ground ginger
1 teaspoon grated nutmeg
2 bay leaves
1 can Italian plum tomatoes (28 ounces)
³/₄ cup red wine
Salt

Béchamel Sauce
5 ounces Parmesan cheese (1¹/₄ cups grated)
3 medium garlic cloves
5 cups milk
5 tablespoons butter
5 tablespoons all-purpose flour
¹/₄ teaspoon grated nutmeg
¹/₂ cup packed parsley leaves

3 medium eggplants (2¹/₂ pounds)
4 medium zucchini (1³/₄ pounds)

PREPARATION AND COOKING: *For the lamb sauce*, peel and chop the onions. Peel and mince the garlic (2¹/₂ tablespoons). Heat the oil in a heavy 5-quart saucepan, add the onions and garlic, cover, and cook over medium heat until the vegetables are softened, about 15 minutes. Add the lamb and sauté until cooked through, about 5 minutes. Stir in the oregano, thyme, cinnamon, cumin, red-pepper flakes, ginger, nutmeg, and bay leaves and saute 5 minutes. Add the tomatoes with their juice, the wine, and 2 teaspoons salt. Bring the liquid to a boil, lower heat, cover and simmer, stirring occasionally, for 30 minutes. Uncover and simmer, stirring occasionally, until the sauce is very thick, about 1¹/₂ hours. Cool. (Can cover and refrigerate sauce up to 3 days.)

For the béchamel *sauce*, grate and set Parmesan aside. Peel and mince garlic (1 tablespoon). Bring milk to a boil; turn off heat. Melt butter in a heavy medium saucepan. Add garlic and cook over low heat until tender but not browned, about 4 minutes. Whisk in flour and whisk constantly until foaming but not browned, about 3 minutes. Remove pan from heat and whisk in hot milk and nutmeg. Return pan to heat and bring sauce to a boil, whisking constantly. Reduce heat and simmer, stirring occasionally, for 20 minutes. Off heat, stir in cheese and transfer sauce to a bowl to cool. Chop and stir in parsley. Press plastic wrap directly onto the surface of the *béchamel* to prevent a skin from forming. (Can set aside at room temperature up to 3 hours, or refrigerate overnight.)

Trim and halve the eggplants lengthwise. Cut each half crosswise into ¹/₂-inch thick slices. Rinse the zucchini and cut them diagonally into ¹/₄-inch thick slices. Sprinkle salt

SPICY MOUSSAKA WITH POTATOES AND PARMESAN

(continued)

Salt
4 large potatoes (2 pounds)
1/2 cup olive oil
5 eggs
2 1/2 ounces Parmesan cheese (2/3 cup grated)

over two 10-inch by 15-inch jelly-roll pans. Put vegetable slices in the pans and sprinkle generously with salt. Cover vegetables with paper towels, then put a heavy pan over towels to press out excess liquid. Let stand 30 minutes, then rinse well and pat vegetables dry, gently pressing to remove all salt and liquid. Peel and slice potatoes 1/4-inch thick. Transfer slices to a large saucepan, cover with cold water, and bring to boil. Turn heat to medium and boil until potatoes are tender, about 5 minutes. Transfer potatoes to a colander and drain. Heat 3 tablespoons of oil in a large skillet. Working in batches and adding oil as needed, sauté eggplant and zucchini over medium-high heat until golden brown, about 4 minutes each side. Drain vegetables on paper towels and set aside.

ASSEMBLY AND COOKING: Adjust oven rack to middle position and heat oven to 350°F. (Bring lamb sauce to room temperature.) Separate 3 eggs into 2 bowls. Whisk whites briefly and stir into lamb sauce. Break remaining eggs into the bowl with the yolks, whisk until liquid, and stir into the *béchamel*. Grate Parmesan.

Using half of the zucchini, eggplant, and potatoes, arrange one layer in each of two 3-quart rectangular baking dishes. Sprinkle the vegetables with 3 tablespoons of the Parmesan cheese. Divide all of the lamb sauce between the two baking dishes, spooning it in an even layer over the vegetables. Arrange the remaining vegetables in an even layer over the lamb and sprinkle with another 3 table-spoons Parmesan cheese. Divide the *béchamel* between the two dishes, gently shaking the pans to settle the layers. Sprinkle the remaining Parmesan cheese over the *béchamel* and bake until the top is puffed and golden brown and the center is set, about 1 hour.

SERVING: Serve *moussaka* hot or tepid. (Can cover and refrigerate up to 2 days. Reheat, covered, in a 350°F oven 30 minutes; uncover and bake 5 minutes until top bubbles.)

Michael McLaughlin
Free-lance writer
Brooklyn, NY

GINGER- AND SESAME-SCENTED RACK OF LAMB

Makes 4 to 6 servings

The rack, or rib roast is a very tender and elegant cut. Ask the butcher to saw through and remove the chine bone and 2 inches from the rib end of each rack, to trim and "french" the ribs, remove the fell, and trim the fat to no more than $1/4$-inch in thickness. To present the racks standing upright, slice a thin wedge of meat off the bottom of the eye. This creates a flat base and simplifies carving.

1 piece of ginger (1 inch long)
2 medium garlic cloves
1 large orange
2 tablespoons all-purpose soy
 sauce
1 tablespoon dark sesame oil
2 racks of lamb, chine bones
 removed and ribs "frenched"
 (about 1$1/4$ pounds each)

PREPARATION: Peel the ginger and garlic. Remove two 1-inch by 3-inch strips of zest from the orange. Squeeze $1/3$ cup orange juice into the workbowl of a food processor fitted with the metal blade. Add the ginger, garlic, soy sauce, and sesame oil, and process until smooth. Put the lamb in a large bowl and rub the meat with the ginger paste. Refrigerate, covered, for 24 hours, turning.

COOKING: Bring meat to room temperature. Adjust oven rack to high position and heat oven to 450°F. Wrap the rib bones in foil to prevent blackening and put the racks meat-side up in a shallow roasting pan. Spread any remaining ginger paste over the meat and roast for 10 minutes. Lower oven to 350°F and roast until the internal temperature of the meat at the thickest point registers 130°F (medium rare), 15 to 20 minutes.

SERVING: Let racks rest 5 minutes, cut into chops, and serve immediately.

Michael McLaughlin
Free-lance writer
Brooklyn, NY

LAMB RIBLETS WITH MAPLE-MUSTARD GLAZE

Makes 4 servings

Often overlooked in favor of pork or beef, lamb riblets offer a delicious change. The preliminary poaching breaks down connective tissue and ensures tenderness; the sweet-and-sour glaze covers the meat with a tasty lacquer.

4 pounds breast of lamb, cut into 6-rib sections, breastbone cracked between each rib
Salt
$1/2$ cup coarse-grain mustard
$1/2$ cup maple syrup
1 tablespoon cider vinegar
Ground black pepper
$1/2$ teaspoon dried thyme

PREPARATION AND COOKING: Trim all visible fat from the breasts and put them in a 5-quart soup kettle with 2 tablespoons salt. Cover with cold water, bring to a boil, reduce heat to low and simmer, partially covered, until tender, about 1 hour. Drain and set aside to cool. In a bowl, stir the mustard with maple syrup, vinegar, $1/2$ teaspoon salt, $1/2$ teaspoon pepper, and thyme. (Can cover and refrigerate breast and glaze separately overnight.)

Adjust oven rack to high position and heat oven to 400°F. Cut the lamb breast into individual riblets and put into a large shallow baking dish in a single layer. Bake riblets, meat side up, frequently draining rendered fat, until crisp and brown, about 35 minutes. Spoon half of the mustard-maple glaze over riblets and bake 8 minutes. Spoon on the remaining glaze and bake until very brown, 5-7 minutes. Serve immediately.

Michael McLaughlin
Free-lance writer
Brooklyn, NY

BRAISED LAMB SHANKS WITH GARLIC AND THYME

Makes 6 servings

Lamb and garlic have a long shared history, particularly around the Mediterranean. Here, a whopping four heads — not cloves — of garlic are braised with lamb shanks for a full-flavored stew. For a particularly graceful presentation, ask the butcher to saw each shank crosswise into three pieces.

6 lamb shanks (about 1
    pound each)
Salt and ground black pepper
4 medium garlic heads
¼ cup olive oil
1 teaspoon dried thyme
1 cup dry white wine
1½ cups chicken stock *or*
    canned chicken broth
1 tablespoon minced parsley

PREPARATION AND COOKING: Adjust the oven rack to the low position and heat the oven to 325°F. Pat the lamb shanks dry with paper towels and sprinkle them with 1 teaspoon salt and ½ teaspoon pepper. Break the garlic into cloves, but do not peel them. Heat the olive oil in a 14- by 11-inch nonreactive roasting pan over 2 burners. Sear the lamb shanks over high heat until they brown on all sides, about 8 minutes. Add the garlic cloves, thyme, wine, and chicken stock, and bring the liquid to a simmer. Cover and transfer the pan to the oven. Braise until the shanks are tender, turning them every 30 minutes, about 2 hours. Remove the shanks from the roasting pan; cover and keep warm. Remove the garlic cloves with a slotted spoon and transfer them to the workbowl of a food processor fitted with the metal blade, or to a food mill fitted with a fine disk; puree. If using the food processor, force the puree through a fine sieve to remove the skins. Skim the pan juices well, then stir in the garlic puree. Adjust seasoning. (Can cool lamb in sauce, cover, and set aside for several hours, or refrigerate overnight.)

SERVING: If shanks have been set aside or refrigerated, warm in a 325°F oven for 25 to 30 minutes. Garnish with minced parsley.

Peter Kump
President
Peter Kump's New York Cooking School
  and James Beard Foundation
New York, NY

BRAISED LAMB SHANKS IN LEMON-DILL SAUCE

Makes 4 servings

Lamb shanks have a high percentage of gelatinous connective tissue, and benefit from slow cooking such as braising or poaching. (Ask the butcher to saw each shank into three parts for a more graceful presentation.) When heating the sauce, keep the temperature below 160°F to avoid curdling the eggs.

2 medium onions
2 medium carrots
2 garlic cloves
1 medium leek
4 large lamb shanks (about 1
  pound each) sawed crosswise
  into thirds
5 tablespoons olive oil
3 bay leaves
3½ cups chicken stock *or*
  canned chicken broth
Salt
3 tablespoons loosely packed
  dill leaves
2 lemons
2 eggs
Ground black pepper

PREPARATION: Peel onions, carrots, and garlic. Chop and put onions (2 cups) and carrots (1 cup) in a bowl with garlic. Rinse, trim, and chop leek (1 cup), (using white portion and about 2 inches of the green), and add to the bowl. Pat shanks dry.

COOKING: Heat 2 tablespoons of oil in a 5-quart Dutch oven until hot but not smoking. Working in batches, sear lamb shanks over high heat until they are browned on all sides, about 7 minutes; set shanks aside. Discard cooking fat and add remaining oil, vegetables, and bay leaves. Cover and sauté over low heat, stirring occasionally, until vegetables are lightly colored, about 15 minutes. Return shanks and accumulated juices to the pot along with stock and 1 teaspoon salt. Bring stock to a boil, reduce heat to low, and simmer, covered, for 45 minutes. Uncover and simmer until lamb is tender, 55-60 minutes. Remove shanks. Strain stock and return it to the pot. Bring to a boil, skimming it well, and reduce to 1¾ cups. (Can cover and refrigerate shanks in the stock for up to 2 days.)

SERVING: If made ahead, heat shanks in foil in oven until hot. Bring stock to a boil. Mince dill. Squeeze ⅓ cup lemon juice into a medium bowl, whisk in eggs, and then slowly whisk in hot stock. Stir in dill and ½ teaspoon pepper. Return the shanks to the pot, add the lemon-egg mixture and cook over low heat, gently stirring and shaking the pot, until shanks are warmed through and sauce has thickened slightly, about 5 minutes. Do not let sauce simmer or eggs may curdle.

Michael McLaughlin
Free-lance writer
Brooklyn, NY

PORK BARBECUE

Makes 8 or more servings

To achieve an authentic barbecue flavor, the roasted pork can be finished on a covered outdoor grill that is made into an improvised smoker by placing soaked and drained hickory, oak, or mesquite wood chips over the coals. Transfer roasted pork to the grill cover and smoke over low heat for about 10 minutes.

4 cups Lexington Barbecue Dip (recipe page 284)
2 boneless pork loins (about 2¼ pounds each)
Salt and ground black pepper
1 dozen hamburger buns

PREPARATION: Make the Lexington Barbecue Dip.

COOKING AND SERVING: Adjust oven rack to lower position. Heat oven to 500°F. Tie the pork loins with string at 1½-inch intervals and rub with salt and pepper. Put pork on a rack in a baking dish and roast for 15 minutes. Reduce heat to 250°F and roast, turning once each hour, until pork loins are very tender, about 5 hours. Set aside for 15 minutes. Cut pork into thin slices or chunks and serve over bottoms of hamburger buns. Top each bun with several spoonfuls of sauce.

Craig Claiborne
Food critic and cookbook author
East Hampton, NY

PORK CHOPS WITH
MOLASSES AND BOURBON BARBECUE SAUCE

Makes 4 servings

This sauce can be served with flank steak, rabbit, grilled Black Forest ham, spare ribs, or swordfish.

1 large onion
3 medium garlic cloves
2 tablespoons red-pepper sauce
Ground black pepper
4 loin pork chops ($^{1}/_{2}$ pound each)

Barbecue Sauce
1 small onion
1 small garlic clove
1 small red bell pepper
$^{1}/_{2}$ small jalapeño chile
$^{1}/_{4}$ cup packed parsley leaves
3 bacon slices ($2^{1}/_{2}$ ounces)
2 medium tomatoes
$^{2}/_{3}$ cup stout
1 tablespoon tomato paste
2 tablespoons dark molasses
$^{1}/_{4}$ cup ketchup
$^{1}/_{2}$ teaspoon Worcestershire
   sauce
$^{1}/_{4}$ teaspoon red-pepper sauce
$^{1}/_{2}$ teaspoon chili powder
$^{1}/_{2}$ teaspoon ground ginger
$^{1}/_{2}$ teaspoon dry mustard
$^{1}/_{4}$ teaspoon dried basil
$^{1}/_{8}$ teaspoon dried oregano
$^{1}/_{8}$ teaspoon cumin
Salt
$1^{1}/_{2}$ teaspoons bourbon
1 tablespoon butter
1 tablespoon vegetable oil

PREPARATION: *For the pork chops,* peel and thinly slice the onion and garlic, and toss with the red-pepper sauce and 1 teaspoon ground black pepper in a 13- by 9-inch baking dish. Turn the pork chops in the marinade and set aside in the baking dish for 2 hours at room temperature. (Can cover pork chops and refrigerate overnight).

For the barbecue sauce, peel and mince the onion; peel the garlic. Stem, quarter, and seed the bell pepper and jalapeño. Put the garlic, bell pepper, chile, and parsley in the workbowl of a food processor fitted with the metal blade and process until minced; set aside.

COOKING: Cut the bacon slices into $^{1}/_{2}$-inch pieces and sauté in a medium saucepan until fat is rendered, about 4 minutes. Discard all but 1 tablespoon of the fat. Add onion and saute until softened and lightly browned, about 5 minutes. Add the minced vegetables and sauté until softened, about 2 minutes. Add tomatoes and the next 13 ingredients including $^{1}/_{2}$ teaspoon salt. Simmer the sauce for 30 minutes, stirring occasionally. Stir in the bourbon. (Can cool, cover, and refrigerate up to 1 week.) Remove pork chops from the marinade and pat dry; discard vegetables. Heat butter and oil in a large skillet. Sauté marinated chops until browned and juices run pale pink, about 7 minutes per side.

SERVING: Bring the bourbon barbecue sauce to a simmer. Spoon sauce onto warm serving plates and put pork chops on the sauce. Additional sauce may be spooned over the pork chops. Serve immediately.

Danny Wisel
Chef
Rocco's
Boston, MA

PORK CHOPS PROVENCAL

Makes 4 servings

These quickly sautéed pork chops are blanketed with a tasty sauce of green olives, lemon, white wine, and rosemary.

1 medium garlic clove
1 teaspoon cornstarch
1 tablespoon vegetable oil
4 loin pork chops, with bone
   (about 2 pounds)
2 tablespoons butter
1 tablespoon minced fresh
   rosemary
$1/4$ cup white wine
$1/2$ cup chicken stock *or* canned
   chicken broth
Ground black pepper
1 small lemon
Salt

PREPARATION: Mince the garlic and slice the olives into thin rounds. Dissolve cornstarch in 1 tablespoon of cold water; set aside.

COOKING AND SERVING: Heat oil in a large skillet. Sauté pork chops over medium-high heat until cooked and browned on both sides, about 12 minutes. Transfer to a plate and cover loosely with aluminum foil to keep warm. Melt the butter in the skillet, add the garlic and rosemary, and sauté until fragrant, 1 to 2 minutes. Add the wine and stock and simmer until liquid reduces to $1/2$ cup, about 5 minutes. Whisk in the cornstarch mixture and simmer until sauce thickens slightly, about 1 minute. Stir in olives and $1/2$ teaspoon pepper, and squeeze in 1 teaspoon lemon juice. Adjust seasoning with salt if necessary. Transfer pork chops to serving plates and top with sauce.

Pam Parseghian
Free-lance writer
New York, NY

COUNTRY PATTY SAUSAGES

Makes 8 sausage patties

This meat should not be overworked or ground in a food processor or it will become too mushy. It freezes well, and if frozen in patties, can be cooked directly from the freezer. Always use plenty of sage, or add a few fennel seeds for a different flavor.

1 pound lean, boneless pork shoulder
$1/2$ pound chilled, fresh pork fatback
Salt and ground black pepper
1 teaspoon dried sage
$1/4$ teaspoon ground allspice
$1/2$ teaspoon hot red-pepper flakes

PREPARATION: Cut the pork and pork fatback into 2-inch pieces and process through the coarse blade of a meat grinder into a large bowl. Or, mince the pork and fatback using 2 knives. Add $1^1/2$ teaspoons salt, $1/2$ teaspoon pepper, sage, allspice, red pepper flakes, and 2 tablespoons cold water and mix well with your hands. Cover with plastic and refrigerate overnight. (Can refrigerate up to 2 days.)

COOKING: Shape pork mixture into eight 3-inch patties. Heat two medium skillets. Fry sausage patties in batches until well-browned on both sides and cooked through, about 8 minutes. Serve immediately.

James Villas
Cookbook author and food editor
Town & Country
New York, NY

PORK STEW WITH SWEET PEPPERS

Makes 8 servings

The intriguing flavor of this satisfying pork stew results from the combination of orange juice, Provençal herbs, and garlic. The bell peppers add a zesty sweetness, and the anchovies a rich, subtle background taste few will identify. The stew is equally good made with lamb.

4 pounds boneless pork shoulder
   or Boston butt
2 onions
1¹/₂ tablespoons chopped fresh
   oregano or 1¹/₂ teaspoons
   dried
1¹/₂ tablespoons chopped fresh
   thyme or 1¹/₂ teaspoons dried
1¹/₂ tablespoons chopped fresh
   basil or 1¹/₂ teaspoons dried
6 cloves garlic
12 anchovy fillets
1 orange
¹/₂ cup olive oil
Salt and pepper
1 bay leaf
¹/₄ cup flour
1¹/₂ cups chicken stock
1 cup dry white wine
3 red bell peppers or a
   combination of green, red,
   and yellow bell peppers
6 ounces imported black olives
   (about 1 cup)

PREPARATION: Cut the pork into 1¹/₂-inch cubes. Chop the onions, oregano, thyme, and basil. Mince the garlic and anchovies. Squeeze juice from orange. Heat oven to 350°F. In a large stockpot, heat 2 tablespoons of the olive oil over medium heat. Brown the pork, working in batches to avoid overcrowding, until golden, about 5 minutes, adding more oil to the pan as needed. Season with salt and pepper. Remove the pork with a slotted spoon. Add 3 tablespoons of the oil to the pot and set over medium heat. Stir in the onions, garlic, oregano, thyme, basil, and bay leaf. Cover and cook, stirring occasionally until onions are softened, about 5 minutes. Uncover, add the flour, and continue cooking, stirring frequently, about 3 minutes more. Stir in the chicken stock, wine, orange juice, anchovies, and pork, including any meat juices that have accumulated. Bring the stew to a boil, cover, and cook in preheated oven for 45 minutes. Stir, and continue cooking until the meat is tender, about 45 more minutes. Meanwhile, core, quarter and seed the bell peppers. Rinse the olives. In a frying pan, heat the remaining 3 tablespoons oil over high heat. Add the bell peppers and sauté until browned, about 5 minutes. Stir the peppers and olives into the stew. Season to taste with salt and pepper. Stew can be made several days ahead.

SERVING: Bring stew to a simmer if made ahead and serve.

Michael McLaughlin
Free-lance writer
Brooklyn, NY

GINGER- AND SHERRY-GLAZED HAM

Makes 12 to 14 servings

A smoked ham requires no special preparation beyond trimming off the fat before baking. Ginger preserves, sherry, and Dijon mustard make a delicious glaze; orange, lime, or grapefruit marmalade can be substituted for the preserves.

1 fully cooked, bone-in smoked ham (13 to 14 pounds)
$2/3$ cup English or Scottish ginger preserves
$1/3$ cup Dijon mustard
1 cup sherry, preferably Amontillado

PREPARATION: Remove and discard rind and all but $1/8$-inch thick layer of fat from the ham. Score the remaining fat diagonally at 1-inch intervals, cutting $1/4$ inch into the flesh, to form diamond shapes. Put ham into a large, shallow roasting pan. Mix the preserves with the mustard.

COOKING: Adjust oven rack to low position and heat oven to 325°F. Pour 1 cup of water in the roasting pan and bake ham for $1^1/_2$ hours. Add sherry to pan. Brush half of the mustard mixture over the ham and bake 10 minutes. Brush remaining mustard mixture over the ham and bake 30 minutes longer, basting frequently with pan juices. Let ham rest 30 minutes in roasting pan; baste frequently. (Can wrap and refrigerate up to 2 weeks.)

SERVING: Thinly slice ham and serve hot, warm, or cold.

Michael McLaughlin
Free-lance writer
Brooklyn, NY

ROASTED FRESH HAM WITH CAMPARI-ORANGE SAUCE

Makes 16 servings

Although Campari is an Italian aperitif whose "secret" recipe includes 69 herbs, spices, barks, and fruits, one can easily detect a hint of orange. The mixture of Campari and orange juice is both a glaze for the ham and, when mixed with the pan juices, a pungent sauce. It may be necessary to order a fresh ham from your butcher since most pork legs are cured. Have the butcher remove the skin, trim off all but $1/8$ inch of fat, bone the leg, and leave the roast untied.

3 large garlic cloves
1 cup loosely packed flat-leaf
  parsley leaves
3 large oranges
1 fresh ham, boned and
  butterflied (about 14 pounds)
Salt and ground black pepper
$3/4$ cup Campari
$1/2$ cup chicken stock *or* canned
  chicken broth

PREPARATION: Peel and mince the garlic. Mince the parsley ($1/2$ cup). Grate $3/4$ cup orange zest and mix it with the parsley and garlic. Squeeze and set aside $1^1/3$ cups orange juice. Put the butterflied leg, fat side down, on a work surface. Spread the orange mixture over the cut surface of the leg and sprinkle with 2 teaspoons salt and 1 teaspoon pepper. Roll and tie the ham with kitchen twine, sprinkle it with salt and pepper, and put it seam side down in a large, shallow roasting pan.

COOKING: Adjust oven rack to low position and heat oven to 350°F. Roast ham $3^1/2$ hours, then carefully transfer cooking juices to a saucepan. Add the Campari and orange juice to the roasting pan and, basting frequently, cook until a meat thermometer inserted into the thickest part of the leg registers 145°F to l50°F, about 20 minutes longer. Transfer ham to a cutting board and cover with foil to keep warm. Bring reserved cooking juices to a simmer and skim to remove fat. Set the roasting pan over 2 burners and bring Campari-orange mixture to a boil; add cooking juices and chicken stock, and bring to a boil, scraping the bottom of the pan with a wooden spoon to deglaze. Season to taste with salt and pepper and strain juices into a sauceboat.

SERVING: Thinly slice the ham and serve with Campari-orange sauce.

Michael McLaughlin
Free-lance writer
Brooklyn, NY

SMITHFIELD HAM WITH BROWN SUGAR GLAZE

Makes 16 to 20 servings

The rind of a Smithfield ham must be scrubbed to remove the pepper coating and mold. The ham is then soaked in cool water for 48 hours to remove as much salt as possible, and then simmered to remove additional salt. Basting with a brown sugar and Madeira glaze during the final minutes of baking gives the ham a dark, glossy finish. A smoked country ham can be substituted for a Smithfield ham.

1 Smithfield or country ham (12 to 13 pounds)
1 cup Madeira
$1/3$ cup firmly packed dark brown sugar

PREPARATION: Immerse the ham in cool water and scrub it with a stiff brush to remove mold and black-pepper coating. Put ham in a 16- to 20-quart stockpot or in the sink, cover with cold water, and soak for 48 hours, changing the water every 6 hours. Drain the ham and scrub it again with a stiff brush to remove remaining mold and coating.

COOKING: Put the ham in a 16- to 20-quart stockpot and cover with cold water. Bring to a boil and simmer gently for 4 hours. Drain and pat ham dry; discard poaching liquid. With a sharp knife, remove the softened rind. Then, carefully remove all but a $1/8$-inch layer of fat from the top of the ham. Adjust oven rack to low position and heat oven to 350°F. Put ham, fat side up, in a large, shallow roasting pan. Bake until fat is rendered and begins to brown, about 30 minutes. Mix the Madeira with the brown sugar; brush ham with one half of the glaze. Bake for 10 minutes and brush with the remaining glaze. Bake for 10 minutes longer, then baste every 5 minutes until ham is glazed and browned, about 15 minutes longer. Let the ham rest for at least 30 minutes, basting frequently. (Can wrap and refrigerate up to 2 weeks.)

SERVING: Thinly slice the ham and serve hot, warm, or cold.

Michael McLaughlin
Free-lance writer
Brooklyn, NY

GRILLED GRUYERE, BLACK FOREST HAM, AND ONION SANDWICHES

Makes 4 sandwiches

Delicious with Black Forest ham, this hearty sandwich can also be made with baked ham leftovers.

8 slices Italian bread (¹/₂ inch thick)
2 tablespoons butter
8 thin slices Gruyère *or* other Swiss cheese (5 ounces)
8 slices Black Forest *or* other smoked ham (8 ounces)
1 cup sautéed onions
Ground black pepper

PREPARATION: Spread butter on each slice of bread. Turn 4 slices buttered sides down, and top each with 1 slice cheese, 2 slices ham, and ¹/₄ cup sautéed onions. Sprinkle each with pepper and top with cheese and a remaining slice of bread, buttered side up.

COOKING: Heat a griddle. Grill sandwiches over medium heat until cheese has melted and sandwiches are golden brown, about 6 minutes. Serve immediately.

Pam Parseghian
Free-lance writer
New York, NY

POULTRY

CHICKEN SALAD WITH
THYME AND RED-ONION VINAIGRETTE

Makes 4 servings

Pungent thyme is a natural accompaniment to sweet red onion in this salad. You can serve the salad warm or prepare it a few hours ahead of time and serve it at room temperature.

1 small red onion
$^1/_2$ head romaine lettuce
$^1/_2$ head red-leaf lettuce
4 large or 6 medium boneless,
   skinless chicken breasts
   (about 1$^1/_2$ pounds)
1 tablespoon minced fresh
   thyme
Salt and pepper
$^1/_3$ cup oil
3 tablespoons balsamic *or*
   red-wine vinegar

PREPARATION: Cut onion into paper-thin slices and separate into rings. Wash and spin-dry lettuces; tear leaves into pieces, and chill. Cut chicken into 1-inch cubes and sprinkle with thyme and salt and pepper.

Heat $^1/_2$ of the oil in a large frying pan over medium-high heat until hot but not smoking. Add the chicken and sauté, stirring frequently, until just cooked through, about 5 minutes. Add the vinegar, stirring with a wooden spoon to deglaze the bottom of the pan. Remove pan from heat and stir in the onion and remaining oil. Season to taste with salt and pepper.

Recipe can be prepared to this point a few hours ahead. Set chicken and vinaigrette aside separately in covered containers.

SERVING: Arrange chilled lettuce on salad plates and top with chicken and red-onion vinaigrette.

Pam Parseghian
Free-lance writer
New York, NY

CHICKEN CAESAR SALAD

Makes 4 servings

This variation on the Caesar salad theme includes grilled or broiled chicken tossed with romaine lettuce and a garlic- and anchovy-kissed Caesar dressing.

2 medium heads romaine lettuce
8 slices French bread
2 whole boneless chicken
   breasts, with skin, split
1 tablespoon olive oil
Salt and ground black pepper

Dressing
$^1/_2$ cup Lemon Vinaigrette
   (recipe page 283)
1 can (2 ounces) flat anchovies,
   drained
1 egg
1 medium garlic clove
$1^1/_2$ teaspoons Worcestershire
   sauce
2 tablespoons grated Romano
   cheese
$^1/_4$ cup grated Parmesan cheese

PREPARATION: Rinse, dry, and tear romaine leaves into bite-size pieces.

COOKING: Adjust oven rack 4 inches from heat source and heat broiler. Cut the bread into $^1/_2$-inch cubes and place on a baking sheet. Broil, turning once, until evenly toasted, about 2 minutes. Or, heat the grill and toast whole bread slices. Cube the bread and set the croutons aside. Brush chicken breasts with olive oil and sprinkle them with salt and pepper. Broil chicken, skin side up, until golden brown, about 4 minutes. Turn and broil until the chicken is cooked, about 4 minutes more. Or, grill chicken, skin side down, for 4 minutes. Turn and continue to grill about 4 minutes longer. Set aside. (Can cool, cover, and refrigerate overnight. Bring the chicken to room temperature at serving time.)

For the dressing, make the Lemon Vinaigrette and reserve $^1/_2$ cup. Chop and put the anchovies in a large salad bowl. Coddle the egg by dipping it into boiling water for exactly 45 seconds. Break the egg into the salad bowl. Peel and mince the garlic and put in bowl along with the Worcestershire sauce and the reserved vinaigrette. Whisk until blended. Set aside $^1/_4$ cup of the dressing. Add lettuce to the salad bowl and thoroughly toss with the dressing. Slice the chicken crosswise into $^1/_2$-inch strips and add to the salad bowl. Sprinkle with the cheeses and croutons and toss again.

SERVING: Transfer the salad to dinner plates and drizzle with the reserved dressing. Serve immediately.

Brooke Dojny and Melanie Barnard
Nationally syndicated food writers and cookbook authors
Fairfield County, CT

CHICKEN FAJITAS WITH TOMATO-CORIANDER SALSA

Makes 4 servings

Thin slices of chicken are rolled with avocado, sour cream, and salsa in a flour tortilla. Refried beans add a real southwestern touch.

1 cup Quick Tomato Sauce (recipe page 285)

Tomato Coriander Salsa
1 jalapeño pepper *or* **¹⁄₈ teaspoon dried red-pepper flakes**
2 tablespoons minced fresh coriander
1 lime
Salt and pepper

1 pound boneless, skinless chicken thighs
2 tablespoons oil
1 teaspoon ground cumin
Salt and pepper
1 lime
8 flour tortillas (8-inches each)
1 avocado
1 cup sour cream

PREPARATION: Make the Quick Tomato Sauce.

For the salsa, split, seed, and mince the jalapeño (take care not to touch your face after working with it). In a bowl, combine the Quick Tomato Sauce, jalapeño or pepper flakes, and coriander. Squeeze the lime, add 1 tablespoon juice to the sauce, and season to taste with salt and pepper. Set aside.

Rub the chicken with the oil and cumin and sprinkle with salt and pepper. Cut the lime into 8 wedges. Recipe can be made to this point 2 hours ahead.

COOKING AND SERVING: Heat the broiler. Set the chicken on a rack about 5 inches from the heat source and cook, turning once, until browned and just cooked through, about 4 minutes on each side. Heat oven to 375°F. Wrap the tortillas in foil and warm in oven for 10 minutes. Meanwhile pit, peel, and cut the avocado into ¹⁄₂-inch cubes. Cut the chicken into thin slices. Divide cooked chicken between the tortillas. Top chicken in each tortilla with 2 tablespoons salsa, 2 tablespoons sour cream, and chopped avocado. Using 1 lime wedge per fajita, squeeze juice over mixture and wrap tortilla around filling.

Elizabeth Riely
Free-lance writer
Newton Centre, MA

SOUTHERN FRIED CHICKEN

Makes 8 servings

To keep fried chicken warm, place it in an ovenproof baking dish, cover with paper towels, and put the dish in a 250°F oven. Or, serve chicken cold or at room temperature.

2 chickens (about 2¹/₂ to 3
   pounds each)
3 to 4 cups milk
¹/₂ teaspoon hot red-pepper
   sauce
2 cups flour
Salt and ground black pepper
1 pound lard *or* 2 cups corn oil
¹/₄ pound butter

PREPARATION: Cut each chicken into 8 pieces and put in a large bowl. Add enough milk to cover and stir in the hot red-pepper sauce. Refrigerate 1 hour. (Can cover and refrigerate overnight.) In a flat dish, mix the flour with 1 tablespoon salt and 4 teaspoons pepper. (Can cover and set flour mixture aside overnight.)

COOKING AND SERVING: In a large frying pan, heat lard and butter to about 225°F, being careful not to burn the butter. Dredge half of the chicken pieces in the flour mixture, add to the hot oil, skin side down, and fry until golden brown on one side, about 8 minutes. Turn the chicken, reduce heat, and continue frying until golden brown, 15 to 20 minutes longer. Repeat with remaining chicken. Serve chicken hot or at room temperature. (Can set cooked chicken aside up to 8 hours.)

Craig Claiborne
Food critic and cookbook author
East Hampton, NY

SPICY FRIED CHICKEN

Makes 4 servings

This taste-of-the-Caribbean fried chicken is highly seasoned, but it is not flaming hot.

1 teaspoon ground allspice
2 teaspoons dried thyme
2 teaspoons red-pepper flakes
2 teaspoons sugar
1 teaspoon salt
4 chicken breasts (about 1½ pounds total)
½ cup flour for dredging
1 cup oil for frying

PREPARATION: In a bowl, combine the allspice, thyme, red-pepper flakes, sugar, and salt and rub into chicken breasts.

Recipe can be made to this point seven hours ahead.

COOKING AND SERVING: Dredge chicken breasts in the flour. Heat oil in a large frying pan over medium-high heat until hot but not smoking. Put the chicken in pan, skin side down, and cook, turning once, until golden brown and cooked through, about 20 minutes total. Drain on paper towels and serve.

Anne Byrn
Food editor
The Atlanta Journal and *The Atlanta Constitution*

ROSEMARY GRILLED CHICKEN
WITH BLACK-PEPPER SHALLOT BUTTER

Makes 4 servings

Rubbing the chicken with rosemary leaves gives it an aromatic fragrance and sharp taste.

**4 large or 6 medium boneless
  chicken breasts, with skin
  (about 1¹/₂ pounds)**
1 tablespoon oil
**2 tablespoons minced fresh
  rosemary**
Salt and pepper

Black-Pepper Shallot Butter
1 shallot
6 tablespoons softened butter
**¹/₂ tablespoon cracked black
  peppercorns**
1 lemon

PREPARATION: Rub chicken breasts with the oil and rosemary; sprinkle with salt and pepper.

For the butter, mince the shallot. Cream the butter, and then beat in the shallot and the cracked black peppercorns. Season to taste with fresh lemon juice. Shape the seasoned butter into a 1-inch log, wrap in plastic, and refrigerate. Recipe can be made to this point several hours ahead. Wrap and refrigerate chicken.

COOKING AND SERVING: Heat the grill or broiler. Grill or broil chicken, turning once, until chicken is cooked through, about 10 minutes. Top each hot chicken breast with a ¹/₄-inch slice of black-pepper shallot butter.

Pam Parseghian
Free-lance writer
New York, NY

CHICKEN MILANAISE

Makes 4 servings

The bread-crumb and Parmesan coating keeps these chicken breasts moist. For a richer dish, use browned butter rather than the squirt of lemon juice suggested here.

1 lemon
1¹/₂ ounces Parmesan cheese
   (about ¹/₃ cup grated)
¹/₃ cup dry bread crumbs
1 egg
4 boneless, skinless chicken
   breasts (about 1¹/₄ pounds
   total)
Salt and pepper
¹/₄ cup flour
3 tablespoons oil

PREPARATION: Cut the lemon into wedges. Grate the cheese. In a small bowl, combine the cheese and bread crumbs. Whisk the egg with 1 tablespoon of water. Sprinkle chicken with salt and pepper and dredge in flour, shaking off excess. Dip chicken in egg and then coat with bread crumbs.

Recipe can be made to this point 2 hours ahead.

COOKING AND SERVING: In a frying pan, heat oil over medium-high heat and cook chicken, turning once, until golden brown, about 10 minutes total. Serve chicken garnished with lemon wedges.

Stephanie Lyness
Free-lance writer
New York, NY

CHICKEN PROVENCAL

Makes 4 servings

In the traditional Provençal stew of chicken with garlic, the chicken is surrounded with unpeeled garlic cloves and very slowly steamed in its juices in a sealed earthenware casserole. Here, garlic is poached to hasten the cooking, and the chicken is steamed in a foil pouch.

1 frying chicken, quartered, backbone removed (about 3 pounds)
2 medium garlic heads
6 tablespoons olive oil
2 jars (6 ounces each) marinated artichoke hearts
Salt and ground black pepper
2 teaspoons dried thyme
1 loaf French or Italian bread

PREPARATION AND ASSEMBLY: Remove and discard the last two wing joints from the chicken. Break the garlic into cloves. Put the unpeeled cloves in a small saucepan with water to cover. Bring to a boil, reduce heat, and simmer until a knife easily penetrates garlic cloves, about 15 minutes. Drain and set aside.

Heat 2 tablespoons oil in a large skillet until hot but not smoking. Pat the chicken pieces dry and brown them for 3 to 4 minutes on each side.

Cut and oil 4 parchment or foil pouches. Center one piece of chicken on one side of each pouch; add 1/4 of the garlic cloves and artichoke hearts. Drizzle 1 tablespoon of olive oil over each piece of chicken; sprinkle lightly with salt, pepper, and 1/2 teaspoon of thyme. Mark outside of pouches to identify leg portions. Seal pouches. (Can refrigerate parchment pouches up to 4 hours, foil pouches overnight.)

COOKING AND SERVING: Adjust oven rack to middle position and heat oven to 400°F. Put pouches on a baking sheet. Bake breast portions 15 minutes and leg portions 18 minutes (18 and 20 minutes if assembled pouches are refrigerated before cooking). Slice and toast the bread. Transfer pouches to plates and carefully pierce each to permit steam to escape. Serve 4 slices of bread with each portion, spreading softened garlic on bread, if desired.

Peter Kump
President
Peter Kump's New York Cooking School
  and James Beard Foundation
New York, NY

ROASTED CHICKEN WITH LEMON-PARSLEY SAUCE

Makes 4 servings

Many cooks prefer flat-leaf Italian parsley for cooking because its flavor is stronger and cleaner than curly parsley and it adds a fresh, bright taste to chicken, especially when combined with the tartness of lemon.

1 lemon
4 tablespoons butter
2 whole chicken breasts, split
Salt and pepper
$1/3$ cup chopped parsley

COOKING AND SERVING: Heat oven to 450°F. Squeeze $1/4$ cup lemon juice. Melt the butter in a small saucepan or in the microwave. Sprinkle chicken with salt and pepper. Put chicken in a baking dish skin side up and drizzle with half of the butter. Bake until skin is crisp and golden brown and juices run clear, about 25 to 30 minutes. Put chicken on a serving platter and keep warm.

Stir the lemon juice and remaining butter into pan juices, scraping the pan with a wooden spoon to deglaze. Add the parsley and season to taste with salt and pepper. Pour sauce over chicken and serve immediately.

Pam Parseghian
Free-lance writer
New York, NY

CHICKEN SAUTE WITH CURRY AND BASIL

Makes 4 servings

Basil is a common ingredient in Indian curries. This dish can be served with a variety of condiments, including chopped peanuts, raisins, chutney, yogurt, or chopped scallions.

1 clove garlic
2 tablespoons butter
4 large or 6 medium, boneless,
   skinless chicken breasts
   (about 1¹/₂ pounds)
Salt and pepper
¹/₃ cup heavy cream
1¹/₂ teaspoons curry powder
   (recipe page 282)
¹/₂ cup lightly packed fresh basil
   leaves

COOKING: Chop the garlic. Melt butter in a large frying pan over medium-high heat. Sprinkle chicken with salt and pepper and cook, turning once, until golden brown, about 4 minutes. Add garlic and continue cooking for 30 seconds. Stir in ¹/₄ cup of the cream and 2 tablespoons water. Reduce heat to medium, cover and simmer until chicken is cooked through, about 10 minutes. Transfer chicken to a serving plate and keep warm. Whisk in remaining cream and curry powder and bring to a simmer. Shred the basil leaves and add them to the pan. Season to taste with salt and pepper

SERVING: Pour sauce over the chicken breasts and serve with rice and curry condiments if desired.

Pam Parseghian
Free-lance writer
New York, NY

SAUTEED CHICKEN WITH TARRAGON AND MUSHROOMS

Makes 4 servings

Tarragon adds a traditional finish to this delicate white wine and cream sauced sauté.

1/4 **pound mushrooms (about** 3/4 **cup)**
8 **chicken thighs (about 2 pounds)**
Salt and pepper
2 **tablespoons butter**
1/3 **cup white wine**
1 **cup heavy cream**
1 **tablespoon minced fresh tarragon**

PREPARATION: Rinse, trim, and slice the mushrooms. Sprinkle the chicken lightly with salt and pepper. Melt the butter in a large, nonreactive frying pan and cook chicken over medium-high heat until seared on all sides, about 4 minutes. Add mushrooms and cook until softened, about 4 minutes. Stir in wine and reduce heat. Cover and simmer until chicken is cooked through, about 20 minutes.

Using a slotted spoon, remove chicken from the pan. Increase heat to high, stir in the cream, and simmer until liquid reduces to 3/4 cup, about 4 minutes. Lower heat to medium, return chicken to pan, and continue cooking until chicken is warmed through. Stir in fresh tarragon and season to taste with salt and pepper.

Recipe can be prepared several hours ahead.

SERVING: Reheat over low heat if made ahead.

Pam Parseghian
Free-lance writer
New York, NY

CHICKEN AND CHILI STEW

Makes 4 servings

Coriander gives this stew an authentic Mexican flavor. Dress it up with your choice of the following garnishes: sour cream, black olives, grated Monterey Jack cheese, chopped jalapeño peppers, tomato, green bell pepper, or scallions.

8 chicken drumsticks (about 2 pounds)
1 small onion
3 cloves garlic
1 16-ounce can cooked beans, such as cannellini (white kidney beans) *or* pinto beans
Salt and pepper
1 tablespoon oil
2 tablespoons chili powder
1 pint cherry tomatoes
1/4 cup chopped fresh coriander leaves

PREPARATION: Cut off the knobby drumstick joint and scrape around the bone to free tendons. Chop the onion. Mince the garlic. Drain and rinse the beans. Sprinkle the chicken with salt and pepper. Heat the oil in a 4-quart soup kettle or Dutch oven. Sauté the chicken over high heat until golden brown on both sides, about 6 minutes. Reduce heat to medium, stir in the onion, garlic and chili powder, and cook until vegetables are softened, about 3 minutes. Add the tomatoes and 1/4 cup water. Cover and simmer, stirring occasionally, until chicken is cooked through and juices have thickened, about 20 minutes. Stir in the beans, return stew to a simmer and season to taste with salt and pepper.

Recipe can be made a couple of days ahead. Cool and refrigerate uncovered until thoroughly chilled.

SERVING: Reheat stew over low heat if made ahead, and stir in coriander. Serve with any or all of the suggested garnishes.

Pam Parseghian
Free-lance writer
New York, NY

STIR-FRIED CHICKEN WITH GINGER AND SNOW PEAS

Makes 4 servings

Harried cooks can be put off by the long list of ingredients that is usually required for stir-fry recipes. This easy recipe uses just a few simple ingredients that complement each other perfectly.

6 ounces snow peas
1 medium garlic clove
1¼ pounds boneless, skinless
    chicken breasts
1½ teaspoons cornstarch
⅓ cup chicken stock *or* canned
    chicken broth
1 tablespoon vegetable oil
Salt and ground black pepper
3 tablespoons minced fresh
    ginger
1½ tablespoons all-purpose soy
    sauce

PREPARATION: Remove the ends and strings from the snow peas. Peel and mince the garlic. Cut the chicken into bite-size pieces. Dissolve cornstarch in the chicken stock.

COOKING AND SERVING: Heat the oil in a wok or a large skillet until it is almost smoking. Sprinkle the chicken with salt and pepper and stir-fry over high heat for 4 minutes. Add the snow peas and stir-fry for an additional 2 minutes. Add the ginger and the garlic and stir-fry until the chicken is just cooked, about 1 minute longer. Push the chicken and snow peas to one side of the wok, then add the cornstarch mixture and the soy sauce and simmer just until the sauce thickens slightly, about 1 minute. Toss together the chicken and vegetables to coat them thoroughly with sauce. Serve immediately with steamed rice.

Pam Parseghian
Free-lance writer
New York, NY

WARM TURKEY SALAD

Makes 4 servings

The chilled salad greens and the warm, crisp-yet-tender turkey are a delicious contrast.

3 slices white bread
1 egg
³/₄ pound boneless turkey breast
    cut into 4¹/₂-inch-thick slices
Salt and pepper
¹/₄ cup flour
1 bunch watercress
2 heads Belgian endive
1 head curly endive

Mustard Vinaigrette
2 tablespoons red-wine vinegar
1 tablespoon Dijon mustard
¹/₂ teaspoon salt
¹/₂ teaspoon pepper
³/₄ cup olive oil

2 tablespoons vegetable oil

PREPARATION: Cut the crusts from the bread. Put bread in a food processor and process to make about 1¹/₂ cups of fine crumbs. Beat the egg. Season slices of turkey with salt and pepper. Dredge in the flour and shake off excess. Dip turkey in the egg and then roll in the bread-crumb mixture to coat evenly. Refrigerate on a rack until dried slightly, at least 30 minutes.

Wash and dry greens, tear into pieces, and chill.

For the vinaigrette, in a small bowl, whisk together the vinegar, mustard, ¹/₂ teaspoon salt, and ¹/₂ teaspoon pepper. Gradually whisk in the olive oil and adjust seasoning to taste.

Recipe can be made to this point several hours ahead.

COOKING AND SERVING: Heat the vegetable oil in a large frying pan over medium heat. Cook the turkey, turning once, until golden brown and crisp, about 6 minutes total. Drain and keep warm.

Toss greens with all but 3 tablespoons of the vinaigrette and arrange on plates. Cut each slice of turkey into ¹/₂-inch strips, keeping the slices intact. Using a spatula, carefully lift each turkey slice onto greens and top with remaining vinaigrette.

Miriam Ungerer
Free-lance writer
Sag Harbor, NY

ROAST TURKEY BREAST WITH HERB STUFFING

Makes 6 servings

Even the most fanatic health nut will find little to object to in this white-meat roast delicately flavored with a layer of fresh-herb and cracked-wheat stuffing. The turkey is easier to slice at room temperature and child's play when cold. It tastes best at room temperature.

Herb Stuffing
8 slices cracked-wheat bread
1 onion
2 cloves garlic
1 tablespoon minced fresh savory *or* **1 teaspoon dried**
1 tablespoon minced fresh thyme *or* **1 teaspoon dried**
1 tablespoon minced fresh sage *or* **1 teaspoon dried**
2 tablespoons minced parsley
1/4 pound butter
1 egg
1 teaspoon salt
1 teaspoon cracked pepper

4 tablespoons softened butter
1 large turkey breast (about 5 pounds)
Salt and pepper
3/4 cup white wine

PREPARATION: *For the stuffing*, trim the bread. Put it in a food processor and process to make about 4 cups of fine crumbs.

Chop the onion. Mince the garlic, savory, thyme, sage, and parsley. Melt the butter in a frying pan over medium heat and cook the garlic and onion until soft, about 5 minutes.

In a bowl, stir together the bread crumbs, onion, garlic, herbs, and egg. Season with 1 teaspoon salt and 1 teaspoon cracked pepper.

Loosen the skin of the breast, leaving about an inch of skin attached around the edge to hold the stuffing in place. Stuff the bird between the skin and breast meat, fastening any loose edges with toothpicks. Rub with 2 tablespoons of the softened butter and transfer to a shallow roasting pan.

Recipe can be made to this point a couple of hours ahead.

COOKING AND SERVING: Heat oven to 350°F. Melt the remaining 2 tablespoons butter. Sprinkle turkey breast with salt and pepper. Add the wine to the pan and roast turkey in preheated oven, basting every 15 minutes with melted butter, until internal temperature reaches l65°F, about 1 1/2 hours. Remove turkey from pan, cover loosely with foil to keep warm, and let rest 1/2 hour.

Carve turkey breast into thin slices, so that each slice shows an edge of stuffing.

Miriam Ungerer
Free-lance writer
Sag Harbor, NY

TURKEY IN MOLE SAUCE
CHOMPIPE EN MOLE

Makes 8 to 10 servings

Chocolate is used here as a seasoning, and it plays a dual role: coloring agent, to darken the sauce; and flavoring, to add a slight bitter chocolate flavor to the dish. This Guatemalan *mole* is first cousin to the Mexican version that is usually made with chicken, and occasionally with pork.

1 turkey (9 to 10 pounds)
4 medium garlic cloves
4 scallions
Salt

Mole Sauce
1 medium *pasilla* chile
1 *guajillo* chile
Salt
¹/₂ cup pumpkin *or* squash seeds (2 ounces)
¹/₂ cup sesame seeds (2 ounces)
1 cinnamon stick (3 inches long)
2 medium tomatoes
1 large onion
1 teaspoon red pepper flakes
Ground black pepper
¹/₂ teaspoon sugar
1 ounce unsweetened chocolate
¹/₄ cup dry bread crumbs

PREPARATION: To bone the turkey, remove the leg and second joints in one piece by cutting through the hip joints. Separate each thigh from the drumstick by cutting through the joint. Wrap and refrigerate or freeze the drumsticks for another use.

Skin and bone the thighs and cut the meat into 2-inch cubes. Put the meat into a bowl and set the bones aside for the broth. Remove the wings from the body at the joint. Cut wings in half and set aside with the thigh bones.

Remove and discard the breast skin. With your fingers and a boning knife, loosen the meat around the breastbone near the neck; then pull the breast meat loose from the carcass in one piece. Cut the breast in half and remove the center cartilage. Remove the fillets from the carcass, cut all of the breast meat into 2-inch cubes, and add it to the bowl along with the thigh meat. Discard the liver and set the carcass, neck, and the remaining giblets aside for the stock.

COOKING: Put turkey meat into a cheesecloth bag; set bag aside. Put the carcass, wings, thigh bones, neck, and giblets into a 6-quart stockpot or Dutch oven. Peel and halve the garlic cloves. Cut the scallions into 2-inch lengths. Add the garlic and scallions to the stockpot along with 2 teaspoons salt and 8 cups water. Bring water to a boil, reduce heat, and simmer, uncovered, for 45 minutes.

Add the cubed turkey meat in the bag and simmer 20 minutes. Strain the stock into a large bowl and set aside. Discard the carcass, wings, neck, thigh bones, and giblets and set the turkey meat aside in a bowl. (Can cool, cover, and refrigerate stock and meat separately up to 3 days.)

For the mole sauce, stem and seed the *pasilla* and

TURKEY IN MOLE SAUCE
CHOMPIPE EN MOLE

(continued)

guajillo chiles. Set the *guajillo* chile aside. Put the *pasilla* chile, 1 teaspoon salt, and $1/2$ cup water into a small saucepan. Bring water to a boil and then simmer until the chile is soft, about 5 minutes. Set saucepan aside off heat.

Put the pumpkin and sesame seeds, *guajillo* chile, and cinnamon stick into a skillet and stir over medium heat until lightly browned, about 10 minutes. Transfer seeds and spices to a food processor and process until finely ground. Coarsely chop the tomatoes and add to the processor.

Adjust the oven rack to highest position and heat the broiler. Peel the garlic and onion and broil 3 inches from the element until charred, about 5 minutes. Transfer vegetables to the food processor along with the *pasilla* chile and its liquid and 1 cup of turkey stock. Puree. Transfer puree to a 6-quart stockpot with the remaining turkey stock, red pepper flakes, $1/4$ teaspoon pepper, sugar, and chocolate. Bring liquid to a boil, and then simmer, stirring frequently, about 30 minutes. Stir in the cubed turkey meat and simmer until tender, about 30 minutes longer. Stir in bread crumbs and simmer until sauce thickens, about 5 minutes longer. (Can cover and refrigerate up to 2 days).

SERVING: If prepared in advance, reheat Turkey in Mole Sauce. Serve warm.

Copeland Marks
Cookbook author
Brooklyn, NY

SEAFOOD

MUSSELS IN WHITE SAUCE
COZZE AL BLANCHETTO

Makes 18 pieces

Cheese and fish is an uncommon combination in the Italian kitchen, but here it works deliciously.

1 bacon slice (1 ounce)
18 large mussels
1 small garlic clove
4 ounces mozzarella (1 cup)
2 tablespoons minced parsley
2 tablespoons dry bread crumbs
2 tablespoons extra-virgin olive oil

PREPARATION: Cook bacon in a small skillet until crisp; drain, and chop it finely. Scrub and clean the mussels. Put mussels in a large skillet; cover and cook over medium-high heat until they begin to open, about 6 minutes. Transfer mussels and their juices to a bowl to cool. Discard the top shells and loosen mussels from the bottom shells. Put the mussels in their half shells on a baking sheet and set aside. Strain reserved liquid through a sieve lined with a coffee filter or paper towels and set aside. (Can cover and refrigerate mussels and liquid up to 4 hours.) Mince the garlic. Shred the mozzarella (1 cup). Mix garlic with parsley, bacon, mozzarella, bread crumbs, and reserved mussel liquid.

COOKING: Adjust oven rack to middle position and heat oven to 375°F. Top mussels with cheese mixture and drizzle with olive oil. Bake until cheese is melted and lightly browned, about 10 minutes.

Anna Teresa Callen
Cookbook author and teacher
New York, NY

GRILLED OYSTERS WITH
LEMON BUTTER AND HOT RED-PEPPER SAUCE

Makes 10 servings

An oyster roast is a great treat. If you are hosting a large party, the meal will move more smoothly if you use two grills and have help with the shucking. Nap oysters with the lemon butter and sprinkle with Old Bay Seasoning, a potpourri of spices specially suited to seafood. Cover a large table with newspaper and be sure to have plenty of paper napkins or paper towels on hand. Serve a flinty chablis.

10 dozen oysters
¹/₂ pound butter
1 medium lemon
**1 small can Old Bay Seasoning
  (6 ounces)**
**1 small bottle hot red-pepper
  sauce (2 ounces)**

PREPARATION: Scrub oysters.

COOKING AND SERVING: Heat the grill. Melt butter in a medium saucepan and squeeze in 3 tablespoons lemon juice; set aside.

Put oysters, with flat shells facing up, 1 inch apart on the grill. Cover the grill, leaving air vents open, and cook oysters until shells open slightly, 8 to 10 minutes.

Remove the oysters from the grill; pry off and discard the flat top shells. Drizzle the oysters with lemon butter and sprinkle lightly with Old Bay Seasoning or hot red-pepper sauce, if desired. Serve immediately on the half shell. Repeat to grill and garnish remaining oysters.

Susan Hermann Loomis
Cookbook author
Seattle, WA

SHRIMP AND PASTA WITH SPICY BEAN SAUCE

Makes 4 servings

This recipe is based on the traditional Italian dish *pasta e fagioli* (pasta and beans). Todd English adds shellfish plus extra vegetables which give an important natural sweetness.

1 carrot
1 onion
1 rib celery
1 clove garlic
1 tablespoon chopped fresh
    rosemary *or* 1 teaspoon dried
1¹/₂ ounces Parmesan cheese
    (about 6 tablespoons grated)
3 tablespoons olive oil
²/₃ cup dried navy *or* pinto beans
3 cups chicken stock
1¹/₂ tablespoons chopped
    flatleaf parsley
³/₄ pound shrimp (about 20) *or*
    1 large langoustine tails
¹/₂ pound penne (quill-shaped
    pasta)
1¹/₂ tablespoons butter
1¹/₂ teaspoons hot red-pepper
    flakes
Fresh rosemary sprigs for
    garnish (optional)

PREPARATION: Chop the carrot, onion, and celery. Mince the garlic. Chop the rosemary. Grate the cheese.

In a large saucepan, heat 1 tablespoon of the oil over low heat. Add the beans, carrot, onion, celery, garlic, and rosemary and sauté until onion is soft, about 4 minutes. Add chicken stock and simmer until beans split, about 1¹/₂ hours.

In a food processor or blender, puree the bean mixture until almost smooth. With the machine running, slowly add remaining 2 tablespoons oil. Season with salt and pepper.

Recipe can be made to this point 1 day ahead.

Chop the parsley and shell and devein the shrimp. Recipe can be made to this point several hours

COOKING AND SERVING: Cook pasta in a pot of boiling, salted water until tender, about 10 minutes. Drain, reserving 1 cup of liquid.

In a large frying pan, melt ¹/₂ tablespoon of the butter over medium heat. Sprinkle the shellfish with salt and pepper and sauté until cooked through, about 2 minutes. Stir in the bean puree and up to 1 cup of the reserved pasta liquid. Add the pasta and heat through. Remove pan from heat. Stir in the cheese, parsley, hot red-pepper flakes, and remaining tablespoon of butter. Season to taste with salt and pepper. Serve pasta in warm bowls garnished with rosemary sprigs if desired.

Todd English
Chef
Michela's
Boston, MA

FISH FILLETS WITH GINGER AND SOY

Makes 12 servings

Mackerel or bluefish are the fish of choice for this dish; however, sea bass, baby Coho salmon, or small black cod can be substituted. Whichever fish you choose, it is important that the skin be left intact.

5 pounds unskinned mackerel fillets (about 10)
1 large onion
2 cloves garlic
6 tablespoons rice vinegar
$^1/_4$ cup sugar
$^1/_3$ cup light soy sauce
$^1/_3$ cup dark soy sauce
$^3/_4$ teaspoon Chinese five-spice powder
2 tablespoons peanut oil
1 tablespoon minced fresh ginger
$^1/_2$ tablespoon Oriental sesame oil
2 scallions

PREPARATION: Cut fish fillets into 3-inch lengths. Slice the onion thinly. Chop the garlic. In a bowl, mix the rice vinegar with the sugar, soy sauces, and five-spice powder and set aside.

Heat the peanut oil in a large nonreactive frying pan. Add the ginger, onion, and garlic and cook over medium-low heat until soft, about 4 minutes. Put the fish pieces, skin side down, in a single layer on top of the vegetables in the pan. Pour the soy mixture over the fish, add enough water just to cover (about 1 cup), and simmer until just cooked through, about 9 minutes. Transfer fish to a large platter and cool.

Bring soy cooking liquid to a boil and cook, stirring occasionally, until reduced to approximately $1^1/_2$ cups, about 10 minutes. Remove from heat, strain, and stir in sesame oil.

Remove skin and arrange fish on a serving platter. Pour liquid over the fish, cover, and refrigerate.

Recipe can be made to this point several hours ahead.

SERVING: Bring fish to room temperature. Slice the scallions into rings and sprinkle over fish.

Florence Fabricant
Food columnist
New York Times
New York, NY

MAHIMAHI WITH MUSTARD AND MINT

Makes 4 servings

The delicate white flesh of mahimahi or dolphinfish is set off perfectly by a simple mustard and mint vinaigrette, and the warmth of the fish heats the room-temperature dressing slightly, heightening its flavor. This combination also can be served tepid, and minced fresh basil, dill, oregano, or tarragon can be used in the sauce if mint is not to your taste.

Mustard and Mint Sauce
**2 tablespoons white wine
  vinegar**
2 tablespoons Dijon mustard
Salt and ground black pepper
1/2 cup corn oil
**1/4 cup firmly packed fresh mint
  leaves**

1 1/2 to 2 pounds mahimahi fillet
2 tablespoons softened butter

PREPARATION: *For the sauce*, whisk together the vinegar, mustard, 1/4 teaspoon salt, and 1/8 teaspoon pepper in a small bowl. Gradually whisk in corn oil. Mince and stir mint leaves into dressing. (Can cover and refrigerate overnight.)

Cut mahimahi fillet on a slight angle to make four 4- to 5-inch long scallops.

COOKING AND SERVING: Bring sauce to room temperature. Adjust oven rack to lowest position and heat oven to 400°F. Butter a baking dish large enough to hold the fish scallops in a single layer. Arrange fish in dish and bake until just done at its thickest point, 10 to 12 minutes. Transfer fish to serving plates. Whisk and spoon sauce generously over fish.

Michael McLaughlin
Free-lance writer
Brooklyn, NY

RED SNAPPER WITH SWEET AND HOT PEPPERS

Makes 4 servings

When peeling, seeding, and slicing hot peppers, remember not to rub the eyes, mouth, or sensitive areas around the nose. Rubber gloves are a good way to keep capsaicin, the substance contained in the interior ribs of the peppers, from causing a burning sensation.

1 1/2 to 2 pounds red snapper fillets (about 4 small fillets)
4 medium jalapeño peppers
1/2 medium red bell pepper
1/2 medium yellow bell pepper
1 medium garlic clove
1/3 cup flour
Salt and ground black pepper
6 tablespoons butter
3 tablespoons sherry wine vinegar
3/4 cup chicken stock

COOKING AND SERVING: Leaving skin intact, remove the thin line of bones from the wide end of each fillet. Core, seed, and cut all the peppers into 1/4-inch-thick strips. Peel and mince the garlic. Put the flour, 1/2 teaspoon salt, and 1/4 teaspoon pepper on a flat dish. Dredge each side of the fillets in the flour mixture. Heat 4 tablespoons of the butter in a medium skillet. Add peppers and sauté, until softened, about 2 minutes. Transfer the peppers to a plate with a slotted spoon. Turn heat to medium-high, add the fish, skin side up, and sauté until just done, about 5 minutes. Turn fish and sauté on the skin side for 1 minute. Transfer fish to warm serving plates. Add the garlic, peppers, vinegar, and stock to the skillet. Bring the liquid to a boil and simmer until liquid reduces to 1/2 cup, about 3 minutes. Remove pan from heat and stir in remaining 2 tablespoons butter. Spoon sauce over fish and serve immediately.

Michael McLaughlin
Free-lance writer
Brooklyn, NY

SALMON STEAKS PUTTANESCA

Makes 4 servings

The term "Puttanesca" is most often associated with a dish of pasta that is thought to have originated on the island of Ischia, off the coast of Naples. The word *puttana* means "streetwalker" in Italian. While Gaeta olives are traditional in the sauce, any brine- or salt-cured black olive can be used. This dish also is good at room temperature.

1 small onion
3 medium garlic cloves
1 pound Italian plum tomatoes
 (about 6 tomatoes)
12 black brine-cured Kalamata
 ***or* Gaeta olives**
6 anchovy fillets
3 tablespoons olive oil
1½ to 2 pounds salmon steaks
 (four 1-inch-thick steaks)
¼ cup dry red wine
2 tablespoons balsamic vinegar
1 tablespoon capers
Salt and ground black pepper

COOKING: Adjust oven rack to middle position and heat oven to 375°F. Peel and mince the onion and garlic. Peel, seed, and cut the tomatoes into 1-inch dice. Pit and coarsely chop the olives. Chop the anchovies. In an ovenproof skillet large enough to hold fish in a single layer, heat the olive oil until hot but not smoking. Pat the salmon steaks dry and sauté until lightly colored, about 2 minutes. Turn fish and cook 1 minute longer. Transfer salmon to a plate. Add the onion and garlic to the skillet and sauté until soft, about 3 minutes. Add the tomatoes and sauté until soft, about 2 minutes. Add the red wine and vinegar and bring to a boil. Return salmon to casserole, cover, and bake until fish is just done, 8 to 10 minutes. Transfer cooked salmon to serving plates. Cover and keep fish warm.

SERVING: Bring sauce in skillet to a boil, lower heat, and simmer until sauce thickens slightly, 1 to 2 minutes. Add olives, anchovies, and capers and simmer just until heated through, about 1 minute. Stir in ¼ teaspoon salt and ⅛ teaspoon pepper. Spoon sauce over fish and serve.

Michael McLaughlin
Free-lance writer
Brooklyn, NY

SOLE MEUNIERE

Makes 4 servings

If you add capers to this classic Sole Meunière and substitute diced lemon for the juice, you will have Sole Grenobloise, or sole cooked in the style of Grenoble.

1 lemon
2 tablespoons chopped parsley
4 fillets of sole, fluke, *or* flounder (about 1¹/₂ pounds total)
Salt and pepper
¹/₂ cup flour
2 tablespoons oil
8 tablespoons butter

PREPARATION: Squeeze 2 tablespoons lemon juice. Chop the parsley.

COOKING AND SERVING: Sprinkle fillets with salt and pepper. Dredge in flour and shake off excess. Using 2 frying pans, heat 1 tablespoon of oil and 1 tablespoon butter in each pan over medium-high heat until hot but not smoking. Add fillets and cook, turning once, until crisp and golden, about 4 minutes total. Transfer fillets to warm plates.

Reduce heat to low. Put the remaining 6 tablespoons butter in the pan and cook until butter bubbles, about 1 minute. Remove pan from heat and stir in lemon juice and parsley.

Pour butter over fillets and serve immediately.

Stephanie Lyness
Free-lance writer
New York, NY

STEAMED SOLE IN GREEN HERB SAUCE
PATRA NI MACCHI

Makes 6 servings

This pungent but elegant preparation can be made from any non-oily fish fillets. Boston lettuce, spinach, or Swiss chard leaves can replace cabbage.

Green Herb Sauce
1/2 cup sweetened shredded coconut
4 small garlic cloves
5 mild *or* hot chiles, such as Anaheims *or* serranos
1 medium lemon
1/2 cup loosely packed fresh coriander leaves
1/4 cup loosely packed fresh mint leaves
Salt

2 medium heads cabbage (to yield 12 large leaves)
2 teaspoons whole *or* crushed cumin seeds
1 ounce ginger (1- by 1-inch length)
2 1/4 pounds grey sole, flounder, haddock, sea bass, salmon, *or* cod fillets (6 filets)
4 tablespoons butter

PREPARATION AND ASSEMBLY: *For the sauce*, rinse coconut under warm running water; drain. Peel garlic. Stem, quarter, and seed chiles. Remove six 3- by 1-inch strips lemon zest; set aside. Squeeze 1/3 cup lemon juice into workbowl of a food processor. Add garlic, chiles, coconut, coriander, mint, and 1/2 teaspoon salt; mince.

For the fish, bring 4 quarts of water to boil in a 6-quart soup kettle. Remove 12 large leaves from the cabbages and cut away the tough center rib from each leaf. Blanch leaves until bright green and tender, 2 to 3 minutes. Drain, refresh under cold running water, and drain again. If using whole cumin seeds, grind in a coffee grinder or with a mortar and pestle; set aside. Cut ginger into 1- by 1/8-inch julienne strips (3 tablespoons); set aside.

Rinse and pat fish dry. Put 2 cabbage leaves on a work surface, overlapping slightly. Center a piece of fish over the leaves. Sprinkle fish with 1/8 teaspoon salt and spread 1 tablespoon green sauce over the top. Top with a strip of lemon zest. Fold leaves over fish to enclose in neat packages. Repeat. Transfer packages to a large wire rack *or* put 2 packages in each of 3 bamboo steamer trays.

COOKING: Bring 1 inch water to boil in a 14- by 11-inch roasting pan or a wok. Put rack directly over simmering water in pan and cover with foil. *Or*, cover and put steamer trays in wok, making sure water is level with bottom edge of wire rack or basket. Steam until fish is tender, 7 to 8 minutes. Heat butter in a small saucepan. Add cumin and ginger, and sauté until ginger is golden, 1 to 2 minutes.

SERVING: Transfer packets to plates. Open leaves, pour butter over each serving, and serve immediately.

Julie Sahni
Cookbook author
New York, NY

SWORDFISH WITH TOMATOES AND BASIL

Makes 4 servings

Saucing a grilled swordfish steak with a riotous tricolored tomato salad may seem slightly extravagant. But the salad marries perfectly with grilled swordfish and the acidity of the tomatoes, in combination with an undertone of garlic and the slight sweetness of the vinegar, complements the fish dramatically.

2 pounds assorted tomatoes (cherry or beefsteak tomatoes, yellow plum tomatoes, *and/or* tomatillos)
3 tablespoons balsamic vinegar
6 tablespoons olive oil
2 medium garlic cloves
1/2 cup firmly packed stemmed basil leaves
Salt and ground black pepper
1 1/2 to 2 pounds swordfish steak (four 1-inch thick steaks)

PREPARATION: Rinse and cut tomatoes into 1-inch chunks (5 cups). Put the tomatoes, balsamic vinegar, and 3 tablespoons of the olive oil in a medium bowl and marinate at room temperature for 30 minutes. (Can marinate up to 2 hours)

COOKING: Heat the grill. Mince the garlic and the basil and stir into the tomatoes with 1/2 teaspoon salt and 1/4 teaspoon pepper. With a small, sharp knife, carefully trim skin from fish steaks. If steaks are very large, cut them into triangular or square portions, 6 to 8 ounces each. Brush the swordfish on both sides with the remaining oil and grill fish, turning steaks once, until just done, 3 to 4 minutes on each side.

SERVING: Transfer fish to serving plates. Divide the tomato mixture over the swordfish and serve immediately.

Michael McLaughlin
Free-lance writer
Brooklyn, NY

CAKE AND COOKIES

APPLE-CARAMEL UPSIDE DOWN CAKE

Makes 8 servings

The trick in this recipe is to melt the sugar over high heat, stirring it often to achieve a delicate caramel color; then remove the warm caramel from the stove and gently, but quickly, arrange the sautéed apple slices in the bottom of the pan. A cast-iron, 9-inch skillet can be used for the upside-down cake, or a heavy duty 9-inch cake pan with straight sides will do in a pinch.

1 large cooking apple (about $\frac{1}{2}$ pound)
10 tablespoons softened unsalted butter
$1\frac{1}{4}$ cups plus 3 tablespoons sugar
1 cup pecans (4 ounces)
1 teaspoon cinnamon
2 cups all-purpose flour
1 teaspoon baking powder
$\frac{1}{2}$ teaspoon baking soda
$\frac{1}{4}$ teaspoon salt
2 eggs
1 cup sour cream
$\frac{1}{2}$ teaspoon vanilla extract

PREPARATION: Peel, core, and thinly slice the apple. Melt 2 tablespoons butter in a 9-inch, cast-iron skillet over medium-low heat. Add apple slices and sauté until wilted, about 3 minutes. Transfer slices to a plate. Increase heat to high; add $\frac{1}{4}$ cup sugar to skillet and cook, stirring frequently, until sugar melts and turns golden, about 3 minutes. Remove skillet from heat and arrange the apple slices in a circular pattern over the bottom. Set skillet aside.

Chop pecans and toss with 3 tablespoons sugar and the cinnamon; set aside. Sift flour with baking powder, baking soda, and salt; set aside. Beat remaining butter in a bowl until lightened. Gradually beat in 1 cup sugar, eggs, one at a time, sour cream, and vanilla. Fold dry ingredients into the batter.

COOKING: Adjust oven rack to middle position and heat oven to 350°F. Sprinkle half of the pecan mixture over the apples. Using your fingers or a spoon, carefully spread half of the cake batter over pecans. Sprinkle the remaining pecan mixture over the batter and carefully spread the remaining cake batter over pecans. Bake the cake until top is golden and a toothpick inserted in the center comes out clean, about 45 minutes. Cool on a rack for 5 minutes. Run a small knife along the edge of the cake and carefully invert cake onto a serving platter. If apples stick to the skillet, loosen with a knife and arrange on the cake. Serve slightly warm or at room temperature. (Can cover and store at room temperature up to 2 days.)

Bert Greene
Cookbook author
New York, NY

RUM AND BROWN-SUGAR APPLESAUCE CAKE

Makes 8 to 10 servings

A wondrous, spicy dessert, here is a cake that old-time cooks claimed was better the day after baking. The cake, incidentally, is best with homemade applesauce.

Applesauce Cake

1$^1/_4$ **cups Rum and Brown-Sugar applesauce (recipe page 239) *or* commercial applesauce**
$^1/_2$ **cup walnut halves (2 ounces)**
$^1/_2$ **cup raisins (3$^1/_2$ ounces)**
$^1/_2$ **cup currants (3 ounces)**
1$^1/_2$ **cups all-purpose flour**
1 **teaspoon baking soda**
$^1/_2$ **teaspoon baking powder**
1 **teaspoon cinnamon**
$^1/_2$ **teaspoon nutmeg**
$^1/_2$ **teaspoon ground cloves**
$^1/_4$ **pound softened unsalted butter**
1 **cup sugar**
1 **egg**

Icing

4 **tablespoons unsalted butter**
1$^1/_2$ **teaspoons vanilla extract**
3 **cups confectioners' sugar**
5 **tablespoons heavy cream**

PREPARATION: Make the applesauce. *For the cake*, chop the walnuts and toss with the raisins, currants, and $^1/_4$ cup flour in a small bowl. Set aside. Sift the remaining 1$^1/_4$ cups flour with the baking soda, baking powder, cinnamon, nutmeg, and cloves and set aside. In a large bowl, beat the butter until lightened. Gradually beat in the sugar, egg, and flour mixture in 3 batches, alternating with the applesauce. Stir in the raisin-nut mixture.

COOKING: Adjust oven rack to middle position and heat oven to 350°F. Butter and flour an 8- to 9-inch springform pan. Spoon batter into prepared pan and bake until a toothpick inserted in the center comes out clean, 50 to 60 minutes. Cool completely on a wire rack and remove springform side.

For the icing, in a large bowl, beat the butter with the vanilla until lightened. Gradually beat in the confectioners' sugar and continue beating until fluffy. Beat in cream, as necessary, to thin the icing to a spreadable consistency. Spread icing over the sides and top of cake.

Bert Greene
Cookbook author
New York, NY

CHOCOLATE-MACADAMIA TORTE

Makes 10 to 12 servings

It might be enough to say that this torte is dense, very rich, and yet, not overly sweet, but that would be selling it short. This flourless cake also has a marvelous, delicate texture, set off by the sinfully rich chocolate and cream ganache.

Ganache
12 ounces semisweet chocolate
1 cup whipping cream
4 tablespoons butter

Torte Layer
Softened butter
3 tablespoons cocoa
1/2 pound shelled macadamia nuts (2 cups)
12 ounces semisweet chocolate
8 eggs
1/4 pound butter
3/4 cup sugar
1/2 cup sour cream
2 teaspoons vanilla extract

PREPARATION: *For the ganache*, chop the chocolate into 1/2-inch pieces and put it in a heatproof mixing bowl. In a medium saucepan, bring cream and butter to a simmer. Strain hot cream mixture through a fine sieve into chocolate. Let stand 2 minutes. Stir until smooth. Cool at room temperature until mixture thickens to frosting consistency, stirring occasionally to prevent the formation of lumps, about 4 hours. Do not refrigerate. (Can cover and let stand overnight.)

For the torte layer, butter the side of a 10-inch springform and a round of parchment paper. Put paper onto springform bottom and dust entire pan with cocoa; refrigerate. Coarsely chop nuts; wrap and reserve 1/2 cup for garnish; set remaining 1 1/2 cups aside. Chop the chocolate (or grind it in a food processor fitted with the metal blade).

Separate the eggs. Stir egg yolks into the chocolate. Set egg whites aside. Heat butter and sugar in a medium saucepan. Stir over low heat until sugar partially dissolves and mixture turns pale, about 2 minutes. Add butter mixture to chocolate and stir until chocolate is melted and smooth. Stir in sour cream and vanilla.

In a large bowl, beat egg whites to firm peaks. Spoon half the chocolate mixture over egg whites and fold mixtures together. Thoroughly fold remaining chocolate and 1 1/2 cups nuts into egg whites.

COOKING: Adjust oven rack to low position and heat the oven to 300°F. Beginning at the outside edge of the pan, pour batter into the pan with a spiral motion. Give the pan several quarter turns to settle the mixture. Bake until a cake tester inserted into the center of the torte is withdrawn clean, about 1 hour. (Cake will soufflé and fall

(continued)
slightly.) Cool on wire rack at room temperature.

Remove pan side and invert cake onto a cardboard cake round or flat serving platter. Remove parchment paper. Generously frost side of cake with *ganache*. Spread remainder over top of cake, using a small metal spatula to create a decorative design. Garnish cake by pressing reserved nuts around the side, then refrigerate cake for 30 minutes to set *ganache*. Remove and set cake aside in a cool place for up to 6 hours.

Jane Freiman
Food columnist and cookbook author
New York, NY

CHOCOLATE-ORANGE CAKE

Makes one 9-inch cake

This cake explores the possibilities of different chocolate textures and appearances in the same dessert.

Candied Orange Zest
1 orange
1¹/₂ cups sugar
¹/₃ cup light corn syrup

Chocolate Génoise
Softened butter for pan
¹/₃ cup plain cake flour
¹/₃ cup cornstarch
3 tablespoons cocoa powder
¹/₈ teaspoon baking soda
4 eggs
Salt
²/₃ cups sugar

Orange Syrup
¹/₃ cup sugar
3 tablespoons orange liqueur
  or **orange juice**

Orange Filling
¹/₃ cup orange marmalade
2 tablespoons orange liqueur *or*
  orange juice

Whipped Ganache Filling
12 ounces semisweet chocolate
1 cup heavy cream

Ganache Glaze
8 ounces semisweet chocolate
1 cup heavy cream

PREPARATION: *For the candied orange zest*, strip off the orange zest with a vegetable peeler or a small knife and slice into ¹/₈-inch-wide strips. Put zest in a small saucepan with boiling water to cover. Boil for 5 minutes to remove bitter taste. Drain and rinse under cold water. Bring 1 cup sugar, ¹/₃ cup water, and corn syrup to a boil in the saucepan. Remove from heat, stir in zest, and let stand 30 minutes. Bring liquid back to a boil; set aside 30 minutes. With a fork, remove orange strips from syrup, one at a time, and put them ¹/₂ inch apart on a rack set over a pan to catch drippings. Let cool. Spread remaining ¹/₂ cup of sugar on a plate and roll cooled orange strips in sugar.

Candied orange zest can be made one week ahead and stored, tightly covered, at room temperature.

For the génoise, adjust oven rack to middle position. Heat oven to 350°F. Butter a 9-inch cake pan or springform pan and line the bottom with buttered parchment or waxed paper. Sift the cake flour with the cornstarch, cocoa powder, and baking soda.

In a medium saucepan, bring 2 inches of water to a simmer over low heat. Combine eggs and a pinch of salt in the bowl of a stand mixer or in a large bowl. Whisk in the sugar. Put the bowl over the pan of simmering water and continue whisking until mixture is warm, about 110°F. Using the whisk attachment of the mixer, whip egg mixture on high speed until cool, lightened in color, and risen in volume, about 5 minutes. If using a hand mixer, whip mixture on high speed, about 8 minutes. Fold the dry ingredients into the egg mixture in 3 batches.

Pour batter into the cake pan. To help cake rise evenly, tilt pan in a circular motion so that batter reaches the rim and then level batter by rapping pan once against work

(continued)

surface. Bake until cake is firm to touch and edges begin to pull away from the side of the pan, about 35 minutes. Run a small, sharp knife along the edge of cake to loosen it. Invert cake layer on a wire rack. Leaving paper on the bottom, turn the layer over and let it cool completely.

For the syrup, in a small saucepan, bring ⅓ cup water and sugar to a boil over medium heat and cook, stirring frequently, until sugar is dissolved. Remove from heat and cool. Stir in the liqueur or juice.

For the orange filling, in small bowl, stir together the marmalade and liqueur or juice.

For the ganache filling, chop chocolate into small pieces. In a large saucepan, bring cream to a simmer. Remove from heat and stir in chocolate. Let the mixture stand for 2 minutes, and then whisk until smooth. Cool ganache at room temperature until thick and set. Store in a cool place, but do not refrigerate.

Génoise, syrup, orange and ganache fillings can be prepared to this point 1 day before assembly. Wrap génoise in aluminum foil; cover ganache loosely; set aside at room temperature.

For the ganache glaze, chop chocolate into small pieces. In a saucepan, bring cream to a simmer. Remove from heat and stir in chocolate. Let mixture stand for 2 minutes, and then whisk until smooth. Ganache Glaze can be made 2 hours ahead. Do not refrigerate.

ASSEMBLY: Beat the ganache filling with a hand mixer or with the paddle attachment of a stand mixer on medium speed until lightened in texture and color, about 2 minutes.

With a serrated knife, split génoise horizontally into 3 equal layers. Put 1 layer on a 9-inch springform bottom or

CHOCOLATE-ORANGE CAKE

(continued)

a 9-inch cardboard disk. Using a pastry brush, moisten layer with $1/3$ of the syrup. Spread with $1/2$ of the orange filling and then with $1/4$ of the whipped ganache. Put a second layer of génoise on top of the ganache and moisten with $1/3$ of the syrup. Spread with the remaining orange filling and then with $1/4$ of the ganache. Put the last layer of génoise on top of the cake and moisten with remaining syrup. Spread the top and sides of the cake thinly with another $1/4$ of the whipped ganache, reserving the remainder for decoration. Refrigerate cake at least 30 minutes or until whipped ganache becomes firm.

Put cake on a rack over a jelly-roll pan to catch drippings. Pour cool ganache glaze over the cake, allowing the glaze to drip down the sides. Smooth with a metal spatula. Refrigerate until glaze has set, at least 30 minutes.

Put the remaining whipped ganache into a pastry bag fitted with $1/4$-inch star tip and pipe out 12 rosettes about 1 inch apart around the top perimeter of the cake. Decorate with candied orange peel.

Cake can be assembled and refrigerated, unwrapped, overnight.

Nicholas Malgieri
Pastry chef and cookbook author
New York, NY

CHOCOLATE SOUFFLE ROLL

Makes about 10 servings

Loosely based on James Beard's Chocolate Roll, this recipe also can be used to make a chocolate soufflé in a 1½-quart gratin dish, or a round cake covered with whipped cream.

Softened butter, for pan
5 eggs
6 ounces semisweet chocolate
2 tablespoons butter
2 tablespoons cognac *or* water
**   plus 1 tablespoon cognac for**
**   whipping cream (optional)**
Salt
¹/₃ cup sugar

1 cup heavy cream
Confectioners' sugar, for
**   garnish**
¹/₂ pint raspberries (optional)

PREPARATION: Heat oven to 350°F. Butter and line a 10- by 15-inch jelly-roll pan with wax paper. Separate eggs. Cut the chocolate into small pieces and combine butter and 2 tablespoons of the cognac in a large bowl. In a medium saucepan, bring 2 inches of water to a simmer over low heat. Remove pan from heat. Set the bowl of chocolate over hot water and stir until mixture is smooth. Remove bowl from hot water and add the egg yolks, one at a time, beating thoroughly. Set aside.

Beat egg whites with a pinch of salt until they just begin to hold soft peaks. Add sugar in a slow stream and continue beating until stiff. Gently stir about ¹/₄ of egg-white mixture into chocolate mixture, and fold in remainder. Pour batter into pan and smooth top with a metal spatula. Bake until firm to the touch, about 15 minutes.

Run a small, sharp knife along the edge of cake to loosen it. Slide cake onto work surface and let cool about 20 minutes. Slide a cookie sheet under the cake layer and cover cake with a sheet of wax paper. Set another cookie sheet on top and carefully invert the cake. Lift off top pan. Peel off the paper and replace with a clean sheet. Put the cookie sheet back on top and invert the cake again. Remove top cookie sheet and paper.

Combine the cream and remaining tablespoon cognac and whip until stiff. Spread the cream over the cake.

To roll the cake, pick up the long edge of paper with both hands and ease cake into a curve. Still holding the paper, simultaneously lift and roll cake directly onto a serving platter, seam side down. Trim edges. Put confectioners' sugar into a sieve and dust over roll. Recipe can be made and refrigerated, covered, several hours ahead.

SERVING: Garnish with raspberries, if desired.

Nicholas Malgieri
Pastry chef and cookbook author
New York, NY

CINNAMON-WALNUT COFFEE CAKE

Makes one 9-inch cake

This classic cake is equally good when made with pecans. It freezes perfectly and thaws quickly so James Villas, who says he is "never without one in the freezer," recommends making three or four at a time.

Cinnamon Topping
1/2 **cup all-purpose flour**
1/4 **cup sugar**
1 teaspoon ground cinnamon
3 tablespoons butter

Coffee Cake
1 tablespoon butter
1 1/2 **cups walnuts (6 ounces)**
2 cups all-purpose flour
1 cup sugar
1 tablespoon baking powder
1 teaspoon salt
1 cup milk
1/4 **cup vegetable shortening** 1 1/2
   teaspoons vanilla
2 eggs

PREPARATION: *For the topping*, mix the flour, sugar, and cinnamon in a small bowl. Cut the butter into 1/2-inch pieces, add them to the bowl, and work with fingertips until the mixture resembles coarse meal; set aside.

For the cake, coat a 9-inch round baking pan with butter. Coarsely chop the walnuts. Sift the flour, sugar, baking powder, and salt into a large mixing bowl. Add the milk, shortening, and vanilla and beat with an electric mixer at medium speed for 3 minutes. Add the eggs and beat 2 minutes longer. Pour the batter into the baking pan. Sprinkle nuts and the cinnamon topping evenly over the top of the batter.

COOKING: Adjust oven rack to middle position and heat oven to 350°F. Bake until a cake tester inserted in the middle comes out clean, about 1 hour. Cool in the pan on a wire rack. (Can wrap in plastic and store at room temperature up to 2 days.)

SERVING: Cut into wedges and transfer to a serving platter.

James Villas
Cookbook author and food editor
Town & Country
New York, NY

HUGUENOT TORTE

Makes 8 servings

One of the South's greatest desserts, this torte was adapted by Bill Neal of Crook's Corner Restaurant in Chapel Hill, North Carolina, from a book called *Charleston Receipts*.

**8 pecan halves (for garnish) plus
  6 ounces pecan halves**
¹/₂ cup all-purpose flour
¹/₄ teaspoon salt
2 teaspoons baking powder
2 large apples (about ³/₄ pound)
3 large eggs
1 cup plus 1 tablespoon sugar
1 teaspoon vanilla extract
²/₃ cup heavy cream

PREPARATION AND COOKING: Adjust oven rack to the center position and heat oven to 325°F. Put the pecan halves in a baking dish and bake until fragrant, about 10 minutes. Set 8 pecans aside. Butter two 9-inch cake pans and line the bottoms with buttered wax paper. Sprinkle the paper with flour and shake off excess. Set pans aside. Mince the remaining pecans (1¹/₂ cups) and put in a mixing bowl. Stir in the flour, salt, and baking powder and blend well. Peel, core, and cut the apples into ¹/₈-inch dice (2 cups). Stir the apples into the dry ingredients. With a whisk or an electric mixer, beat the eggs until frothy, about 2 minutes. Gradually beat in the sugar and vanilla until a ribbon forms, about 5 minutes. Gently fold in the flour mixture. Pour the batter into prepared cake pans and smooth the tops. Bake until cake tester inserted in the center comes out clean, about 35 minutes. Cool the cakes in the pans for 10 minutes. Loosen cakes by running a sharp knife along the rim of each layer. Unmold layers onto a wire rack. Cool. (Can wrap in plastic and set aside at room temperature overnight.)

SERVING: Whip cream to stiff peaks. Spread the bottom cake layer with about three quarters of the whipped cream, and then top with second cake layer. Put the remaining whipped cream into a pastry bag fitted with a No. 32 star tip. Pipe 8 rosettes around rim of cake. Top each rosette with a toasted pecan.

Craig Claiborne
Food critic and cookbook author
East Hampton, NY

LEMON MOUSSE CHEESECAKE

Makes 10 to 12 servings

Soft and creamy, this cake combines the texture of a mousse with the lusciousness of classic cheesecake. Because the cake is so creamy, it will be easier to slice if frozen. A slicing knife can be heated with warm or hot water and wiped dry.

Wafer Crust
5 tablespoons softened butter
6 ounces vanilla wafers (about 43)
$1/4$ cup sugar

Lemon Mousse Filling
3 large lemons
4 eggs
24 ounces softened cream cheese
$1^1/2$ cups sugar
$1/3$ cup all-purpose flour
Candied Lemon Zest (recipe page 286) (optional)

PREPARATION: *For the crust*, coat a 9- by 3-inch or $10^1/2$- -by 2-inch springform pan with 1 tablespoon butter. Seal the outside of the pan with foil. Put the wafers and sugar in the workbowl of a food processor and process to crumbs. Melt the remaining butter and process it into the crumbs. *Or*, put wafers between 2 layers of wax paper and crush them with a rolling pin; transfer crumbs to a bowl and stir in sugar and melted butter. Press crumb mixture evenly over the bottom of the pan.

For the filling, grate 1 tablespoon lemon zest and squeeze $3/4$ cup lemon juice; set aside separately. Separate eggs. Put cream cheese in a bowl and beat until smooth. Gradually add $1^1/4$ cups sugar and beat until light and fluffy, 5 minutes. Add flour, egg yolks, lemon juice, and zest and beat until smooth, 1 minute. Whip the egg whites to soft peaks. Gradually add the remaining sugar while whipping whites to firm peaks. Fold egg whites thoroughly into the lemon batter.

COOKING: Adjust oven rack to middle position and heat oven to 325°F. Pour batter into the springform pan. Put springform in a baking dish just large enough to contain it. Put dish in oven and add hot tap water to come 1 inch up the side. Bake until cake is set and golden, 55 to 65 minutes. Transfer pan to a rack; cool. Cover cake and refrigerate until chilled, at least 4 hours. (Can refrigerate 3 days or freeze 1 month.)

SERVING: Run a knife along the edge of cake to loosen. Carefully remove pan rim. Garnish slices of cake with Candied Lemon Zest (optional).

Marlene Sorosky
Cookbook author
Towson, MD

LEMON-YOGURT COFFEE CAKE

Makes 12 servings

Yogurt and lemon have long been paired in salads, but the combination is seen less frequently in baked goods. In this bundt cake, the two ingredients produce a moist, dense crumb and tangy glaze.

Cake
**1/2 pound plus 1 tablespoon
  softened butter**
**2 cups plus 1 tablespoon
  all-purpose flour**
4 eggs
2 small lemons
1 1/2 cups sugar
1 cup plain yogurt (8 ounces)
2 teaspoons baking powder
3/4 teaspoon baking soda
1/2 teaspoon salt

Lemon-Yogurt Glaze
1 cup confectioners' sugar
1 small lemon
3/4 cup plain yogurt (2 ounces)

PREPARATION: *For the cake*, coat a 3-quart bundt or tube pan with 1 tablespoon of the butter and dust pan with 1 tablespoon flour.

Separate and set eggs aside. Grate 2 teaspoons lemon zest and squeeze 1/3 cup juice. Beat remaining butter and the sugar in a bowl until mixture is light and fluffy. Beat in egg yolks, one at a time. Beat in lemon zest, lemon juice, and yogurt. Sift remaining flour with baking powder, baking soda, and salt.

Turn mixer to low and beat in dry ingredients until just incorporated. Turn mixer to medium; beat for 2 minutes. With clean beaters, whip whites to firm peaks and fold into batter. Pour batter into pan.

COOKING: Adjust oven rack to middle position and heat oven to 350°F. Bake until a cake tester inserted in the center of the cake comes out clean, about 50 minutes. Cool cake in the pan for 10 minutes, then invert onto a wire rack to cool completely. (Can wrap and store at room temperature overnight, or freeze up to 1 month.)

ASSEMBLY: *For the glaze*, sift confectioners' sugar into a medium bowl or large measuring cup. Squeeze in 1 tablespoon lemon juice and stir in yogurt until glaze is smooth. If necessary, return cake to a wire rack set over a pan to catch drippings. Pour glaze over the cake, allowing it to drip down the sides. Let cake stand at room temperature until glaze sets, about 10 minutes. (Can cover and store at room temperature up to 2 days.)

Marlene Sorosky
Cookbook author
Towson, MD

YULE LOG CAKE
BUCHE DE NOEL

Makes 1 Yule Log

This combination of sponge cake and chocolate and coffee buttercreams is not only delicious, but makes a stunning holiday centerpiece

Buttercream
**14 ounces bittersweet *or*
    semisweet chocolate**
4 egg yolks
1¹/₃ cups confectioners' sugar
³/₄ pound softened butter
**2 tablespoons instant espresso
    powder**
2 teaspoons boiling water

Sponge Cake
14 tablespoons softened butter
**1 cup plus 3 tablespoons plain
    cake flour**
1¹/₂ teaspoons baking powder
¹/₈ teaspoon salt
1 cup sugar
3 eggs

**Meringue Mushrooms (recipe
    page 289)**
**2 ounces bittersweet *or*
    semisweet chocolate**
Cocoa powder
Confectioners' sugar

PREPARATION: *For the buttercream*, chop the chocolate into small pieces and put them in a heatproof bowl. Bring 2 inches of water to a boil in a small saucepan. Remove the saucepan from the heat. Set the bowl over the pan of hot water and stir until the chocolate is melted and smooth; cool.

Put the egg yolks and sugar in a medium bowl and beat with an electric mixer until very pale, about 2 minutes. Add the butter, a tablespoon at a time, beating well after each addition. Continue beating until the buttercream is very smooth, about 5 minutes longer. Remove half the buttercream to a separate bowl. Stir melted chocolate into one batch of the buttercream. Dissolve the instant espresso powder in the boiling water, and stir it into the plain buttercream. (Can cover and set aside at room temperature up to 2 hours, or cool, cover, and refrigerate up to 48 hours.)

For the sponge cake, coat a 16- by 11-inch jelly-roll pan with 1 tablespoon butter, and line it with parchment or wax paper. Coat the paper with 1 tablespoon butter; set aside. Sift flour with baking powder and salt. Beat the remaining butter and the sugar in a medium bowl with an electric mixer until very pale, about 2 minutes. Beat in the eggs, one at a time, beating well after each addition. Add the flour mixture and beat until smooth, about 2 minutes.

COOKING: Adjust oven rack to middle position and heat oven to 375°F. Evenly spread the batter in the pan. Bake until the cake layer is lightly browned and springy, about 10 minutes. Run a small knife along the rim of the cake to loosen it. Slide the cake onto a work surface and trim off the crisp, brown edges. Cover cake with a large, damp

(continued)

dish towel (edges should extend at least 2 inches beyond cake). Slide a baking sheet under cake and cover dish towel with another baking sheet. Carefully invert cake. Remove top baking sheet and peel off paper. Position cake with long side facing you. Fold bottom edge of towel up over bottom edge of cake. Tightly roll cake and set aside, seam-side down, until cool, about 30 minutes.

ASSEMBLY: (Bring buttercreams to room temperature and stir until smooth.) Set aside $1/2$ cup coffee buttercream. Unroll cake, spread with remaining coffee buttercream, and roll tightly. Cut a diagonal slice from 1 end of roll, about 1 inch long at the longest point. Put cake roll on a baking sheet, seam-side down. Set the slice on top of roll to form a stump, and spread ends of roll and top of stump with reserved coffee buttercream. Spread chocolate buttercream over the rest of exterior of the roll. Draw tines of a fork along length of cake and around stump to imitate bark. (Can refrigerate overnight or freeze up to 1 month.)

Make the mushrooms. Chop chocolate into pieces and put in a heatproof bowl. Bring 2 inches water to boil in a small saucepan. Remove from heat. Set the bowl over the hot water; stir until chocolate melts. Fit a pastry bag with a writing tip. Fill bag with melted chocolate and pipe spirals on the end of stump to represent rings.

SERVING: Transfer chilled cake to a platter. Lightly sift cocoa over tops of mushrooms. Put 8 or 9 mushrooms on top of, and around cake. Put confectioners' sugar in a sieve and dust lightly over top of cake.

Peter Kump
President
Peter Kump's New York Cooking School
  and James Beard Foundation
New York, NY

APRICOT-ALMOND DANOISES

Makes 30 pastries

This light, flaky pastry, wrapped around a tart filling, has an irresistibly buttery flavor and a gentle crunch.

Pastry
1/4 **pound chilled, unsalted butter**
1/2 **cup cottage cheese (4 ounces)**
1 **cup all-purpose flour**
1/8 **teaspoon salt**

Apricot Filling
2/3 **cup dried apricots (4 ounces)**
1/3 **cup sugar**

1 **egg white**
1/2 **cup sliced almonds (2 ounces)**
1/2 **cup confectioners sugar**

PREPARATION: *For the pastry*, cut butter into 1-inch pieces and put into the workbowl of a food processor, along with cottage cheese, flour, and salt. Process until dough forms a ball. Flatten dough into a disk, wrap in plastic, and refrigerate at least 1 hour. (Can refrigerate overnight or freeze up to 1 month)

For the apricot filling, put apricots, sugar, and 1/2 cup water in a small saucepan and bring to boil. Simmer, stirring occasionally, until apricots are softened, 5 to 8 minutes. Mash apricots with a wooden spoon or potato masher and set aside to cool. (If cooled mixture is too thick to spread, stir in up to 2 teaspoons of water, or enough to give mixture the consistency of jam.)

Lightly beat egg white with a fork and set aside. Line 2 baking sheets with parchment paper. On a lightly floured surface, roll out pastry dough to a 10- by l2-inch rectangle. Using a pastry cutter, cut dough into thirty 2-inch squares. Spoon 1 teaspoon apricot filling in a 1/4-inch wide diagonal line from 1 corner of the square to opposite corner. Fold 1 blank corner to the center, over the jam. Brush opposite blank with egg white and bring to the center, stretching it slightly to wrap around the pastry. Press lightly to seal. Transfer pastries to baking sheets. Brush tops with egg white and sprinkle with almonds. Cover and refrigerate at least 1 hour, or overnight.

COOKING: Adjust oven rack to middle position; heat oven to 350°F. Sift confectioners' sugar over pastries. Bake until golden, 25 to 30 minutes. Transfer to wire rack and cool. (Can refrigerate 2 days or freeze up to 1 month.)

SERVING: If pastries have been frozen, heat in a 350°F oven until warmed through, about 5 minutes. Serve at room temperature.

Marlene Sorosky
Cookbook author
Towson, MD

BLACK AND WHITE BARS

Makes about 48 bars

Call these bars great deceivers. With the first bite, guests will discover these are not just ordinary squares of cheesecake. A full pound of imported white chocolate suffuses each one with a subtle undertone that is sensational and surprising.

Chocolate Wafer Crust
1 box chocolate wafer cookies (8¹/₂ ounces)
8 tablespoons unsalted butter
1 tablespoon sugar

Cheesecake Filling
4 large eggs
10 ounces white chocolate
¹/₂ cup whipping cream
1 pound cream cheese
4 teaspoons vanilla
¹/₈ teaspoon salt

White Chocolate Topping
6 ounces white chocolate
¹/₄ cup whipping cream
2 tablespoons white crème de cacao

PREPARATION: *For the chocolate wafer crust*, line the bottom and sides of a 9- by 13-inch baking pan with heavy duty aluminum foil. Coat the foil with 2 tablespoons of the butter. Put the chocolate wafers in the workbowl of a food processor fitted with the metal blade and process crumbs. Or, put wafers between two layers of wax paper and use a rolling pin to crush them. Melt the remaining butter and stir thoroughly into the crumbs along with the sugar. Press crumb mixture evenly over the bottom of the foil-lined pan.

For the cheesecake filling, separate and set the eggs aside. In a medium saucepan, bring 2 inches of water to a simmer and remove pan from heat. Chop the chocolate into 1-inch pieces and put in a heatproof bowl. Set the bowl over the hot water, stirring until chocolate melts; set pan aside. Gradually stir in the cream. Set aside to cool slightly. Beat the cream cheese until smooth. Beat in egg yolks, one at a time, scraping side of bowl frequently with a spatula. Add chocolate, vanilla, and salt, and beat filling for 2 minutes. Using clean beaters, beat egg whites to firm peaks and fold them into the chocolate mixture. Pour filling evenly over the crust.

COOKING: Adjust oven rack to middle position and heat oven to 300°F. Bake until filling has risen and is almost set, about 30 minutes. Transfer pan to a wire rack and cool cake to room temperature.

For the white chocolate topping, reheat 2 inches of water in the saucepan and remove from heat. Chop the chocolate into 1-inch pieces and put into a heatproof bowl. Set bowl over the hot water, stirring until the chocolate melts. Gradually stir in the cream and creme de cacao. Pour the white chocolate topping over the cool cheesecake. When

BLACK AND WHITE BARS

(continued)

cool, cover and freeze the bars for 1 hour. (Can freeze up to 1 month.)

SERVING: Using the foil corners as handles, lift the frozen cheesecake from the pan and set on a flat surface. With a chefs knife dipped in very hot water, cut the frozen cheesecake into $1/2$ inch squares. Keep bars frozen until ready to garnish.

Top with reserved crumbs; drizzle with melted semisweet chocolate or decorate with semisweet chocolate curls. Serve immediately, or store in refrigerator and serve chilled. Makes about 48 bars.

Marlene Sorosky
Cookbook author
Towson, MD

CHOCOLATE ALMOND TRIANGLES

Makes 12 servings

In the first bite, you discover oozing chocolate hidden in the luscious almond and cream cheese filling. If you're a serious chocolate lover, add a bit more than is called for in the recipe.

Almond Filling
**2 ounces semisweet *or*
    bittersweet chocolate**
1 lemon
6 ounces cream cheese
¹/₂ pound almond paste
1¹/₂ teaspoons almond extract
1 tablespoon flour

¹/₄ pound butter
8 sheets phyllo

PREPARATION: *For the filling*, cut the chocolate into 12 equal pieces. Grate 1 teaspoon zest from the lemon and squeeze 1 tablespoon juice. In a bowl, stir together the cream cheese and almond paste. Add the lemon juice and zest, almond extract, and flour and stir until smooth. Chill for at least 1 hour.

Melt the butter. Butter a baking sheet. Lay out 1 sheet of phyllo on a work surface with the short side at the bottom and brush with the melted butter. Top with another sheet of phyllo and brush with butter. Cut the layered phyllo lengthwise into 3 strips. Put a generous tablespoon of the chilled filling in the bottom left-hand corner of each strip and top with a piece of chocolate. Fold the bottom right-hand corner of each strip over the filling to make a triangle. Continue folding the strip as you would a flag, keeping the triangular shape.

Put the pastry on the prepared pan and brush with butter. Repeat 3 more times using the remaining phyllo sheets and filling to make 12 pastries.

Pastries can be prepared to this point a day ahead.

COOKING AND SERVING: Heat the oven to 375°F. Bake the Chocolate Almond Triangles in preheated oven until crisp and golden brown, about 20 minutes. Serve warm or at room temperature.

Bonnie Tandy LeBlang
Free-lance food writer
Hamden, CT

CHOCOLATE ARABIANS

Makes 24 pieces

Nutmeat-studded chocolate cushions, laced with espresso coffee and liqueur, are tiny exotic gems that are moist and rich enough for a sultan.

1/4 **pound unsalted butter**
1/2 **cup semisweet chocolate**
   chips (3 ounces)
2 **large eggs**
1 **tablespoon coffee liqueur**
1/2 **cup all-purpose flour**
3/4 **cup sugar**
1 **teaspoon instant espresso**
   powder
1/2 **cup pecans (2 ounces)**
24 **large pecan halves**

PREPARATION: In a medium saucepan, bring 2 inches of water to a simmer and remove from heat. Cut butter into 1-inch pieces and put into a heatproof bowl with the chocolate. Set the bowl over the hot water and stir until smooth. Cool slightly. Whisk in the eggs and liqueur, then stir in the flour, sugar, and espresso. Chop and stir 1/2 cup of the pecans into the batter.

COOKING: Adjust oven rack to middle position and heat oven to 350°F. Line two mini-muffin tins (each with twelve 1 3/4-inch-diameter cups) with paper muffin cups. Spoon batter into cups, filling them three-quarters full, and placing a pecan half in the center of each cup of batter. Bake until batter is set and a toothpick inserted into the center comes out clean, about 20 minutes. Cool 2 to 3 minutes in muffin tins, then transfer each piece to a wire rack. (Can store in an airtight container for 3 days or freeze up to 1 month). Arabians can be served in the paper cups, or removed from the papers before serving.

Marlene Sorosky
Cookbook author
Towson, MD

CHOCOLATE-FILLED MACADAMIA WAFERS

Makes about 4 dozen cookies

If you can only find salted Macadamia nuts, soak them in hot water for 5 minutes, rinse well under hot, running water, and then crisp in a 300°F oven for 5 minutes.

Macadamia Wafers
10 tablespoons softened
   unsalted butter
6 tablespoons all-purpose flour
1 cup unsalted macadamia nuts
   (4¹/₂ ounces)
¹/₂ cup sugar
2 egg whites

Chocolate Filling
6 ounces semisweet chocolate
4 tablespoons butter

PREPARATION: *For the wafers*, coat 2 baking sheets with 2 tablespoons butter and dust with 2 tablespoons flour. Put nuts and sugar in the workbowl of a food processor; pulse until mixture resembles coarse meal. *Or*, finely chop nuts with a large, heavy knife. Mix chopped nuts with sugar in a small bowl; set aside. Beat remaining butter in a bowl with an electric mixer until light and creamy, 3 to 4 minutes. Add nut-sugar mixture and beat until very light, about 5 minutes longer. Add egg whites, 1 tablespoon at a time, and beat until batter is shiny and smooth, about 3 minutes. Sift and lightly stir in the remaining flour.

COOKING: Adjust oven racks to middle and low positions and heat oven to 300°F. Put batter in a pastry bag fitted with a ¹/₂-inch tip and pipe ³/₄-inch mounds of batter 2 inches apart on baking sheets. Bake until edges are lightly browned, 8 to 10 minutes. (Switch baking sheets after 5 minutes to ensure even cooking.) Cool for 3 minutes on baking sheets, then carefully loosen with a spatula, transfer to a wire rack, and cool completely.

For the filling, bring 2 inches of water to a simmer in a medium saucepan; remove from heat. Cut chocolate and butter into 1-inch pieces and put in a medium heatproof bowl. Set the bowl over the hot water and stir until the chocolate and the butter melt. Cool to room temperature. (Can cover and refrigerate for several weeks.)

ASSEMBLY: (Bring filling to room temperature, stirring occasionally until it reaches a spreadable consistency. If it still remains stiff, stir in 1 or 2 teaspoons of heavy cream.) Spread the flat side of half the wafers with a thin layer of chocolate. Top with remaining wafers, flat side against the chocolate. (Can store up to 3 weeks in an airtight container or freeze up to 1 month).

Nicholas Malgieri
Pastry chef and cookbook author
New York, NY

CHOCOLATE-ORANGE PINWHEELS

Makes about 5 dozen cookies

This versatile dough need not be confined to pinwheels. The dough may be rolled out and cut into a variety of shapes, brushed with beaten egg, and decorated with chopped nuts or colored sugar.

$1/2$ **pound softened unsalted butter**
2 teaspoons vanilla extract
$1/2$ **cup sugar**
3 egg yolks
$2^1/4$ **cups plain cake flour**
$1/4$ **teaspoon salt**
1 small orange
3 tablespoons cocoa powder
$1/2$ **teaspoon instant espresso coffee powder**

PREPARATION: Beat butter with an electric mixer until creamy, 2 to 3 minutes. Beat in vanilla, then add sugar in a slow stream, and continue beating until mixture is light, about 5 minutes. Add yolks, 1 at a time, beating thoroughly. Divide mixture between 2 bowls. Sift $1^1/4$ cups flour with salt and fold into mixture in 1 bowl; grate in $1^1/2$ teaspoons orange zest. Sift cocoa powder and espresso with remaining flour; fold into second bowl.

Spread a 6-inch square of orange-flavored dough, about $1/4$ inch thick, on plastic wrap. Cover with plastic wrap and refrigerate until firm, about 1 hour. Repeat with chocolate-flavored dough. (Can refrigerate overnight.)

On a lightly floured sheet of parchment paper, roll out orange-flavored dough to a 9-inch square, about $3/8$-inch thick; chill. Repeat with chocolate-flavored dough. (If doughs become very soft, return to refrigerator.) Lightly brush orange-flavored dough with water. Ease chocolate dough from paper onto orange-flavored dough. Gently roll to press layers together. Cut layered square into two 9- by $4^1/2$-inch rectangles. Lightly brush each rectangle with water. Arrange 1 piece of dough with long side facing you. Use parchment paper to ease dough into a curve, then using the paper as a guide, simultaneously lift and roll dough into a cylinder. Repeat with remaining rectangle. Wrap and refrigerate until firm, at least 1 hour. (Can refrigerate up to 3 days.) Line 2 baking sheets with wax paper. Slice dough $1/2$-inch thick and put slices on baking sheets.

COOKING: Adjust oven racks to middle and low positions and heat oven to 325°F. Bake until firm, but pale, 10 to 15 minutes. (Switch baking sheets after 5 minutes to ensure even cooking.) Transfer cookies to a wire rack and cool.

Nicholas Malgieri
Pastry chef and cookbook author
New York, NY

CHOCOLATE PECAN SQUARES

Makes sixteen 2-inch square bars

This is a perfect treat for casual entertaining or for taking along on picnics.

Softened butter, for pan
6 ounces pecans (about 1¹/₂ cups chopped)
¹/₂ cup flour
2 eggs
Salt
1 tablespoon rum (optional)
3 ounces semisweet chocolate
3 tablespoons butter
¹/₄ cup sugar
¹/₂ cup dark corn syrup
Confectioners' sugar for garnish

PREPARATION: Heat oven to 325°F. Butter an 8- by 8-inch baking pan and line bottom with a piece of parchment or wax paper. Chop pecans. In a bowl, mix the pecans with the flour. In a separate bowl, beat eggs with a pinch of salt and the rum.

Chop the chocolate into small pieces. Put chocolate and the butter in a bowl. In a medium saucepan, bring 2 inches of water to a simmer. Remove pan from heat. Set the bowl over the hot water and stir until mixture is melted; cool.

In a small saucepan, bring sugar and corn syrup to a boil. Remove pan from heat and stir in the cooled chocolate mixture, then stir in the beaten eggs. Stir in pecan mixture.

Pour batter into prepared pan and bake until set, about 35 minutes. Cool in the pan, about 10 minutes, and then turn out onto a wire rack to cool. Put confectioners' sugar in a sieve and dust over bars. Cut into 16 squares. Chocolate-pecan squares can be made 3 days ahead and stored in an air-tight container.

Nicholas Malgieri
Pastry chef and cookbook author
New York, NY

COCOA- AND RUM-MARBLED MADELEINES

Makes 5 dozen madeleines

Egg-rich *madeleines*, usually flavored with vanilla or lemon, are a French classic. This unusual version marbles rum- and cocoa-flavored batters in mini madeleine molds. The molds are sold in gourmet cookware stores.

15 tablespoons plus 3
    tablespoons unsalted butter
$1^1/_4$ cups plus 3 tablespoons
    all-purpose flour
3 eggs
1 tablespoon dark rum
$^2/_3$ cup sugar
2 tablespoons cocoa powder

PREPARATION: Coat three *madeleine* molds (each with 20 imprints measuring $1^3/_4$- by $1^1/_4$-inches) with 3 table-spoons of the butter and dust with 3 tablespoons of the flour.

Heat remaining 12 tablespoons butter in a small saucepan over low heat; set aside. Lightly beat the eggs with an electric mixer. Beat in the rum, then add sugar in a slow stream, and continue beating until the mixture is very light in texture and color, 3 to 4 minutes. Sift and fold in the remaining $1^1/_4$ cups flour. Fold in the melted butter.

Transfer $^1/_2$ cup of the batter to a small bowl; sift and fold in the cocoa powder. Spoon the chocolate batter over the rum batter and marbleize with 5 or 6 turns of a spatula; do not overmix.

COOKING: Adjust oven rack to low and middle positions and heat oven to 350°F. Spoon or pipe the batter into the mold imprints, filling them two-thirds full. Put the *madeleine* molds on 2 baking sheets and bake until the cookies are firm, 7 to 8 minutes. (Switch the baking sheets after 4 minutes to ensure even baking). Cool *madeleines* 5 minutes in the molds. Then transfer the *madeleines* to a wire rack and cool completely. (Can wrap and refrigerate *madeleines* for up to 4 days, or freeze up to 1 month.)

Nicholas Malgieri
Pastry chef and cookbook author
New York, NY

DARK FRUITCAKE BARS

Makes about 4 dozen bars

This dark, moist fruitcake is cut into small bars so that its richness is not too overwhelming. For a more intense flavor, the bars may be soaked in rum and aged for 2 to 3 weeks.

1/2 **cup dried figs (4 ounces)**
1/2 **cup dates (3^1/2 ounces)**
1/2 **cup dried apricots (3^1/4 ounces)**
1/2 **cup prunes (3^1/4 ounces)**
1/2 **cup pecans (2 ounces)**
1/2 **cup walnuts (2 ounces)**
1/2 **cup almonds (2 ounces)**
1/2 **cup dark raisins (3 ounces)**
1/2 **cup white (sultana) raisins (3 ounces)**
1/2 **cup dark rum**
13 **tablespoons softened unsalted butter**
1 **cup firmly packed dark brown sugar**
3 **eggs**
1/2 **teaspoon ground cinnamon**
1/2 **teaspoon ground cloves**
1/2 **teaspoon ground nutmeg**
1/2 **teaspoon ground ginger**
1/2 **teaspoon baking powder**
1/2 **teaspoon baking soda**
1/4 **teaspoon salt**
2 **cups all-purpose flour**

PREPARATION: Removing stems or pits as necessary, cut the figs, dates, apricots, and prunes into 1/4-inch dice. Coarsely chop the pecans, walnuts, and almonds. Mix the chopped fruit and nuts in a medium bowl, add the raisins and 1/4 cup rum, cover, and set aside at room temperature overnight. (Can cover and refrigerate for up to 2 weeks.)

Coat a 10- by 15-inch jelly-roll pan with 1 tablespoon of the softened butter and line with a sheet of parchment paper. Beat the remaining butter in a medium bowl with an electric mixer until light and creamy, 3 to 4 minutes. Add the brown sugar and continue beating until the mixture is very light, about 5 minutes longer. Add the eggs, one at a time, beating thoroughly after each addition.

Mix cinnamon, cloves, nutmeg, ginger, and baking powder with baking soda and salt. Sift the spices with the flour. Stir the dry ingredients into the batter and then fold the batter into the reserved fruit-nut mixture. Use a spatula to spread the batter evenly in the pan and cover with a sheet of parchment paper.

COOKING: Adjust oven rack to middle position and heat oven to 350°F. Bake the cake until it is firm, 25 to 30 minutes. Cool the cake in the pan on a wire rack. Cover with plastic wrap and refrigerate overnight.

Remove the top sheet of parchment from the cake layer. Brush the cake layer with 1/4 cup rum, cover tightly with plastic wrap, and refrigerate 2 to 3 days (optional). Invert the cake layer onto a cutting board, remove the bottom sheet of parchment, and trim off hard edges. Cut the cake into 1^1/2- by 2-inch bars. (Can store the bars between sheets of wax paper in an airtight container for up to 3 weeks.)

Nicholas Malgieri
Pastry chef and cookbook author
New York, NY

GINGER AND PINEAPPLE SWIRLS

Makes about 28 swirls

Spirals of ginger cake surround mellow pineapple cream in a tropical pinwheel of fruit and spice.

Ginger Cake
Softened butter
$^1/_2$ cup all-purpose flour
$^1/_2$ teaspoon baking soda
$^1/_2$ teaspoon baking powder
1 tablespoon ground ginger
1 teaspoon ground cinnamon
$^1/_2$ teaspoon ground nutmeg
$^1/_4$ teaspoon ground cloves
4 large eggs
$^1/_2$ cup packed dark brown sugar
3 tablespoons molasses

Pineapple Filling
1 can crushed pineapple (8 ounces)
$^2/_3$ cup heavy cream
2 tablespoons confectioners' sugar

PREPARATION AND COOKING: *For the ginger cake*, adjust oven rack to middle position and heat oven to 350° F. Butter a 10- by 15-inch jelly roll pan, line it with parchment or wax paper, and butter the paper. Sift the flour with the baking soda, baking powder, ginger, cinnamon, nutmeg, and cloves. Set the mixture aside.

Separate eggs into 2 bowls. Set whites aside. Beat yolks with an electric mixer on medium speed. Gradually add brown sugar and beat until light and fluffy, about 2 minutes. Beat in molasses. Turn mixer to low speed and beat in dry ingredients until just incorporated. Turn mixer to medium and beat 30 seconds. With clean beaters, whip whites to firm peaks and fold into batter. Pour batter into prepared pan and bake until cake springs back when lightly pressed, about 15 minutes, Cover cake immediately with a damp kitchen towel and cool to room temperature in the pan.

For the pineapple filling, drain pineapple, and mash it slightly with a spoon. Whip cream to soft peaks, add confectioners' sugar, and beat cream to firm peaks. Fold pineapple into whipped cream, cover, and refrigerate until ready to use. (Can refrigerate up to 4 hours.)

ASSEMBLY: Remove towel from the cake and run a sharp knife around the edge, to loosen it; transfer cake to a flat work surface. Cut the cake in half lengthwise. Cut each half crosswise. Peel off the paper, using a small knife to detach it from the cake. Spread one quarter of the filling over each cake quarter. Arrange one cake rectangle with a short side facing you and roll the cake as tightly as possible. Wrap securely in plastic. Repeat to roll the remaining cake rectangles and refrigerate at least 2 to 3 hours. (can refrigerate up to 2 days or freeze up to 1 month.

SERVING: Use a serrated knife to cut cake rolls into $^3/_4$-inch-thick slices.

Marlene Sorosky
Cookbook author
Towson, MD

HAZELNUT PIZZELLE

Makes 5 dozen

These delicate wafer cookies are a special treat when paired with ice cream or gelato. There are two basic types of *pizzelle* makers available at gourmet and specialty stores. One resembles a tortilla press. Another is an electric machine that makes two wafers. *Pizzelle* makers are available from Williams-Sonoma.

1 cup hazelnuts (about 4 ounces)
   (optional)
$^1/_2$ pound butter
6 eggs
1$^1/_2$ cups sugar
1 tablespoon vanilla extract
3$^1/_2$ cups all-purpose flour
4 teaspoons baking powder

PREPARATION: (If using hazelnuts, heat oven to 350°F and adjust oven rack to middle position. Spread the hazelnuts in a cake pan and toast until browned, about l0 minutes. While still warm, rub off the skins with a clean towel. Cool and chop.) Melt the butter. In a large bowl, beat eggs lightly. Stir in sugar, butter vanilla, flour, baking powder, and nuts. (The batter will be thick.)

COOKING: Heat the pizzelle iron. Drop one teaspoon of batter onto the center of each cookie imprint. Press down the lid and cook 30 seconds. Remove cookies. Immediately quarter each cookie or shape each into a cone around a cone-shaped mold. Cookies also can be placed flat to cool. Repeat with remaining batter, dipping the spoon in water as necessary if the batter sticks.

Anna Teresa Callen
Cookbook author and teacher
New York, NY

LEMON AND PISTACHIO BARS

Makes 2 to 3 dozen bars

Rich lemon custard is sandwiched between two layers that are both enhanced by lemon and pistachios.

Pistachio Pastry
2 medium lemons
$^1/_3$ cup sugar
1 cup shelled pistachio nuts ($5^1/_2$ ounces)
$^1/_4$ pound butter
$^3/_4$ cup all purpose flour

Lemon filling
4 tablespoons butter
4 eggs
$^3/_4$ cup sugar
$1^1/_2$ teaspoons all-purpose flour

PREPARATION: *For the pastry*, line bottom and sides of an 8- or 9-inch square baking dish with heavy-duty aluminum foil. Strip off lemon zest, put in the workbowl of a food processor fitted with the metal blade, and process until coarsely chopped. Reserve lemons for filling. Add sugar and pistachios to machine; process until zest is minced. Wrap and reserve $^1/_2$ cup of the mixture for topping. Cut butter into pieces; add to the processor along with flour. Pulse until mixture just holds together.

COOKING: Adjust oven rack to middle position; heat oven to 350°F. Press dough evenly over bottom of pan. Bake until crust is golden, 20 to 25 minutes.

For the filling, melt butter. Squeeze 6 tablespoons juice from reserved lemons into the workbowl of a food processor fitted with the metal blade. Add eggs, sugar, butter and flour; process to mix. *Or*, whisk in a bowl. Pour filling over crust.

Bake until filling is almost set, 10 to 12 minutes. Sprinkle evenly with reserved pistachio-lemon mixture. Bake until filling is completely set, 8 to 10 minutes longer. Transfer to a wire rack and cool to room temperature.

SERVING: Using the corners of the aluminum foil as handles, lift the square out of the pan and put it on a work surface. Trim off the edges and cut it into $1^1/_2$-inch squares. (Can cover and refrigerate squares up to 4 days or freeze up to 1 month.)

Marlene Sorosky
Cookbook author
Towson, MD

PISTACHIO-ORANGE SLICES

makes 3 dozen cookies

A bright pavé of pale-green pistachios and snippets of orange zest distinguish these crisp slices. The special marriage of citrus and nuts recalls the sunny Mediterranean and designates the cookies as sublime partners for a glass of chilled Late Harvest Riesling or Barsac. The recipe was inspired by Victoria Morena of San Francisco's Square One restaurant.

1 cup shelled pistachios (about 4 ounces)
1 small orange
10 tablespoons softened, unsalted butter
$1/2$ cup sugar
1 tablespoon plus 1 teaspoon milk
$1/4$ teaspoon vanilla
2 tablespoons orange liqueur
$1^{1}/_{4}$ cups all-purpose flour
$1/8$ teaspoon salt

PREPARATION: Adjust oven rack to middle position and heat oven to 300°F. Spread the shelled pistachios in a shallow baking pan and toast, stirring once or twice, until they are golden and fragrant, about 10 minutes. Grate the orange zest; set aside. (Reserve the orange for another use.)

In a medium bowl or in the workbowl of a food processor fitted with the metal blade, cream 8 tablespoons of the butter with the sugar until light and fluffy. Add the milk, vanilla, orange liqueur, flour, and salt, and mix or process until well blended. Mix or process in the toasted pistachios along with 2 teaspoons of the grated orange zest. Shape the cookie dough into a 2-inch cylinder, wrap in plastic wrap, and freeze until firm, about 1 hour. (Can refrigerate cylinder up to 2 days or freeze up to 1 month.)

COOKING: Adjust two oven racks to middle and low positions and heat oven to 350°F. Use the remaining butter to lightly coat two baking sheets. Using a serrated knife, slice the cylinder of dough into $1/4$-inch thick rounds and put the rounds on the baking sheets. (The cookies should be placed about $1/2$ inch apart.) Bake the cookies until lightly browned but still soft, 15 to 18 minutes. (If baking two sheets at the same time, shift bottom baking sheet to top rack and the top baking sheet to the bottom rack after 7 minutes to ensure even browning). Transfer cookies to a wire rack to cool. (Can store cookies in an airtight container for 1 week or freeze up to 1 month.)

Marlene Sorosky
Cookbook author
Towson, MD

RASPBERRY-ALMOND CAKES

Makes 2¹/₂ dozen cakes

These delicate, festive cakes are a variation on the classic *petits fours*. The cakes are iced with fondant tinted with a raspberry puree, which gives the icing a brilliant rose color and a fresh berry flavor. Prepared fondant or a good dry fondant mix can be ordered by mail from Maid of Scandinavia Co., 3244 Raleigh Ave., Minneapolis, MN 55416, (612) 927-7996. Almond paste is available in supermarkets.

Raspberry Fondant
3 cups sugar
¹/₂ teaspoon cream of tartar
1 package frozen raspberries (10 ounces)

Almond Cake
9 tablespoons softened unsalted butter
1 can almond paste (8 ounces)
¹/₂ cup sugar
4 eggs
³/₄ cup all-purpose flour
¹/₄ cup seedless raspberry reserves
1 ounce semisweet chocolate
¹/₂ teaspoon vegetable oil

PREPARATION: *For the fondant*, fill a heatproof bowl with ice water; set aside. Bring sugar, cream of tartar, and 1 cup water to a boil in a medium saucepan, stirring frequently to dissolve sugar. Skim off foam and wash down any sugar crystals from the sides of the pan with a brush dipped in cold water. Cook the syrup to the soft-ball stage (240°F). Immediately plunge the bottom of the saucepan into the ice water to stop the cooking; pat bottom dry.

Pour the syrup onto a clean marble surface or a non-stick jelly-roll pan and cool 1 minute. Use 2 stainless-steel spatulas to work the syrup by folding the sides of the mixture into the center until it becomes opaque and crumbly, about 15 minutes. Break the fondant into 3 pieces and knead each until soft and pliable, 3 to 5 minutes. Put the softened fondant in a bowl, cover with plastic wrap, and refrigerate overnight. (Can sprinkle with 1 teaspoon water, put plastic wrap directly on the surface to prevent drying, and refrigerate up to 1 month.)

Thaw and put raspberries in a heavy-bottomed medium saucepan and bring to a boil over very low heat. Simmer 10 minutes. Transfer raspberries to the workbowl of a food processor fitted with the metal blade and puree. Strain puree through a fine sieve, discard seeds, and cool. Measure ¹/₄ cup puree (wrap and freeze remainder for another use), and work into the fondant with your hands. Fondant should be thin enough to pour easily, but thick enough to coat a surface opaquely. (Can sprinkle with 1 teaspoon water, put plastic wrap directly on surface of fondant to prevent drying, and refrigerate up to 1 month.)

(continued)

For the cake, coat a 15- by 10-inch jelly-roll pan with 1 tablespoon butter and line with parchment or wax paper. Beat almond paste, sugar, and 1 egg in a bowl with an electric mixer until smooth. Add the remaining butter and continue to beat until lightened in texture and color, 3 to 4 minutes. Beat in the remaining eggs one at a time. Sift and stir in flour. Spread batter evenly in the pan.

COOKING: Adjust oven rack to middle position and heat oven to 400°F. Bake cake until firm to the touch and the edges begin to pull away from the sides of the pan. Invert cake onto a wire rack; cool. (Can return cake to pan, wrap in plastic, and refrigerate overnight.) Transfer cake to a cutting board, and cut into two 10- by 7^1/$_2$-inch pieces. Spread one half with the preserves, and top with the remaining half, paper side up. Peel off and discard both papers. (Can wrap and refrigerate cake up to 3 days, or freeze up to 1 month.)

ASSEMBLY: Bring cake to room temperature, if refrigerated. Cut the cake into 1^1/$_2$-inch squares and put them 1 inch apart on a wire rack set over a baking sheet to catch the drippings. Bring 2 inches of water to a simmer in a medium saucepan. Put fondant in a heatproof bowl. Set bowl over simmering water, and stir fondant until warm, about 100°F. (Do not overheat or icing will become dull and grainy.) Spoon the liquid fondant over the cake squares to coat completely; set aside until set, about 30 minutes. Cut the chocolate into small pieces and put in a small heatproof

RASPBERRY-ALMOND CAKES

(continued)

bowl. Bring 2 inches of water to a boil in a small saucepan. Remove the pan from heat. Set the bowl of chocolate over the hot water and stir until melted. Stir in the oil. To make a parchment paper cone, cut out a triangle of parchment paper. Twist the paper triangle into a loose cone. Tighten the outside layer of paper against the cone, forming a sharp tip. Fold the upper ends of the paper inside the cone to prevent it from unraveling. Fill the cone with the melted chocolate. Pipe the top of each cake with a ribbon and bow design or with a chocolate zigzag. (Can wrap and refrigerate Raspberry-Almond Cakes up to 3 days.)

Nicholas Malgieri
Pastry chef and cookbook author
New York, NY

RASPBERRY-ALMOND LINZER COOKIES

Makes 2¹/₂ to 3 dozen cookies

The classic Viennese nut dough, *Mandelmuerbteig*, is used here to make a two-layer cookie filled with raspberry preserves.

1 cup blanched almonds (4
   ounces)
1¹/₂ cups all-purpose flour
12 tablespoons softened
   unsalted butter
¹/₂ cup sugar
1 tablespoon grated lemon zest
2 teaspoons vanilla extract
1 egg white
¹/₈ teaspoon salt
¹/₃ cup sliced, blanched almonds
   (about 1¹/₂ ounces)
1 cup seedless raspberry jam
Confectioners' sugar

PREPARATION: Put almonds and flour in the workbowl of a food processor; process until finely ground; set aside. Beat butter in a medium bowl with an electric mixer until lightened in color, 2 to 3 minutes. Add sugar and continue beating until mixture is very light, about 5 minutes longer. Beat in lemon zest along with vanilla extract. Stir in flour mixture; don't overmix. Form dough into a ¹/₂-inch-thick disk. Wrap in plastic and refrigerate until firm, about 1 hour (Can refrigerate overnight.)

Line 2 baking sheets with parchment or wax paper. Cut dough into 4 pieces; set 3 aside. Roll out dough ¹/₈ inch thick on a lightly floured work surface. Cut 1¹/₂-inch circles with a plain or fluted cookie cutter. Press scraps into a ball; roll and cut more circles. To form cookie tops, cut out centers of half the dough circles with a ¹/₂-inch round canapé cutter or bottom of a metal pastry tip. Put rings and bottoms ¹/₂-inch apart on baking sheets. Repeat to cut out circles and rings from three remaining pieces of dough.

COOKING: Adjust oven racks to low and middle positions and heat oven to 325°F. Whisk the egg white with the salt. Coarsely chop the almonds or crush with a rolling pin. Brush the cookie tops with egg wash and sprinkle with crushed almonds. Bake until cookies are dry and very lightly browned, 12 to 15 minutes. (Switch the baking sheets after 6 minutes to ensure even cooking.)

Bring ¹/₂ cup jam to a boil in a small saucepan and simmer until slightly thickened, 5 to 8 minutes. Brush cookie bottoms with the jam; top with cookie rings. Dust with confectioners' sugar. Use a small spoon or pastry bag fitted with a ¹/₄-inch tip to fill the holes with remaining jam. (Can store cookies in an airtight container between layers of wax paper up to 3 weeks or freeze up to 1 month.)

Nicholas Malgieri
Pastry chef and cookbook author
New York, NY

VENETIAN CORNMEAL COOKIES

Makes about 5 dozen cookies

These cookies are based on a classic Venetian pastry called *zaleti*. Although the original recipe calls for cookies to be formed individually, these are rolled, baked, and then sliced.

$^3/_4$ **cup shelled pistachios (3$^3/_4$ ounces)**
1$^1/_2$ **cups yellow cornmeal**
1$^1/_2$ **cups all-purpose flour**
$^1/_2$ **cup sugar**
$^1/_4$ **teaspoon salt**
1 **teaspoon baking powder**
l5 **tablespoons unsalted butter**
$^3/_4$ **cup white (sultana) raisins (4$^1/_2$ ounces)**
1 **medium lemon**
2 **eggs**
2 **teaspoons vanilla extract**

PREPARATION: Put pistachios in a small saucepan with water to cover. Bring water to a boil; drain pistachios and rub in a towel to remove skins. Put skinned nuts in a single layer in a cake pan and bake until dry, about 5 minutes; cool.

Line 2 baking sheets with wax paper; set aside. Mix the cornmeal, flour, sugar, salt, and baking powder in a large bowl. Cut the butter into $^1/_2$-inch pieces and work into the dry ingredients with your fingertips until mixture resembles coarse meal. Stir in pistachios and raisins. Grate 1 teaspoon lemon zest into a small bowl and whisk with eggs and vanilla extract. Work the egg mixture into the dry ingredients with a fork and press into a ball. Transfer dough to a lightly floured work surface and cut into 4 pieces: Roll pieces into 1- by 12-inch cylinders. (Can refrigerate up to 3 days.)

COOKING: Adjust oven rack to middle position and heat oven to 350°F. Put the cylinders on baking sheets and bake until golden and dry, about 15 minutes. Transfer cylinders to a work surface and cut diagonally with a serrated knife into $^3/_4$-inch slices. Return cookie slices to the baking sheets, cut sides down, and bake until slightly dried (do not overbake), about 5 minutes longer. Transfer cookies to a wire rack to cool.

Nicholas Malgieri
Pastry chef and cookbook author
New York, NY

WALNUT SQUARES

Makes 10 dozen squares

Pecan halves, blanched almonds, or toasted hazelnuts can be substituted for the walnuts in these rich, gooey squares. Do not overcook the sugar mixture or it will harden. Chilling will make the pastry easier to cut. In addition to squares, the pastry can be cut into diamonds, triangles, or rectangles.

Sweet Pastry Dough
2 cups all-purpose flour
$1/2$ cup sugar
$1/4$ teaspoon salt
$1/2$ teaspoon baking powder
9 tablespoons chilled unsalted butter
2 eggs

Caramel-Walnut Filling
3 cups walnuts ($10^1/2$ ounces)
$1/2$ cup light corn syrup
$1^1/4$ cups firmly-packed, light brown sugar
4 tablespoons butter
$1/2$ cup heavy cream
2 teaspoons vanilla extract
1 tablespoon dark rum

PREPARATION: *For the dough*, put the flour, sugar, salt, and baking powder in the workbowl of a food processor fitted with the metal blade, or in a medium bowl. Cut 8 tablespoons of the butter into $1/2$-inch pieces and add to the bowl or processor with dry ingredients. Pulse or work mixture with fingertips until it resembles coarse meal. Beat the eggs lightly and add to the mixture. Pulse, or toss mixture with a fork, until dough holds together when pinched.

Transfer dough to a lightly floured surface and lightly knead the dough until smooth. Flatten dough into a 6- by 4-inch rectangle, 1-inch thick. Cover with plastic wrap and refrigerate 1 hour. (Can refrigerate overnight.)

Coat a 15- by 10-inch jelly-roll pan with remaining butter. Roll the dough into a 17- by 12-inch rectangle on a lightly floured work surface. Transfer dough to the pan and press firmly into the bottom and up the sides, doubling the dough on the sides. Freeze crust for 10 minutes. (Can wrap and freeze overnight.)

COOKING: *For the filling*, coarsely chop the walnuts; set aside in a heatproof bowl. Bring the corn syrup and the brown sugar to a boil in a medium saucepan, stirring frequently to dissolve the sugar crystals. Add the butter and cream and bring to a boil. Simmer for 3 minutes, remove from heat; stir in the vanilla and rum. Mix the hot syrup with the walnuts; set the filling aside.

Adjust the oven rack to low position and heat the oven to 375°F. Butter a 15- by 10-inch sheet of aluminum foil. Line the frozen dough with the buttered foil, buttered side down, and fill with dried beans or pie weights. Bake for 10

WALNUT SQUARES

(continued)

minutes. Remove foil and beans and return crust to oven for 5 minutes. Lower oven temperature to 350°F. Remove crust from oven, spread evenly with the filling, and bake for 15 minutes. Turn the pan in the oven to ensure even baking. Then bake until filling bubbles and crust is lightly browned, about 15 minutes longer. Cool the pastry completely in the pan on a wire rack. Cover with aluminum foil and chill.

SERVING: Run a small, sharp knife around the edge of the chilled crust. Set the pan over low heat for a few seconds to melt caramel which may make crust adhere to the pan. Transfer the walnut pastry to a cutting board. (If the pastry sticks to the jelly-roll pan, carefully invert the walnut pastry onto a baking sheet and then slide it onto a cutting board.) Remove thick side crusts and cut the pastry into 1-inch squares or diamonds. (Can store squares between layers of wax paper in an airtight container up to 3 weeks, or freeze up to 1 month.)

Nicholas Malgieri
Pastry chef and cookbook author
New York, NY

OTHER SWEETS

APPLE-CRANBERRY LATTICE TART

Makes 6 servings

A smashing dessert, this makes a perfect ending for any holiday meal. Since the tart is not overly sweet, it can be served with vanilla ice cream on the side.

Pastry
¹/₂ cup chilled lard
2 cups all purpose flour
2 teaspoons sugar
¹/₂ teaspoon salt
**¹/₄ cup chilled vegetable
    shortening**
2 eggs
1¹/₂ teaspoons red-wine vinegar
3 tablespoons cold water

Apple-Cranberry Filling
¹/₄ cup walnut halves (1 ounce)
1 orange
2 large pie apples (1 pound)
1 cup cranberries (4 ounces)
¹/₂ cup raisins (3¹/₂ ounces)
**1 cup plus 1 tablespoon
    granulated sugar**
**¹/₂ cup firmly packed dark brown
    sugar**
1 tablespoon instant tapioca
¹/₂ teaspoon cinnamon
¹/₈ teaspoon ground cloves

PREPARATION: *For the pastry*, cut the lard into ¹/₂-inch pieces. If making the dough by hand, put the flour, sugar, and salt in a bowl. Cut the lard and shortening into the dry ingredients with a pastry blender, or work quickly with fingertips until mixture resembles a coarse meal with some pea-sized pieces remaining. Lightly beat 1 egg with the vinegar and 1 tablespoon of the cold water and add it to the bowl, tossing with a fork. Add water, 1 tablespoon at a time, until dough just holds together. If using a food processor, put lard, flour, sugar, salt, and shortening into the workbowl fitted with the metal blade and process until mixture resembles a coarse meal. Lightly beat 1 egg with the vinegar and 1 tablespoon cold water. Add the egg mixture and pulse until dough holds together. Divide the dough into 2 equal disks. Wrap in plastic and refrigerate for 1 hour. (Can refrigerate overnight, or wrap in plastic and freeze up to 1 month.)

For the filling, chop and set walnuts aside. Grate 2 teaspoons orange zest into a large bowl and squeeze in 2 tablespoons orange juice. Peel and grate apples into the bowl. Stir in cranberries, raisins, 1 cup sugar, brown sugar, tapioca, cinnamon, and cloves.

COOKING: Butter a 9-inch fluted tart pan with a removable bottom. In a small bowl, lightly beat the remaining egg with 1 tablespoon cold water. On a lightly floured work surface, roll out 1 disk of dough to an 11-inch circle and ease it into the tart pan. Trim the edge, leaving a ¹/₂-inch border, and brush edge of crust with egg. Pour filling into the crust and pack it evenly with the back of a spoon.

Roll out the remaining dough to an 11-inch square. With

(continued)

a sharp knife or serrated pastry wheel, cut dough into ten $^3/_4$-inch-wide strips. To form the lattice, put 5 strips horizontally across the top of the tart at 1-inch intervals. Working carefully, weave 5 vertical strips over and under the horizontal strips, taking care not to break the strips as you work. Trim and flute the edge. Brush the pastry with egg. Sprinkle walnuts in the spaces between the lattice-work and dust the top of the pie with the remaining tablespoon granulated sugar. Adjust oven rack to middle position and heat oven to 425°F. Put the pie on a foil-lined baking sheet and bake 15 minutes. Reduce heat to 350°F. and bake until crust is golden and filling is bubbling, about 35 minutes. Serve at room temperature.

Bert Greene
Cookbook author
New York, NY

DUTCH APPLE SOUFFLE PANCAKE WITH APRICOT SAUCE

Makes 4 to 6 servings

Make this pancake in an ovenproof baking dish with low sides, and remember to work fast when the pancake is assembled. A lovely apricot-apple syrup is a good accompaniment, but any topping of your choice will do.

Apricot Sauce (recipe page 278)

**1 large cooking *or* pie apple
   (about 1/2 pound)
5 tablespoons unsalted butter
1/4 cup apricot preserves
2 tablespoons sugar
1 orange
3 eggs
3/4 cup milk
3/4 cup all-purpose flour
1/8 teaspoon nutmeg
1/4 cup confectioners' sugar**

PREPARATION AND COOKING: Make the Apricot Sauce. Peel, core, and thinly slice the apple. Melt 1 tablespoon of the butter in a large, heavy skillet. Add the apple slices and apricot preserves, sprinkle with sugar, and toss over medium-low heat until apples wilt and release their juices, about 3 minutes. Raise heat to medium and cook until apples are just tender, and the juices have thickened, about 8 minutes. Cover and keep warm over very low heat.

Squeeze 2 tablespoons orange juice into the workbowl of a food processor fitted with the metal blade. Add the eggs, milk, flour, and nutmeg and process until smooth. Adjust oven rack to middle position and heat oven to 425°F. Put the remaining 4 tablespoons butter in a 2-quart baking dish that is no more than 3 inches deep. Put dish in the oven until butter melts, about 5 minutes. Carefully tilt the dish to coat the bottom and sides with butter. Spoon the apples and their cooking juices into the dish and pour the batter over the apples. Bake until golden and puffed, l5 to 20 minutes. Rewarm Apricot Sauce.

SERVING: Immediately dust Apple Pancake with confectioners' sugar and serve with Apricot Sauce.

Bert Greene
Cookbook author
New York, NY

APPLE STRUDEL

Makes 12 servings

This apple strudel couldn't be easier — tart apples, sweet raisins, and rich pecans, all in a crisp phyllo wrapping.

Strudel Filling

1¹/₂ cups chopped pecans (6¹/₂ ounces)
1 lemon
2 pounds Granny Smith *or* other tart apples (about 4)
³/₄ cup granulated sugar
2 teaspoons ground cinnamon
¹/₂ cup raisins

¹/₂ pound butter
10 sheets phyllo

PREPARATION: *For the filling*, chop the pecans. Squeeze 2 tablespoons lemon juice. Peel and core the apples and cut into thin slices. Put apples in a bowl and toss with the lemon juice. Add the sugar, cinnamon, and raisins and mix.

Butter a baking sheet. Melt the ¹/₂ pound butter. Put a damp dish towel on a work surface and then cover it with a piece of plastic wrap. Brush one sheet of phyllo with the melted butter and sprinkle with about 2 tablespoons of the pecans. Lay a second sheet of phyllo on top, brush with butter, and sprinkle with 2 tablespoons of pecans. Repeat the layering with seven more sheets of phyllo. Add one more sheet, but do not brush the top with butter or sprinkle with nuts.

Spread an even 3-inch-wide strip of the apple mixture, about 1 inch in from the bottom edge of the phyllo and 2 inches in from each side. Fold in the sides and bottom of the phyllo and roll up the strudel like a jelly-roll, using a towel to help you roll. Put the strudel on the prepared baking sheet and brush the top and sides with the remaining melted butter.

The strudel can be made one day ahead.

COOKING AND SERVING: Heat oven to 375°F. Bake the strudel in oven until crisp and golden, about 30 minutes. Cool 10 minutes and then slice with a serrated knife.

Bonnie Tandy LeBlang
Free-lance food writer
Hamden, CT

GOLDEN SUGAR-CRUSTED BAKED APPLES

Makes 4 servings

These days, baked apples are beloved as a comfort food; to be consumed with lots of cream after, or in lieu of, a light supper. What gives this baked apple its distinction is the paucity of outside peel. Crushed seasoned walnuts make an admirable edible exterior instead.

$^1/_2$ **cup walnut halves (2 ounces)**
$^1/_4$ **cup granulated sugar**
$^1/_2$ **teaspoon cinnamon**
6 tablespoons unsalted butter
$^1/_4$ **cup packed dark brown sugar**
$^1/_4$ **cup raisins (1$^3/_4$ ounces)**
4 baking apples (about 2 pounds)
1 lemon
4 small cinnamon sticks
$^3/_4$ **cup apple juice**
1 cup heavy cream (optional)

PREPARATION: Adjust oven rack to middle position and heat oven to 375°F. Put the walnuts, sugar, and cinnamon in the workbowl of a food processor fitted with the metal blade and process until nuts are ground. Transfer nut mixture to a small bowl and set aside. In a small saucepan, melt 4 tablespoons of the butter and set aside. Cut the remaining butter into $^1/_4$-inch cubes and put in a small bowl with the brown sugar. Mix with a fork until well blended. Stir in raisins and set aside.

Use a paring knife to remove the core of each apple in one rectangular piece. Remove the top two-thirds of the peel. Halve the lemon. Rub the tops and sides of the apples with lemon juice and squeeze juice into the cored centers. Brush the apples with the melted butter and press the walnut mixture evenly over the tops and peeled sides of the apples.

COOKING: Transfer apples to a shallow 8-inch baking dish and fill the centers with the brown sugar-raisin mixture. Place a cinnamon stick into the center of each apple and drizzle with remaining melted butter. Pour the apple juice into the dish and bake until the apples are tender, 50 to 60 minutes. Cool 15 minutes on a rack.

SERVING: Serve warm or at room temperature in shallow bowls accompanied by the pan juices, and heavy cream, if desired.

Bert Greene
Cookbook author
New York, NY

RUM AND BROWN-SUGAR APPLESAUCE

Makes about 1 quart

Use this applesauce as the base of the Rum and Brown-Sugar Applesauce Cake (recipe page 199) or eat it on its own as a simple, homey sweet.

6 large cooking apples (about 3 pounds)
1 lemon
³/₄ cup packed dark brown sugar
3 tablespoons dark rum
2 tablespoons unsalted butter

PREPARATION: Peel, core and thinly slice apples (8 cups) and put slices into a large saucepan. Grate ¹/₂ teaspoon lemon zest into the pan; set lemon aside. Cover and stew the apples over low heat until very tender, 30 minutes. Mash the apples with a potato masher and squeeze in 2 teaspoons lemon juice. Stir in sugar, rum, and butter, and over medium heat, simmer, uncovered, until thickened, 10 minutes. (Can cover and refrigerate up to 5 days.)

Bert Greene
Cookbook author
New York, NY

CHOCOLATE MINT MOUSSE

Makes 6 servings

For an elegant summer dessert, layer this mousse in individual goblets and top with a sprig of mint.

8 ounces semisweet chocolate
4 egg yolks
$^1/_3$ cup white crème de menthe
$^1/_2$ package unflavored gelatin
   ($1^1/_2$ teaspoons)
2 cups heavy cream
Mint sprigs for garnish
   (optional)

PREPARATION: Chop the chocolate into small pieces and put into a bowl. In a medium saucepan, bring 2 inches of water to a simmer. Remove pan from heat. Set the bowl of chocolate over the hot water, stirring frequently until just melted. Remove bowl from hot water. Cool.

Bring the water in the saucepan back to a simmer. In a large bowl or in the bowl of a standing mixer, combine the egg yolks, sugar, and crème de menthe. Set bowl over simmering water and whisk constantly until egg mixture is slightly thickened, about 3 minutes. Remove bowl from hot water. With mixer on medium speed, whisk the egg mixture until light and cool, about 4 minutes.

In a small saucepan, bring about 1 inch of water to a simmer. Put $^1/_4$ cup of water in a small bowl, sprinkle with gelatin, and let stand until softened, about 2 minutes. Remove pan of simmering water from heat and set bowl of softened gelatin in hot water until gelatin has melted, about 2 minutes. Whip cream to soft peaks. Whisk gelatin into cool egg mixture, and then divide egg-gelatin mixture evenly between two bowls. Stir melted chocolate into second bowl and then fold in remaining whipped cream.

To layer the mousse, divide $^1/_2$ of the chocolate-mint mousse between individual goblets. Spoon all of the mint mousse on top. Make a final layer using the remaining chocolate-mint mousse. Refrigerate until set, at least 2 hours.

Recipe can be prepared and refrigerated 1 day ahead.
SERVING: Decorate with mint sprigs, if desired.

Nicholas Malgieri
Pastry chef and cookbook author
New York, NY

CHOCOLATE MARBLE TERRINE

Makes about 10 servings

This striking presentation utilizes two different chocolate mousses, one made with semisweet chocolate and the other with white chocolate. To slice the terrine perfectly, use a very sharp, thin knife that has been rinsed in warm water and wiped dry. Slices of the terrine can be served on pools of dark-chocolate sauce; count on 3 to 4 tablespoons of sauce per serving.

Softened butter, for pan

Dark Chocolate Mousse
8 ounces semisweet chocolate
4 tablespoons butter
$^1/_2$ cup heavy cream
1 tablespoon cognac

White-Chocolate Mousse
12 ounces white chocolate
6 tablespoons butter
$^2/_3$ cup heavy cream
1 tablespoon cognac

Chocolate Sauce
$^1/_2$ pound semisweet chocolate
1 cup sugar
$^1/_3$ cup light corn syrup

Meringue
3 egg whites
$^1/_3$ cup sugar

PREPARATION: Butter a $1^1/_2$-quart terrine mold or loaf pan and line with plastic wrap.

For the Dark-Chocolate Mousse, cut chocolate and butter into small pieces and combine in a bowl. In a medium saucepan, bring about 2 inches of water to a simmer. Remove pan from heat. Set the bowl of chocolate over the hot water and stir until chocolate has melted. Cool, and then add the cream, 2 tablespoons at a time, stirring well. Stir in the cognac. Cover mixture with plastic and let stand at room temperature until firm and cool, at least 2 hours. Do not refrigerate.

For the White-Chocolate Mousse, follow the procedure above, using white chocolate.

For the chocolate sauce, cut chocolate into small pieces. In a saucepan, combine sugar, corn syrup, and 1 cup water, and bring to a boil. Remove from heat and stir in chocolate. Let chocolate mixture stand 2 minutes, and then whisk until smooth. Set aside to cool. Recipe can be prepared to this point a day ahead.

For the meringue, in a medium saucepan, bring about 2 inches of water to a simmer. Combine egg whites and sugar in the bowl of an electric mixer or in large bowl. Set bowl over the simmering water and gently whisk until egg whites are warm and sugar is dissolved, about 3 minutes. Remove bowl from simmering water, and using the whisk attachment of mixer, whip until meringue is cool and stiff peaks form, about 7 minutes. Set aside.

Beat white-chocolate mousse on medium speed until lightened in texture and color, about 3 minutes. Repeat with dark-chocolate mousse. Immediately fold $^1/_3$ of the

CHOCOLATE MARBLE TERRINE

(continued)

meringue into the dark-chocolate mousse; $^2/_3$ of the meringue into the white-chocolate mousse.

Spoon the dark-chocolate mousse on top of the white-chocolate mousse in 1 bowl. Using a spatula, marbleize the mixtures with about 6 turns of the spatula, being careful not to overmix. Gently pour mixture into the mold. Give mold several raps against a towel-covered surface to level the mousse, and then cover with plastic wrap. Refrigerate for 8 hours or up to 2 days.

SERVING: Wrap the mold in a hot, wet cloth. Invert pan onto a cutting board and cut in 1-inch thick slices with a warm, dry knife. Spoon Chocolate Sauce onto dessert plates and gently lay slices on top.

Nicholas Malgieri
Pastry chef and cookbook author
New York, NY

DARK-CHERRY PACKETS

Makes 4 servings

Filled with sweet cherries and hazelnuts, this flaky pastry turns over a new leaf with its easy phyllo wrapping. Substitute blueberries for an equally sumptuous pastry.

1 16-ounce can dark, sweet, pitted cherries
1½ ounces hazelnuts (½ cup chopped)
¼ cup confectioners' sugar plus more for sprinkling
¼ teaspoon vanilla extract
¼ pound butter
4 sheets phyllo

PREPARATION: Drain the cherries. Chop the hazelnuts. In a bowl, combine the hazelnuts and confectioners' sugar. In another bowl, toss together the cherries and vanilla.

Butter a baking sheet. Melt the ¼ pound butter. Lay out 1 sheet of the phyllo on a work surface with the long side at the bottom; brush with the melted butter. Center ¼ of the cherry mixture on the phyllo about 2 inches from the bottom edge and sprinkle with 2 tablespoons of the nut mixture. Fold the bottom 2 inches of phyllo over the filling. Fold the left and right sides of phyllo over the filling and then gently roll up. Brush with butter and put on prepared pan. Repeat 3 more times using the remaining ingredients.

The pastries can be assembled a day ahead.

COOKING AND SERVING: Heat the oven to 375°F. Bake pastries in preheated oven until crisp and golden, about 20 minutes. Cool at least 10 minutes and sprinkle with confectioners' sugar before serving.

Bonnie Tandy LeBlang
Free-lance food writer
Hamden, CT

SPICED CRANBERRY-PEAR COBBLER

Makes 6 servings

Tart cranberries contrast with sweet pears in this warm winter dessert. Fresh or frozen cranberries may be used; frozen berries need not be thawed before cooking. Bosc, d'Anjou, and comice pears are good choices for this cobbler.

Pastry
1¾ cups all-purpose flour
½ teaspoon salt
5 tablespoons chilled butter
⅓ cup chilled vegetable shortening
¼ cup ice water

Cranberry-Pear Filling
4 medium pears
3½ cups fresh *or* frozen
cranberries (12 ounces)
1½ cups sugar
¼ cup all-purpose flour
¼ teaspoon ground allspice
⅛ teaspoon ground cardamom
(optional)
1 tablespoon butter
3 cups vanilla ice cream
(optional)

PREPARATION: *For the pastry*, put the flour and salt in the workbowl of a food processor fitted with the metal blade, or in a medium bowl. Cut the butter into ½-inch pieces and add them and the shortening to the dry ingredients. Pulse or work quickly with your fingertips until the mixture resembles coarse meal. Sprinkle with ice water and pulse or toss with a fork until dough holds together when pinched. Flatten dough into a disk, wrap in plastic, and refrigerate 20 minutes. (Can refrigerate overnight.)

For the filling, peel, core, and slice the pears lengthwise, ¼ inch thick. Put pears and cranberries into a medium bowl. Sprinkle the sugar, flour, allspice, and cardamom over the fruit and mix thoroughly. Spread cranberry-pear mixture in a 7- by 11-inch baking dish or a 4- to 5-cup gratin dish. Dot with butter.

On a lightly floured work surface, roll out pastry about ⅛ inch thick and 1 inch larger than the outside rim of the baking dish. Ease dough over fruit mixture, trim, and press against the sides of the dish to form a crimped border. Cut three 2-inch slits in the pastry.

COOKING: Adjust oven rack to middle position and heat oven to 400°F. Bake cobbler until pastry is lightly browned and fruit is bubbling, 35 to 45 minutes. Cool 15 to 20 minutes. (Can cover and set aside at room temperature overnight.)

SERVING: Serve cobbler warm (can heat cobbler in a 300°F oven until warm, about 15 minutes) or at room temperature, with ice cream, if desired.

Marlene Sorosky
Cookbook author
Towson, MD

FRUIT FOOL

Makes 4 servings

Gooseberry is probably the best known, but you can make a fool with almost any fruit. Papaya is quick because you don't need to cook it first as you must gooseberries. The lime juice and zest balance the papaya's sweetness.

2 ripe papayas
2 limes
$^1/_4$ cup sugar
1 cup heavy cream

PREPARATION: Skin and seed the papayas and cut into 1-inch chunks. Remove zest from 1 lime and cut it crosswise into thin julienne strips. Squeeze $^1/_4$ cup lime juice. In a food processor, combine the papayas, sugar, and lime juice and process until smooth.

Recipe can be made to this point several hours ahead.

SERVING: Beat heavy cream to soft peaks and fold it into the papaya puree, leaving swirls of orange and white. Serve the fool garnished with julienned lime zest.

Stephanie Lyness
Free-lance writer
New York, NY

MACERATED GRAPEFRUIT, CRANBERRIES, AND KIWI WITH GINGER

Makes 8 servings

This colorful mixture can be made with almost any fruits that are in season. The ginger adds an unexpected spark of flavor to the dish.

12 ounces cranberries
1 cup sugar
2 large grapefruits
3 medium kiwi fruits
$^1/_2$ cup orange liqueur
1 piece ginger (about 1 inch long)

PREPARATION: Bring the cranberries, sugar, and 1 cup water to a boil in a small saucepan. Simmer until cranberries pop, about 3 to 5 minutes; cool and transfer to a large serving bowl. Peel and section the grapefruits into the serving bowl. Peel and slice the kiwi into $^1/_4$-inch rounds and add them to the bowl. Pour in the liqueur and toss gently to mix. Cover with plastic wrap and refrigerate for at least 1 hour. (Can refrigerate overnight.)

SERVING: Peel and grate 1 tablespoon ginger over the fruit and serve.

James Villas
Cookbook author and food editor
Town & Country
New York, NY

LEMON MERINGUES

Makes about 60 meringues

Shallow meringue wells filled with ambrosial lemon curd are an artful and clever play on the classic American pie.

Meringue Shells
Softened butter
3 large egg whites
1 cup sugar
1/2 teaspoon white vinegar
1/2 teaspoon vanilla

Lemon Curd
10 tablespoons unsalted butter
5 large egg yolks
1 cup sugar
2 tablespoons grated lemon zest
1/2 cup lemon juice
1 lime
Candied violets

PREPARATION AND COOKING: *For the meringue shells*, butter 2 large baking sheets. Adjust oven racks to middle and low positions and heat oven to 200°F. Beat egg whites to firm peaks, about 3 minutes. Add 1 tablespoon sugar and beat 3 minutes. Gradually add remaining sugar and beat until whites are stiff and shiny, about 10 minutes. Add vinegar and vanilla and beat 1 minute.

Fit a large pastry bag with a 1/4-inch star tip. Pipe egg whites onto baking sheets into 1 1/2-inch-diameter pinwheels. Pipe a border around outer edge of each pinwheel to form small cups. Bake until shells are lightly colored and firm, about 50 minutes. (Switch sheets after 25 minutes to ensure even cooking). Carefully loosen meringues with a spatula and cool completely. (Can cover and set aside at room temperature up to 2 days, or freeze up to 1 month.)

For the lemon curd, cut the butter into tablespoon-size pieces; set aside. In a medium saucepan, bring 2 inches water to a simmer. Whisk yolks and sugar in a heatproof bowl until blended. Stir in lemon zest and juice. Put bowl over saucepan and stir constantly until lemon mixture expands, thickens, and lightens, about 10 minutes. Remove from heat and stir in butter. Put plastic wrap directly on surface of curd and refrigerate until chilled. (Can refrigerate up to 2 days.)

Using a pastry bag fitted with a 1/2-inch star tip, fill each meringue shell with curd. (Can freeze up to 1 month, but do not refrigerate or shells will become soggy.)

SERVING: (Remove meringues from freezer 10 minutes before serving.) Cut lime zest into tiny "leaf" shapes. Break violets into small pieces. Garnish meringues with 1 violet and 2 leaves. Top with confectioners' sugar.

Marlene Sorosky
Cookbook author
Towson, MD

LEMON POTS DE CREME

Makes 6 servings

These lush and creamy baked custards are charmingly enclosed in individual dishes or *pots* from which they take their name.

2 medium lemons
²/₃ cup sugar
1 egg
4 egg yolks
1¹/₄ cups heavy cream
5 teaspoons confectioners' sugar
6 candied violets (optional)

PREPARATION AND COOKING: Heat oven to 325°F. Grate 1 teaspoon lemon zest. Squeeze ¹/₂ cup lemon juice. Whisk in sugar, egg, and yolks, then whisk in cream until sugar dissolves. Pass mixture through a strainer; stir in zest.

Put six ¹/₂-cup *pots de crème* or soufflé dishes in a deep baking dish. Divide the lemon mixture evenly between the *pots*. Put dish in the oven and fill it with hot tap water to come within ¹/₂ inch of the top of the *pots*. Bake, uncovered, until custards are just set in the centers, 35 to 40 minutes. Carefully remove *pots* from water and set aside to cool completely.

SERVING: Dust surface of custard with confectioners' sugar and garnish with a candied violet.

Marlene Sorosky
Cookbook author
Towson, MD

LEMON TART BRULEE

Makes 6 to 8 servings

Crème Brûlée is the inspiration for this tart, which wraps delicate pastry around luscious lemon filling. The top is adorned with a crackling sugar glaze.

¹/₄ cup dark brown sugar

Pastry
¹/₄ pound frozen unsalted butter
1 cup unbleached all-purpose flour
¹/₂ teaspoon salt
¹/₄ to ¹/₃ cup ice water

Filling
2 medium lemons
1 small lime
³/₄ cup sugar
5 large eggs
¹/₄ pound unsalted butter

PREPARATION: Spread brown sugar in a thin layer in a cake pan. Dry near oven pilot light until sugar is dehydrated, about 24 hours. Or, set sugar aside, at room temperature for 48 hours, raking it frequently with fingers. Sift the dried brown sugar to remove any lumps. (Can store in an air-tight container up to 1 week.)

For the pastry, cut butter into 8 pieces and add to the workbowl of a food processor fitted with the metal blade, along with the flour and salt. Process until mixture resembles coarse meal. Add ¹/₄ cup ice water and process until dough starts to form a ball. If dough is dry, pulse in remaining water. If making dough by hand, combine flour and salt in a medium bowl. Cut chilled (not frozen) butter into dry ingredients with a pastry blender or work quickly with fingertips until mixture resembles coarse meal. Add ¹/₄ cup cold water, tossing with a fork. If needed, add remaining water until dough just holds together. Press dough into a disk. Wrap in plastic and chill for at least 20 minutes. (Can refrigerate overnight.)

On a lightly floured work surface, roll dough to a 13-inch circle. Transfer to a 9-inch tart pan with a removable bottom. Ease dough into pan, trimming off excess. Freeze dough 10 minutes. (Can wrap and freeze up to 10 days.)

Adjust oven rack to low position and heat oven to 375° F. Line dough with aluminum foil and fill with beans, rice, or pie weights. Bake until firm, about 35 minutes. Cool 5 minutes, remove foil and weights, and return crust to oven until crisp and golden, 5 to 7 minutes longer. Cool in pan on wire rack.

For the filling, remove zest from one of the lemons and the lime and put zest into the workbowl of a food processor

LEMON TART BRULEE

(continued)

fitted with the metal blade. Add sugar and process until zest is finely chopped. Squeeze $1/2$ cup juice from the lemons and add to the workbowl, along with the eggs. Process just until mixed. Melt butter in a 2-quart nonaluminum saucepan over very low heat. Add lemon mixture and cook over low heat, stirring constantly, until curd thickens to a pudding-like consistency, about 6 minutes. Strain into a medium bowl, cover with plastic wrap directly touching top of curd, and cool to room temperature. Spread curd evenly into cooked pastry crust and freeze until set, about 30 minutes. (Can cover and keep frozen up to 3 days.)

COOKING: Adjust oven rack to high position and heat broiler. Sprinkle 3 tablespoons of brown sugar on tart in a thin, even layer. Cover edge of tart crust with narrow strips of aluminum foil. Put tart under broiler, turning it constantly until sugar caramelizes evenly. Let tart stand at room temperature for 30 minutes before serving. (Can refrigerate up to 2 hours before serving, but sugar glaze may not be crisp.)

Jane Freiman
Food columnist and cookbook author
New York, NY

LEMON-ALMOND TART

Makes 8 servings

Lemons and almonds combine beautifully in this tart, which is redolent of the sunny Mediterranean. Almond paste, or marzipan, stabilizes the pastry crust, making it unnecessary to chill before baking or to bake blind (pre-bake with pie weights).

Almond Pastry
1 cup all-purpose flour
Salt
2 tablespoons sugar
2 ounces almond paste (¹/₄ cup)
6 tablespoons chilled butter
1 egg yolk

Lemon Filling
2 medium lemons
4 tablespoons butter
2 eggs
¹/₄ cup sour cream
³/₄ cup sugar

2 tablespoons confectioners' sugar

PREPARATION AND COOKING: *For the pastry*, adjust the oven rack to low position and heat the oven to 350°F. Put the flour, ¹/₂ teaspoon salt, the sugar, and the almond paste in the workbowl of a food processor fitted with a metal blade, or into a medium bowl. Pulse the mixture, or work it with your fingertips, until it resembles coarse meal. Cut the butter in with your fingertips, until the mixture again resembles coarse meal. Add the egg yolk and pulse, or toss with a fork, until dough holds together when pinched.

Press the dough evenly over the bottom and up the side of a 9-inch tart pan with a removable bottom. (Can wrap the crust in the pan and freeze up to 2 days; defrost the crust before baking). Transfer the tart pan to a baking sheet and bake until the crust is golden brown, about 20 minutes,

For the filling, grate 2 teaspoons lemon zest and squeeze ¹/₃ cup of lemon juice into a medium bowl. Melt the butter and whisk it into the bowl with the eggs, the sour cream, and the sugar. Pour the filling into the pre-baked crust and return the pan to the oven, baking until set, 12 to 15 minutes. Transfer the tart, in the pan, to a wire rack and cool to room temperature. (Can cover and refrigerate overnight.)

SERVING: Dust tart lightly with confectioners' sugar and serve at room temperature.

Marlene Sorosky
Cookbook author
Towson, MD

LEMON-PINEAPPLE TRIFLE

Makes 8 servings

In this irresistible dessert, part of the lemon custard is mixed with crushed pineapple, lightened with whipped cream, and layered with lemon-flecked ladyfingers.

Lemon Custard
2 medium lemons
1 teaspoon cornstarch
$^1/_4$ pound butter
$1^1/_4$ cups sugar
5 eggs

Lemon Ladyfingers
3 eggs
9 tablespoons sugar
1 medium lemon
$^2/_3$ cup all purpose flour
$^1/_4$ cup confectioners' sugar

1 can crushed pineapple (8 ounces)
$1^1/_2$ cups heavy cream
3 tablespoons vodka
Candied Lemon Zest (recipe page 286)

PREPARATION AND COOKING: *For the custard*, grate 1 tablespoon lemon zest and squeeze $^1/_2$ cup lemon juice into a saucepan. Stir in cornstarch. Add butter and sugar, and heat until butter melts. Off heat, whisk in eggs. Return mixture to heat and whisk until it thickens. Transfer to a bowl and put plastic wrap directly on surface. When cool, refrigerate until chilled, at least 2 hours.

For the ladyfingers, adjust oven racks to middle and high positions and heat oven to 350°F. Line 2 baking sheets with parchment or wax paper. Separate eggs. Gradually beat 6 tablespoons of sugar into yolks and beat until light and fluffy, about 2 minutes. Grate 2 teaspoons zest and squeeze 3 tablespoons juice into mixture and stir well. Whip egg whites to soft peaks. Gradually add remaining sugar and whip whites to fine peaks. Sift half the flour over mixture, add half the whites, and fold mixtures together. Fold in remaining flour and egg whites. Fit a pastry bag with a $^1/_2$-inch round tip. Pipe 3- by 1-inch ladyfingers about 1 inch apart on baking sheets. Dust ladyfingers with confectioners' sugar and bake until golden, 12 to 14 minutes. (Switch sheets after 7 minutes to ensure even browning.) Cool on baking sheets for 5 minutes, then transfer to a rack to cool completely.

ASSEMBLY: Drain pineapple and reserve $^1/_3$ cup juice. Divide custard between 2 bowls. Fold pineapple into 1 batch. Reserve $^1/_3$ cup cream and whip remainder to firm peaks. Fold whipped cream into pineapple mixture. Stir vodka into the reserved juice and brush ladyfingers with the mixture.

Line bottom and sides of a 2-quart serving bowl with

(continued)

ladyfingers. Spread half of the plain lemon custard over the ladyfingers. Top with half the pineapple-lemon cream. Cover with a layer of ladyfingers. Layer half of the remaining custard over ladyfingers. Cover with remaining pineapple-lemon cream. Spread top with remaining custard, making a smooth surface. (Can cover and refrigerate overnight).

SERVING: Whip reserved cream to firm peaks. Transfer to a pastry bag fitted with a $1/4$-inch star tip. Pipe 8 rosettes around the perimeter of the trifle. Top each rosette with Candied Lemon Zest.

Marlene Sorosky
Cookbook author
Towson, MD

ORANGE-FILLED TARTLETS

Makes 3 dozen tartlets

A refreshing change from the perennial lemon curd, this orange curd is especially good when made with the juice of blood oranges.

Candied Orange Zest
1 medium orange
1^1/$_2$ cups sugar
^{1}/$_3$ cup light corn syrup

Pastry Dough
1^1/$_2$ cups all-purpose flour
^{1}/$_4$ teaspoon salt
14 tablespoons chilled unsalted butter
4 tablespoons ice water

Orange Curd
8 egg yolks
2 large oranges
1 medium lemon
^{1}/$_4$ pound butter
^{1}/$_2$ cup sugar
Candied violets (optional)

PREPARATION: *For the candied orange zest*, remove zest from orange with a vegetable peeler or a small, sharp knife and slice into ^{1}/$_4$-inch strips. Put zest in a small saucepan with water to cover and boil for 5 minutes to remove bitter taste. Drain and rinse under cold water.

Bring 1 cup of the sugar, the corn syrup, and ^{1}/$_3$ cup water to a boil in the saucepan. Remove from heat, stir in zest, and let stand 30 minutes. Bring liquid back to a boil; let stand 30 minutes. Remove orange strips with a fork and transfer to a wire rack set over a pan to catch drippings; cool.

Put remaining sugar on a plate and roll cooled orange strips in sugar. (Can store in an airtight container at room temperature up to 1 week.)

For the dough, put flour and salt in the workbowl of a food processor fitted with the metal blade, or in a medium bowl. Cut 10 tablespoons of the butter into ^{1}/$_2$-inch pieces and add to the bowl. Pulse or work mixture quickly with fingertips until it resembles coarse meal. Sprinkle ice water over mixture and pulse or toss with a fork until dough holds together when pinched. Flatten dough into 2 disks, wrap in plastic, and refrigerate at least 20 minutes. (Can refrigerate overnight.)

Coat 36 tartlet tins (1^1/$_2$ inches in diameter) with remaining butter. On a lightly floured work surface, roll dough disks to 12-inch squares, about ^{1}/$_8$-inch thick. Transfer to 2 large, lightly floured baking sheets and refrigerate until firm, about 20 minutes. Cut out 36 rounds of dough with a 2-inch cookie cutter. Press into tartlet tins, and pierce 2 or 3 times with a fork. Put tins on a jelly-roll pan and freeze 10 minutes.

COOKING: Adjust oven rack to middle position and heat

(continued)

oven to 350°F. Bake tartlet shells until dry and lightly browned, about 20 minutes; cool in tins. Carefully invert tins to remove tartlet shells. (Can store shells in an airtight container at room temperature up to 2 days, or freeze up to 1 month.)

For the curd, lightly whisk the egg yolks in a heatproof, nonreactive bowl; set aside. Grate $1/4$ cup zest from the oranges into a nonreactive saucepan. Squeeze and strain in $1/4$ cup orange juice and $1/4$ cup lemon juice. Cut the butter into $1/2$-inch pieces and add it to the juice along with the sugar. Bring to a boil, stirring occasionally. Carefully whisk $1/3$ of the boiling liquid into the yolks. Return the yolk mixture to the saucepan and stir constantly over low heat until the curd begins to simmer and thicken, about 3 minutes. Transfer curd to a nonreactive bowl and put a sheet of plastic wrap directly on the surface to prevent a skin from forming. Cool. (Can cover and refrigerate up to 2 days.)

SERVING: Put shells on a serving platter. Use a pastry bag fitted with a $1/4$- to $1/8$-inch tip to pipe a mound of curd into each shell. Garnish with candied orange peel and violets (optional).

Nicholas Malgieri
Pastry chef and cookbook author
New York, NY

PASTRY CREAM

Makes 1³/₄ cups

Pastry cream is the basis for hundreds of desserts. In addition to its versatility, pastry cream is easy to make and can be prepared well ahead of time.

4 egg yolks
6 tablespoons sugar
Pinch of salt
4¹/₂ tablespoons flour
1¹/₂ cups milk
**¹/₂ vanilla bean *or* 1¹/₂ teaspoons
    vanilla extract**
1 tablespoon butter

PREPARATION: In a bowl, beat the egg yolks with the sugar and salt until the mixture is a very pale yellow and a ribbon forms when yolks are trailed from the beater. Beat in flour and ¹/₂ cup milk.

Put the remaining 1 cup milk into a nonreactive saucepan. If using a vanilla bean, slit it in half lengthwise and scrape the seeds into the saucepan with the point of a knife. Add the pod as well. Bring to a simmer over medium heat. Remove the vanilla pod.

Slowly whisk the milk into the yolks to temper them. Pour the egg and milk mixture back into the saucepan and cook over medium heat, stirring constantly, until mixture is thick and large bubbles break the surface, about 3 minutes. Continue cooking 1 more minute.

Remove from heat and whisk in butter and vanilla extract, if using. Pour into a bowl and press plastic wrap directly onto the surface of the cream to prevent a skin from forming. Cool and refrigerate until ready to use.

Pastry Cream can be made a few days ahead.

Susan Spicer
Chef
The Bistro at Hotel Maison de Ville
New Orleans, LA

PEAR CREAM TART

Makes one 9-inch tart

This luscious pear tart is quick and easy, especially if the crust and pastry cream are made ahead.

$1/2$ **cup apricot preserves**
Pastry Cream (recipe left)
Pie pastry for single crust (use your favorite recipe)
4 firm, ripe pears, such as Bosc (about 1 pound total)

PREPARATION: Heat the apricot preserves in a small saucepan over low heat until dissolved. Strain. This glaze can be made weeks in advance and reheated.

Make Pastry Cream and chill. Make the pie pastry dough and chill. Recipe can be made to this point a few days ahead.

Roll out chilled dough to measure slightly larger than a 9-inch tart pan. Gently press the dough on the bottom of the pan toward the middle. Press down the dough around the sides so that just a fraction of an inch extends. Roll the rolling pin across the top to cut off excess dough. Chill at least 20 minutes or even overnight. Heat oven to 375°F. Press a double thickness of aluminum foil into the pan and up against the sides. Bake in preheated oven 10 minutes and then lower temperature to 350°F. Bake 10 minutes more and remove foil. Return to oven until dough is dry and lightly browned, about 10 additional minutes. Remove from oven and cool. Fill cooled pie shell with Pastry Cream.

Peel, halve, and core the pears. Cut crosswise into thin slices, keeping each sliced pear half intact. Press gently to flatten the slices of each pear half like a stack of dominoes. Use a knife or metal spatula to lift pears and arrange on top of the cream in a star design. Bake tart in preheated oven until pears are tender, about 30 minutes. Remove from oven and cool. Reheat the glaze. Brush pears with glaze.

Recipe can be made to this point several hours ahead.

SERVING: Serve at room temperature.

Susan Spicer
Chef
The Bistro at Hotel Maison de Ville
New Orleans, LA

SKILLET PEAR DESSERT WITH BRANDY

Makes 8 servings

Some last-minute desserts are worth the fuss. This is one of them. The lavish result, full of deep winter flavors, ends the meal with panache. Red Bartlett pears add special visual appeal, although any ripe but still somewhat firm pear such as Bosc or Anjou will do as well.

24 fresh *or* canned chestnuts
6 pears
6 tablespoon butter
$^{1}/_{4}$ cup sugar
$^{3}/_{4}$ cup Armagnac *or* cognac
$^{3}/_{4}$ cup heavy cream

PREPARATION: If using fresh chestnuts, heat oven to 400°F. With a small, sharp knife, cut a slit in each chestnut. Spread in a shallow baking pan and roast for 15 to 20 minutes. While still warm, peel off outer and inner skins. If the chestnuts cool and become difficult to peel, simply reheat them briefly.

Recipe can be made to this point several days ahead.

COOKING AND SERVING: Peel the pears if the skins are tough or spotty; otherwise, leave them unpeeled. Halve, core, and cut each half, lengthwise, into 3 pieces.

In a large frying pan, melt the butter over medium heat until foaming. Add the pears and sauté until lightly colored, about 5 minutes. Turn the pears and lower the heat. Gently stir in the chestnuts, sugar, and Armagnac and simmer, basting pears once or twice with pan juices, until tender, about 5 minutes.

With a slotted spoon, transfer pears and chestnuts to serving plates. Add the heavy cream to the pan and bring to a boil. Cook over high heat until the cream is slightly reduced, about 3 minutes. Pour Armagnac and cream sauce over pears and serve.

Michael McLaughlin
Free-lance writer
Brooklyn, NY

OLD-FASHIONED STRAWBERRY COBBLER

Makes 4 servings

This quick cobbler is delicious with a dollop of whipped cream.

1 quart fresh strawberries
$^1/_4$ pound butter
1 cup milk
1 cup flour
1$^1/_2$ teaspoons baking powder
$^1/_2$ teaspoon salt
1 cup sugar
$^1/_4$ teaspoon ground cinnamon
Whipped cream (optional)

PREPARATION: Hull the strawberries.

COOKING: Heat oven to 400°F. Melt butter in an 8- by 12-inch baking dish in preheated oven, about 4 minutes. Remove dish from oven. Add milk, flour, baking powder, salt, sugar, and cinnamon to the baking dish and stir until just mixed. Arrange strawberries, tips pointed up, on top of the batter. Bake cobbler in oven until golden brown, about 25 minutes.

SERVING: Serve cobbler warm or at room temperature, topped with a dollop of whipped cream, if you like.

Anne Byrn
Food editor
The Atlanta Journal and *The Atlanta Constitution*

BRANDY ALEXANDER CREAM PIE

Makes one 9-inch pie

With whipped cream folded into the custard, this is a light, airy pie with a punch of brandy flavor.

Graham Cracker Crust
5¹/₂ tablespoons butter
4 ounces graham crackers (1 cup crumbs)
3 tablespoons sugar

Brandy Custard
1¹/₂ cups milk
¹/₂ cup sugar
¹/₄ teaspoon salt
3 egg yolks
¹/₂ cup half-and-half
6 tablespoons cornstarch
¹/₂ cup brandy *or* Cognac
¹/₂ cup crème de cacao
1 tablespoon butter

1 cup heavy cream
1 tablespoon sugar

1 ounce semisweet chocolate

PREPARATION: *For the crust*, melt the butter in a small saucepan. Break the graham crackers into the workbowl of a food processor fitted with the metal blade and process to crumbs, about 20 seconds. Add the sugar and process 5 seconds. With the machine running, add the melted butter. Transfer the crumbs to a 9-inch pie pan. Using your fingers, press the crumbs firmly into the bottom of the pan and up the side. Form a smooth top edge by pressing crumbs between your fingers and thumb. Freeze the crust for 10 minutes.

COOKING: Adjust oven rack to low position and heat oven to 350°F. Bake the crust until lightly browned and set, about 7 minutes. Cool completely on a wire rack.

For the custard, bring the milk, sugar, and salt to a simmer in a medium saucepan. Bring 2 inches water to a simmer in a separate saucepan. Whisk egg yolks with half-and-half and cornstarch in a heatproof bowl. Slowly whisk the warm milk mixture into the egg yolks. Put bowl over simmering water and whisk constantly until custard begins to thicken, 5 to 7 minutes. Bring brandy and crème de cacao to a simmer and whisk mixture into the custard. Cook until custard thickens to a pudding-like consistency, about 5 minutes longer. Remove bowl from heat, stir in butter, and strain custard through a fine sieve into a bowl. Put a sheet of plastic wrap directly on the surface of the custard and cool to room temperature.

ASSEMBLY: Whip the cream with the sugar to firm peaks. Lightly stir one-third of the cream into the cooled custard. Fold in the remaining cream, pour the custard into the pie crust, and smooth the top. Refrigerate 2 to 3 hours.

SERVING: Draw a small knife across the chocolate to make shavings. Sprinkle shavings over the top of the pie and serve immediately.

Betsy Schultz
Food consultant
New York, NY

CLASSIC BANANA CREAM PIE

Makes one 9-inch pie

Ripe bananas are set off by a smooth vanilla custard, sweetened whipped cream, and a flaky crust in this favorite cream pie recipe.

Pastry Crust
1 cup all-purpose flour
2 tablespoons sugar
$^1/_2$ teaspoon salt
4 tablespoons chilled butter
**2 tablespoons vegetable
   shortening**
1 egg yolk
2 tablespoons ice water

Vanilla Custard
2 cups milk
$^1/_3$ cup sugar
$^1/_4$ teaspoon salt
3 egg yolks
1 cup half-and-half
6 tablespoons cornstarch
1 tablespoon butter
1 teaspoon vanilla extract

1 cup heavy cream
1 tablespoon sugar

2 medium bananas

PREPARATION: *For the crust*, put the flour, sugar and salt in the workbowl of a food processor fitted with the metal blade and process 5 seconds. Cut butter into 1-inch pieces and add to the processor along with the vegetable shortening. Process until mixture resembles coarse meal, about 5 seconds. Add the egg yolk and ice water and pulse 3 to 4 times until dough begins to hold together. Press dough into a disk, wrap in plastic, and refrigerate at least 1 hour (or overnight). Roll out dough to a 13-inch circle on a lightly floured surface. Transfer to a 9-inch pie pan and trim away excess pastry. Use the tip of a metal spoon to decorate the edge of the rim with half-moon indentations. Freeze 10 minutes.

COOKING: Adjust oven rack to low position and heat oven to 425°F. Line the crust with buttered aluminum foil, shiny side down, and fill with dried beans or pie weights. Bake for 10 minutes. Lower oven temperature to 350°F. Remove foil and beans and return crust to oven until golden-brown, about 10 minutes. Cool completely on a wire rack.

For the custard, bring the milk, sugar, and salt to a simmer in a medium saucepan, stirring frequently, until sugar dissolves. Bring 2 inches water to a simmer in a separate saucepan. Whisk the egg yolks with the half-and-half and cornstarch in a heatproof bowl. Slowly whisk the milk mixture into the egg yolks, set the bowl over the simmering water, and whisk constantly until mixture thickens to a pudding-like consistency, 7 to 10 minutes. Remove custard from heat, whisk in butter and vanilla, and strain though a fine sieve into a bowl. Put plastic wrap

CLASSIC BANANA CREAM PIE

(continued)

directly on the surface of the custard and cool to room temperature.

ASSEMBLY: Whip the cream with the sugar to firm peaks. Spread one-third of the custard over the crust. Slice and distribute 1 of the bananas evenly over the custard; top with half of the remaining custard. Cut off and reserve one quarter of the second banana for garnish. Slice and evenly distribute the remaining banana over the custard; top with the remaining custard and whipped cream. Refrigerate for 2 to 3 hours.

SERVING: Cut three slices from the reserved banana quarter. Arrange slices in the center of the pie and serve immediately.

Betsy Schultz
Food consultant
New York, NY

DEEP-DISH PUMPKIN
ICE CREAM PIE WITH BUTTERSCOTCH SAUCE

Makes one 9-inch pie

Spicy pumpkin puree is combined with vanilla ice cream to make a wonderful frozen filling. Wrapped in graham cracker crust, the pie is served in a luscious pool of warm butterscotch sauce.

Graham Cracker Crust

4 tablespoons chilled butter
8 ounces graham crackers (2 cups crumbs)
3 tablespoons sugar
1/2 teaspoon ground cinnamon

Pumpkin Filling

2 1/4 cups canned pumpkin puree
3/4 cup brown sugar
1/4 teaspoon ground cinnamon
1 1/4 teaspoon ground ginger
1 1/4 teaspoon grated nutmeg
1/2 teaspoon cloves
1 1/2 quarts vanilla ice cream
1 cup Butterscotch Sauce (recipe page 280)

PREPARATION: *For the crust*, melt the butter in a small saucepan. Break the graham crackers into the workbowl of a food processor fitted with the metal blade and process to crumbs. Add the sugar, cinnamon, and butter and process 10 seconds. Transfer crumbs to a 9-inch springform pan. Using your fingers, press the crumbs firmly into the bottom of the pan and up the side, to within 1 inch of the top. Freeze crust 10 minutes.

COOKING: Adjust oven rack to low position. Heat oven to 350°F. Bake until crust is set, about 7 minutes; cool on a wire rack.

For the filling, cook the pumpkin puree with the brown sugar, cinnamon, ginger, nutmeg, and cloves in a heavy-bottomed saucepan over low heat, stirring occasionally, until sugar dissolves and puree thickens slightly, 5 minutes. Refrigerate until well-chilled. (Can refrigerate up to 3 days).

ASSEMBLY: Freeze the baked, cooled crust for 10 minutes. Soften 1 quart ice cream, but do not allow it to melt. Put the pumpkin mixture and the softened ice cream in the workbowl of a food processor fitted with the metal blade and process 1 minute. Spread the pumpkin mixture evenly in the frozen pie crust. Put pie in freezer until firm, at least 2 hours. (Can freeze up to 3 days.) Soften the remaining ice cream, put it in the food processor, and process until smooth. Spread ice cream over the pumpkin mixture and return pie to freezer for 2 hours. (Can wrap and freeze up to 3 weeks.) Make the Butterscotch Sauce.

SERVING: Slice and serve on a circle of warm Butterscotch Sauce.

Betsy Schultz
Food consultant
New York, NY

LEMON CREAM PIE

Makes one 9-inch pie

This tangy filling is made by lightening a classic lemon curd with whipped cream. The pastry crust is finished with an easy, but impressive rope border of twisted pastry, and the garnish of candied lemon zest adds an elegant touch.

Candied Lemon Zest
1 lemon
$1/3$ cup plus $1/4$ cup sugar
1 tablespoon light corn syrup

Pastry Crust
1 cup all-purpose flour
2 tablespoons sugar
$1/2$ teaspoon salt
4 tablespoons chilled butter
2 tablespoons vegetable shortening
1 egg
2 tablespoons ice water

Lemon Curd
3 eggs
3 egg yolks
6 ounces unsalted butter
$1^1/4$ cups sugar
3 large lemons

$1^1/2$ cups heavy cream
1 tablespoon sugar

PREPARATION: *For the candied zest,* strip off the lemon zest with a vegetable peeler or a small knife and slice into $1/8$-inch wide strips. Put zest in a small nonreactive saucepan with water to cover. Bring water to a boil and drain. Repeat process 4 more times.

Bring $1/3$ cup sugar, corn syrup, and 1 tablespoon water to a boil in the saucepan; boil until sugar dissolves. Add the zest and boil 5 minutes. With a fork, remove strips of zest from syrup and put them on a rack set over a pan to catch drippings. Cool 3 hours. Spread remaining $1/4$ cup sugar on a plate and roll cooled strips individually in sugar. (Can store strips, tightly covered, up to 1 week at room temperature.)

For the crust, put the flour, sugar, and salt in the workbowl of a food processor fitted with the metal blade and process 5 seconds. Cut butter into 1-inch pieces and add to the processor along with the vegetable shortening. Process until mixture resembles coarse meal, about 5 seconds. Separate the egg. Beat the egg white lightly with a fork; set aside. Add egg yolk and ice water to processor and pulse 3 to 4 times, just until the dough holds together. Form dough into a disk, wrap in plastic wrap, and refrigerate at least 1 hour.

Roll dough to a 13-inch circle on a lightly floured surface. Transfer dough to a 9-inch pie pan and trim away excess pastry. With the palms of your hands, roll extra pastry into two $1/4$-inch thick ropes, each 32 inches long. Twist the two ropes together to form a cord. Brush the rim of the crust with the egg white and put the cord around the rim, pressing the two ends together to form a circle. Brush the cord with egg white and freeze crust for 10 minutes.

(continued)

COOKING: Adjust oven rack to low position and heat oven to 425°F. Line the crust with buttered aluminum foil and fill with dried beans or pie weights. Bake for 10 minutes. Lower oven temperature to 350°F. Remove foil and beans and return crust to oven until golden brown, about 10 minutes longer. Cool completely on a wire rack.

For the lemon curd, bring 2 inches water to a simmer in a medium saucepan. Whisk the whole eggs and egg yolks in a medium heatproof bowl. Cut the butter into 1-inch pieces and add to the eggs, along with the sugar. Grate in the zest from the lemons ($1^1/_2$ tablespoons), and squeeze in 7 tablespoons lemon juice. Set the bowl over the simmering water and whisk until curd thickens, about 20 minutes. Put a sheet of plastic wrap directly on the surface of the curd. Refrigerate until chilled. (Can refrigerate up to 48 hours.)

ASSEMBLY: Whip cream and sugar to firm peaks. Stir one-third of the whipped cream into the lemon curd. Fold in the remaining cream and pour the mixture into the cooled pastry crust. Refrigerate 2 to 3 hours.

SERVING: Sprinkle candied lemon zest over the pie and serve immediately.

Betsy Schultz
Food consultant
New York, NY

MAPLE-PECAN AND PRALINE CREAM PIE

Makes one 9-inch pie

Lightly toasted pecans give this crust an extra-good, nutty flavor that sets off the maple-meringue filling. The crunchy maple-praline topping can be made well in advance and stored in an airtight container.

³/₄ cup pecans (2¹/₂ ounces)

Pecan Pastry Crust
1 cup all-purpose flour
**2 tablespoons firmly packed
    light brown sugar**
¹/₂ teaspoon salt
4 tablespoons chilled butter
**1 tablespoon vegetable
    shortening**
1 egg yolk
2 tablespoons ice water

Maple Custard
³/₄ cup maple syrup
2 cups milk
¹/₄ teaspoon salt
3 eggs
1 cup half-and-half
6 tablespoons cornstarch
¹/₄ cup sugar

Praline Topping
1 tablespoon vegetable oil
¹/₄ cup maple syrup
¹/₂ teaspoon light corn syrup
1 tablespoon sugar

PREPARATION AND COOKING: *For the crust*, adjust oven rack to high position and heat oven to 350°F. Spread pecans on a pie pan and toast until fragrant, about 5 minutes; cool. Set aside ¹/₄ cup for the topping.

Process the remaining toasted pecans in a food processor fitted with the metal blade until finely ground, about 20 seconds. Add the flour, brown sugar, and salt and process 10 seconds. Cut the butter into 1-inch pieces and add them to the processor along with the vegetable shortening. Process until mixture resembles coarse meal, about 10 seconds. Add egg yolk and ice water and pulse 3 to 4 times until dough just holds together. Wrap dough in plastic and refrigerate at least 1 hour. (Can cover and refrigerate dough overnight.)

Roll dough to a 13-inch circle on a lightly floured surface. Transfer dough to a 9-inch pie pan, flute the edge, and freeze for 10 minutes.

Adjust oven rack to low position and heat oven to 425°F. Line the crust with buttered aluminum foil, shiny side down, and fill with dried beans or pie weights. Bake for 10 minutes. Lower oven to 350°F. Remove foil and beans and return crust to oven until pastry is dry and edges are lightly browned, about 10 minutes longer. Cool crust completely on a wire rack.

For the custard, in a large, heavy-bottomed saucepan, simmer the maple syrup over low heat until it registers 225°F on a candy thermometer and reduces to ¹/₃ cup, about 10 minutes. Remove saucepan from heat and slowly whisk in milk and salt. Return saucepan to low heat until mixture is warm but not simmering; set aside.

Bring 2 inches of water to a simmer in a separate

(continued)

saucepan. Separate the eggs, putting the yolks into a heatproof bowl; reserve the whites. Whisk the egg yolks with the half-and-half and cornstarch, then whisk in the warm milk mixture. Set the bowl over the simmering water and cook, stirring constantly, until mixture thickens to a pudding-like consistency, about 7 to 10 minutes. Strain the custard through a fine sieve into a bowl. Put plastic wrap directly on the surface of the custard to prevent a skin from forming; cool to tepid.

Whip the egg whites to soft peaks, then add the sugar by tablespoons until meringue is firm and glossy. Lightly stir one third of the meringue into the warm custard. Fold in the remaining meringue and immediately pour the mixture into the prepared pastry crust. Refrigerate for 2 to 3 hours.

For the topping, lightly oil a metal pie pan or baking sheet. Put the maple and corn syrups and sugar in a small, heavy-bottomed saucepan and cook over low heat until the syrup registers 300°F on a candy thermometer, about 5 to 7 minutes. Stir in the reserved pecans and immediately pour mixture onto the oiled pan. When cool, break the praline into pieces and chop it coarsely. (Can store topping in an airtight container up to 1 month.)

Betsy Schultz
Food consultant
New York, NY

TRIPLE CHOCOLATE CREAM PIE

Makes one 9-inch pie

This pie is filled with a bittersweet chocolate custard and topped with a layer of white chocolate cream.

Chocolate Pastry Crust
1 cup all-purpose flour
6 tablespoons unsweetened cocoa
2 tablespoons sugar
1/2 teaspoon salt
4 tablespoons chilled butter
2 tablespoons vegetable shortening
1 egg yolk
1 tablespoon white vinegar
2 tablespoons ice water

White Chocolate Topping
7 ounces white chocolate
1 1/2 cups heavy cream
3 tablespoons sugar
2 teaspoons white crème de cacao

Chocolate Custard
1 1/2 cups milk
3/4 cup sugar
1/4 teaspoon salt
3 1/2 ounces bittersweet chocolate
4 egg yolks
1 cup half-and-half
4 tablespoons cornstarch
2 tablespoons butter
1 teaspoon vanilla
2 tablespoons crème de cacao
1/2 lemon

1 ounce semisweet chocolate

PREPARATION: *For the crust*, put the flour, 2 tablespoons cocoa, sugar, and salt in the workbowl of a food processor fitted with the metal blade; process 5 seconds. Cut butter into 1-inch pieces and add to the processor along with the vegetable shortening. Process until mixture resembles coarse meal, about 5 seconds. Add egg yolk, vinegar, and ice water and pulse 3 to 4 times until dough forms a ball. Wrap in plastic and refrigerate 1 hour. (Can refrigerate dough overnight.)

Dust work surface with remaining cocoa and roll out dough to a 13-inch circle. Transfer to a 9-inch pie pan. Make a scalloped edge by pinching the dough rim between thumb and forefinger. Freeze crust 10 minutes.

COOKING: Adjust oven rack to low position and heat oven to 425°F. Line the dough with buttered aluminum foil, shiny side down, and fill with dried beans or pie weights. Bake for 10 minutes. Lower the oven temperature to 350°F. Remove foil and beans and return crust to oven until pastry is dry and edges are lightly browned, about 10 minutes longer. Cool completely on a wire rack.

For the topping, chop the white chocolate into pea-sized pieces and put into a bowl. Put the cream, sugar, and crème de cacao in a small, heavy-bottomed saucepan, and warm to 90°F, stirring to dissolve sugar (do not allow cream to simmer). Pour cream over chocolate and stir until chocolate has melted. Cover loosely and refrigerate until very cold. (Can refrigerate 2 days).

For the custard, heat milk, sugar, and salt in a saucepan, stirring frequently, until sugar dissolves. Chop and stir in chocolate. Bring 2 inches water to a simmer in a separate saucepan. Whisk egg yolks with half-and-half and cornstarch in a heatproof bowl. Slowly whisk the warm

(continued)

chocolate milk into the egg yolk mixture; set the bowl over the simmering water and cook, whisking constantly, until mixture thickens to a pudding-like consistency, 7 to 10 minutes. Remove custard from heat, whisk in butter, vanilla, and crème de cacao, and squeeze in 2 teaspoons lemon juice. Strain custard through a fine sieve into a bowl. Put plastic wrap directly on surface of custard to prevent a skin from forming; cool to room temperature.

ASSEMBLY: Spread the chocolate evenly in pastry crust. Whip the chilled white-chocolate cream to soft peaks (do not over-whip) and spread it over custard. Refrigerate at least 2, or up to 3, hours.

SERVING: Draw a small knife across the block of chocolate to make shavings. Sprinkle shavings over pie; serve immediately.

Betsy Schultz
Food consultant
New York, NY

GRANDMOTHER'S MILE-HIGH PIE

Makes 8 servings

The flaky crust, made from a combination of vegetable shortening and butter, has a rich, buttery taste. Use Granny Smith apples for this pie.

Pie Pastry

¼ pound chilled unsalted butter
2 cups all-purpose flour
½ teaspoon salt
¼ teaspoon sugar
3 tablespoons chilled vegetable shortening
5 tablespoons cold water

Pie Filling

5 large pie apples (about 2½ pounds)
1 lemon
1½ tablespoons all-purpose flour
1 cup sugar
1 tablespoon cinnamon
⅛ teaspoon grated nutmeg
½ teaspoon vanilla extract
⅛ teaspoon salt
1 egg
1½ tablespoons unsalted butter

PREPARATION: *For the pastry*, cut chilled butter into ¼-inch pieces. To make dough by hand, put flour, salt, and sugar in a medium bowl. Cut butter and shortening into dry ingredients with a pastry blender, or work quickly with fingertips until mixture resembles a coarse meal with some pea-sized pieces remaining. Add ¼ cup cold water, tossing with a fork. Add 1 more tablespoon water, if necessary, so dough just holds together. Or, put flour, salt, sugar, butter, and shortening into the workbowl of a food processor; pulse until mixture resembles a coarse meal. Add water and pulse until dough holds together. Divide the dough into two disks, one slightly larger than the other. Wrap in plastic and chill for at least 20 minutes. (Can wrap and refrigerate overnight, or freeze up to 1 month.)

For the filling, peel, core, and slice the apples over a large bowl. Grate the zest from the lemon into the bowl and squeeze in 1 tablespoon lemon juice. Sprinkle the apples with the flour, sugar, cinnamon, nutmeg, vanilla, and salt and toss to combine.

COOKING: Adjust oven rack to middle position and heat oven to 425°F. In a small bowl, beat egg lightly. On a lightly floured work surface, roll out larger disk of dough to an 11-inch round and ease it into a 9-inch pie pan. Pile apple filling into pie shell and dot with butter. Roll out remaining dough and put over the apples. Seal, trim, and flute the crust. Cut decorative slashes in top pastry and brush with beaten egg. Transfer pie to a foil-lined baking sheet; bake for 15 minutes. Reduce heat to 350°F and continue baking until pie crust is golden and apples are tender, about 50 minutes. (Can cool, cover, and refrigerate up to 3 days. Reheat for 20 minutes in a 300°F. oven.)

Bert Greene
Cookbook author
New York, NY

ESPRESSO GELATO

Makes 1¹/₂ quarts

Select the best-quality Espresso, French, or Viennese roast coffee beans, which should be used to make gelato as soon as possible after roasting. The flavor of the ice cream will be only as good as that of the coffee beans.

3 ounces espresso beans (about 1 cup)
2²/₃ cups half-and-half
³/₄ cup sugar
6 egg yolks
1¹/₃ cups heavy cream
¹/₈ teaspoon salt

PREPARATION: Spread the espresso beans on a baking sheet and crush with the bottom of a heavy pan.

COOKING: Put the half-and-half, sugar, and crushed espresso beans into a medium nonreactive saucepan. Bring liquid to a simmer, stirring to dissolve the sugar. Remove pan from heat, cover and let mixture steep for 30 minutes. Strain through a fine sieve and discard coffee beans. In a heatproof mixing bowl, whisk the egg yolks with the cream and salt. Slowly whisk the warm half-and-half into the egg yolk mixture and then return the partially cooked custard to the saucepan. Stir constantly over medium-low heat until mixture begins to thicken slightly and coats the back of a spoon, about 5 minutes. Strain through a fine sieve into a bowl. Put a sheet of plastic wrap directly on the surface of the custard to prevent a skin from forming. Set custard aside at room temperature to cool. (Can cover and refrigerate as long as 48 hours.)

FREEZING: Pour custard into an ice cream maker and freeze according to manufacturers instructions.

Betsy Schultz
Food consultant
New York, NY

GIANDUIA GELATO

Makes about 1¹/₂ quarts

The combination of ground hazelnuts and chocolate is known as *gianduia* (pronounced john-doo-ya). The flavor is extremely popular in Italy, and here the flavor of the ground nuts is reinforced by liqueur.

1 cup hazelnuts (about 6¹/₄ ounces)
4 ounce semisweet chocolate
6 egg yolks
1¹/₃ cups heavy cream
¹/₈ teaspoon salt
2²/₃ cups half-and-half
³/₄ cup sugar
3 tablespoons hazelnut liqueur

PREPARATION AND COOKING: Heat the oven to 350°F. Spread the hazelnuts in a cake pan and toast, stirring once or twice, until browned, about 10 minutes. While still warm, rub off the skins with a clean towel. Cool, and then finely grind nuts in a food processor or grinder; set aside. Chop the chocolate into ¹/₂-inch pieces. In a heatproof mixing bowl, whisk the egg yolks with the cream and salt. Put the half-and-half and sugar in a medium nonreactive saucepan. Bring liquid to a simmer, add the chocolate, cover, and set aside 5 minutes, or until the chocolate is melted when the mixture is stirred.

Slowly whisk the hot chocolate half-and-half into the egg yolk mixture. Then return the partially cooked custard to the saucepan. Stir constantly over medium heat until mixture begins to thicken slightly and coats the back of a spoon, about 5 minutes. Strain custard through a fine sieve into a bowl. In a small saucepan, reduce hazelnut liqueur to 1 teaspoon over low heat. Stir the reduced liqueur and the ground hazelnuts into the custard. Put a sheet of plastic wrap directly on the surface of the custard to prevent a skin from forming. Set custard aside at room temperature to cool.

FREEZING: Pour custard mixture into an ice cream maker and freeze according to manufacturer's instructions.

Betsy Schultz
Food consultant
New York, NY

GRAPPA-RAISIN GELATO

Makes about 1¹/₂ quarts

Grappa-soaked raisins are easy to prepare and store in a covered jar. Their flavor improves with age. Grappa (a colorless spirit that is a first cousin to brandy) can be purchased in liquor stores. Good-quality brandy is a substitute for grappa, but it may darken the color of the gelato.

**1 cup white sultana raisins *or*
  dark raisins**
**1¹/₂ cups grappa, marc, *or*
  brandy**
6 egg yolks
1¹/₃ cups heavy cream
¹/₈ teaspoon salt
2²/₃ cups half-and-half
³/₄ cup sugar
1 teaspoon vanilla extract

PREPARATION: Soak the raisins in ¹/₂ cup of the grappa for several hours until raisins are soft and plump and most of the liquid is absorbed.

COOKING: Whisk the egg yolks with the cream and salt in a heatproof mixing bowl. Put the half-and-half and sugar in a medium nonreactive saucepan. Bring liquid to a simmer, stirring to dissolve the sugar; do not boil. Remove pan from heat. Slowly whisk the hot half-and-half into the egg yolk mixture. Then return the partially cooked custard to the saucepan. Stir constantly over medium-low heat until mixture begins to thicken slightly and coats the back of a spoon, about 5 minutes. Add the vanilla and strain custard through a fine sieve into a bowl. In a small saucepan, reduce the remaining 1 cup of grappa to 2 tablespoons over low heat. Add the reduced grappa to the custard. Put sheet of plastic wrap directly on the surface of the custard to prevent a skin from forming and set custard aside to cool. (Can cover and refrigerate as long as 48 hours.)

FREEZING: Transfer the custard to an ice cream maker and freeze according to the manufacturer's instructions until custard is two-thirds frozen. Add the soaked raisins and any remaining grappa, and finish freezing.

Betsy Schultz
Food consultant
New York, NY

NOCCIOLA

Makes about 1 quart

Nocciola means hazelnut in Italian and this delicious hazelnut gelato is made by stirring a slightly sweet hazelnut praline paste into the ice cream custard. The praline paste is available in gourmet food stores.

6 egg yolks
1¹/₃ cups heavy cream
¹/₈ teaspoon salt
2²/₃ cups half-and-half
¹/₂ cup sugar
2 tablespoons plus 2 teaspoons
  hazelnut praline paste
6 tablespoons hazelnut liqueur

PREPARATION AND COOKING: Whisk the egg yolks with the cream and salt in a heatproof mixing bowl. Put the half-and-half and sugar in a medium nonreactive saucepan. Bring liquid to a simmer, stirring to dissolve the sugar. Remove pan from heat. Slowly whisk the hot half-and-half into the egg yolk mixture. Then return the partially cooked custard to the saucepan. Stir constantly over medium-low heat until mixture begins to thicken slightly and coats the back of a spoon, about 5 minutes. Stir the praline paste into the custard. Strain custard into a bowl through a fine sieve lined with a double thickness of cheesecloth. In a small saucepan, reduce the hazelnut liqueur over low heat to 2 teaspoons. Stir the reduced hazelnut liqueur into the custard. Put a sheet of plastic wrap directly on the surface of the custard to prevent a skin from forming and set custard aside at room temperature to cool. (Can cover and refrigerate as long a 48 hours.)

FREEZING: Transfer the custard mixture to an ice cream freezer and freeze according to the manufacturer's instructions.

Betsy Schultz
Food consultant
New York, NY

GLACE AUX PRUNEAUX
PRUNE ICE CREAM WITH MARC

Makes 8 servings

Cognac or other brandy can be substituted if marc is not available. Serve any leftover marc as an after-dinner drink. A simple, rich cookie is the perfect accompaniment.

1/2 **pound pitted prunes (1**1/4 **cups)**
1 3/4 **cups marc *or* other brandy**
3 **cups milk**
1 **cup heavy cream**
1 **vanilla bean**
8 **egg yolks**
1 **cup sugar**

PREPARATION: Cut the prunes in half and put in a saucepan. Add the marc and put over low heat until marc is just warm. Cover and let macerate in a warm place for at least 2 hours or up to several weeks.

Combine the milk and cream in another saucepan. Split the vanilla bean in half lengthwise with a sharp knife and scrape the seeds into the saucepan. Add the pod and bring to a simmer over medium heat. Remove from heat, cover, and let steep for 10 minutes.

Whisk together the egg yolks and sugar until thick and pale yellow, about 4 minutes. Slowly whisk the warm cream mixture into the yolks. Return the mixture to the saucepan and cook over very low heat, stirring constantly with a wooden spoon, until the custard thickens enough to coat the back of the spoon lightly, about 10 minutes (160°F). Be careful not to boil, or the custard will curdle. Strain and cool completely.

Strain prunes, reserving the marc, and puree in a food processor. Stir the prune puree into the milk mixture and chill.

Transfer to an ice-cream maker and freeze according to the manufacturer's instructions.

Ice cream can be made several days ahead.

SERVING: Soften ice cream in the refrigerator for about 30 minutes if hard.

Anne Willan
Founder
La Varenne Ecole de Cuisine
Paris, France

ZABAGLIONE

Makes 4 servings

Crunchy Italian macaroons are a perfect foil for this frothy dessert but it is also delicious over fruit or plain cake. It is very important that it be cooked on the lowest possible heat so that the eggs don't overcook and curdle. It's simple with a double boiler or a bowl set over a pan of water. Be sure the bottom of the bowl doesn't touch the water and keep the water temperature well below the boiling point.

4 egg yolks
3 tablespoons sugar
$^1/_2$ lemon
$^1/_3$ cup Marsala

COOKING: In a saucepan, bring 1 inch of water to a simmer over low heat.

In a bowl, beat egg yolks with the sugar until they are pale yellow and a ribbon forms when they are trailed from beater. Grate about a teaspoon of lemon zest into the Zabaglione and then stir in $^1/_3$ cup Marsala.

Put the egg mixture over the pan of simmering water, being careful that the water doesn't touch the bottom of the bowl. Beat the mixture to soft peaks, about 5 minutes.

SERVING: Serve immediately in wine glasses or small bowls.

Stephanie Lyness
Free-lance writer
New York, NY

Sauces and Sundries

APRICOT SAUCE

Makes 3/4 cup

1 orange
3/4 cup apricot preserves
1/2 cup apple juice

PREPARATION AND COOKING: Grate 1 teaspoon of orange zest into a medium saucepan. Stir in the preserves and apple juice and bring to a boil. Reduce heat and simmer until slightly thickened, about 10 minutes. Serve warm.

Bert Greene
Cookbook author
New York, NY

BLACK-OLIVE PESTO

Makes 2 cups

A flavorful, inky pesto, made of minced olives and seasoned with garlic and shallots, is brightened with skinny snippets of lemon zest and chives.

1 can large, pitted black olives
   (9 ounces)
1 fresh, hot red chile (2 inches
   long)
2 small garlic cloves
2 small shallots
2 tablespoons minced parsley
   leaves
$3/4$ teaspoon minced thyme
   leaves
$3/4$ teaspoon red-wine vinegar
Salt
$1/2$ cup extra-virgin olive oil
1 lemon
1 small bunch fresh chives

PREPARATION: Rinse, drain, and pat the olives dry. Put them into the workbowl of a food processor fitted with the metal blade and process until chopped. Stem, seed, and mince the chile. Peel and mince the garlic and shallots and add them to the processor along with the chile, parsley, thyme, vinegar, and $1/4$ teaspoon salt. Pulse in the oil and adjust seasoning to taste. (Can cover and refrigerate sauce overnight.)

SERVING: If refrigerated, bring sauce to room temperature. Remove and cut lemon zest into fine julienne strips (or use a lemon zester). Snip chives into 1-inch lengths. Serve 3 to 4 tablespoons of sauce on each portion. Garnish with lemon and chives.

Jane Freiman
Food columnist and cookbook author
New York, NY

BUTTERSCOTCH SAUCE

Makes 1 cup

This can be a delicious substitute for caramel sauce in many desserts. Be sure to add the tablespoon of hot water very carefully to the hot caramel to avoid splattering.

1/2 sugar
2 teaspoons light corn syrup
3/4 cup heavy cream
1 tablespoon butter
1/2 teaspoon vanilla

COOKING: Put the sugar and corn syrup in a small, heavy-bottomed saucepan with 1/4 cup cold water. Simmer until caramelized and amber-colored, about 10 minutes. Remove saucepan from heat and carefully stir in 1 tablespoon hot water. Stir in cream, return pan to low heat, and stir until smooth. Bring to a boil, then reduce heat and simmer until sauce thickens, about 4 minutes. Remove from heat and stir in butter and vanilla. (Can cover and refrigerate up to 2 weeks. Warm over low heat before serving.)

Betsy Schultz
Food consultant
New York, NY

COCONUT MILK
LECHE DE COCO

Makes about 2¹/₂ cups

1 small ripe coconut (about 1¹/₄ pounds)
2¹/₂ cups hot water

PREPARATION: Adjust oven rack to lowest position and heat oven to 375°F. Bake the coconut 20 to 25 minutes to loosen the meat from the shell. Transfer the coconut to the sink and use a hammer to crack it open in several places. (The liquid that drains out is the coconut water, not used in this recipe.) Use a dull-tipped knife to pry the coconut meat from inside the shell. Cut the coconut meat into 1-inch strips (2 cups) and put it into a food processor fitted with the metal blade. Add the hot water and process for about 1 minute to release the coconut milk.

Strain the coconut milk through a fine sieve into a bowl, pressing the coconut shreds against the sieve to release the remaining milk. Set coconut milk aside until sediment settles, about 10 minutes. Carefully pour off the milk and discard the sediment at the bottom. (Can cover and refrigerate for 3 days, or freeze up to 3 months.)

Copeland Marks
Cookbook author
Brooklyn, NY

CURRY POWDER

Makes ⅓ cup

Curry powder, or *kari podi*, is a southern Indian *masala* originally made with kari leaf and other spices. The imperial British called this *masala* curry powder and used it as a standard ingredient.

3 tablespoons ground coriander seeds
1 tablespoon turmeric
1½ teaspoons cayenne pepper
½ teaspoon ground yellow mustard
½ teaspoon ground cumin
½ teaspoon ground fenugreek

PREPARATION: Mix the spices in a small bowl. Transfer to an airtight container (Can store up to 3 months.)

GARAM MASALA

Makes ¼ cup

In India, spice mixtures are known collectively as *masala* (ma SA la — which translates roughly as spice blend). Spices may be dry or pasty, and many blends contain fresh herbs, garlic, and ginger. Dry *masala* are often made in advance, and these mixtures are frequently pan-roasted or sautéed. The most widely used blend is *Moghul garam masala*, a combination of cardamom, cinnamon, cloves, and black pepper. The addition of coriander and cumin makes a more potent mixture that is popular in northern India.

1 tablespoon whole cumin seeds
1 tablespoon whole coriander seeds
1 tablespoon whole cardamom seeds
½ cinnamon stick
1½ tablespoons black peppercorns
½ teaspoon whole cloves

PREPARATION AND COOKING: Put the spices in a non-stick skillet and toast until fragrant and lightly colored, about 3 minutes. Cool and grind in a coffee grinder or with a mortar and pestle. Transfer to a jar with an airtight lid. (Can store up to 3 months.)

Julie Sahni
Cookbook author
New York, NY

LEMON VINAIGRETTE

Makes 1¹/₂ cups

This versatile dressing imparts a tangy flavor to sandwiches as well as salads.

1 medium lemon
¹/₄ cup balsamic *or* red wine
    vinegar
1 teaspoon Dijon mustard
Salt and ground black pepper
1 cup olive oil

PREPARATION: Squeeze ¹/₄ cup lemon juice into a small mixing bowl. Whisk in vinegar, mustard, ¹/₂ teaspoon salt, and ³/₄ teaspoon pepper. Slowly whisk in the olive oil. (Can cover and refrigerate for 1 week.)

Brooke Dojny and Melanie Barnard
Nationally syndicated food writers and cookbook authors
Fairfield County, CT

LEXINGTON BARBECUE DIP

Makes 1³/₄ cups

This spicy sauce, sharpened with vinegar, is a traditional accompaniment to pork barbecue.

³/₄ **cup distilled white *or* cider vinegar**
³/₄ **cup ketchup**
³/₄ **teaspoon dried red pepper flakes**
1 **teaspoon sugar**
Salt and ground black pepper

PREPARATION AND COOKING: Combine all ingredients except the salt and pepper in a small saucepan. Add ¹/₄ cup water and bring to a simmer. Remove from heat, season to taste with salt and pepper and cool. (Can refrigerate up to 3 days.)

Craig Claiborne
Food critic and cookbook author
East Hampton, NY

QUICK TOMATO SAUCE

Makes 3 cups

This basic tomato sauce can be made ahead and used for a variety of dishes, such as the Spicy Tomato-Sausage Sauce (recipe page 92).

1 onion
1 large clove garlic
2 28-ounce cans Italian plum
    tomatoes
2 tablespoons oil
Salt and pepper

PREPARATION: Chop the onion. Mince the garlic. Drain and seed the tomatoes, reserving the tomato juice for other uses.

COOKING: Heat the oil in a large, nonreactive frying pan. Sauté the onion until soft, about 3 minutes. Add the garlic and cook 1 minute. Add the tomatoes and cook, uncovered, over medium-high heat, breaking tomatoes into chunks with the side of a spoon, until almost all liquid has evaporated, about 10 minutes. Season to taste with salt and pepper.

Quick Tomato Sauce can be made 3 days ahead.

Elizabeth Riely
Free-lance writer
Newton Centre, MA
Brooke Dojny
Free-lance writer
Westport, CT

CANDIED LEMON ZEST

Makes 8 diamonds or enough strips to garnish 1 Lemon Mousse Cheesecake

Desserts may be attractively garnished with Candied Lemon Zest that is easily cut into thin julienne strips, decorative diamonds, or any number of fanciful shapes.

1 large lemon
1¹/₂ cups sugar
¹/₃ cup light corn syrup

PREPARATION AND COOKING: Carefully remove zest from the lemon in 1-inch wide strips and cut into 1- by ¹/₄-inch julienne strips. *Or,* cut out eight ¹/₂-inch diamond shapes. Put zest in a small nonreactive saucepan with water to cover and boil for 5 minutes. Drain and rinse with cold water. Bring 1 cup of the sugar, the corn syrup, and ¹/₃ cup water to boil in the saucepan. Remove from heat, stir in zest, and let stand 30 minutes. Bring liquid back to a boil and let stand 30 minutes. Using a fork, remove diamonds (or strips) from the syrup and transfer to a wire rack set over a pan to catch the drippings; cool. Discard syrup.

Put remaining sugar onto each piece. *Or,* roll strips in sugar to coat the surface. (Can store at room temperature up to 1 week.)

Marlene Sorosky
Cookbook author
Towson, MD

CHEESE AND EGGS WITH JALAPENOS

Makes 8 servings

This is a recipe that has been in James Villas' family for at least four generations and it takes, as he says, "patience, patience, patience." Make sure the milk, butter, and bread are mashed until they are absolutely smooth, and that the cheese and egg mixture is stirred constantly and cooked very slowly.

8 slices white bread
2 pounds extra-sharp cheddar
   cheese
1 medium jalapeño pepper
10 eggs
1/4 pound butter
2 cups milk
Salt and ground black pepper

PREPARATION: Trim and cut bread into 1-inch cubes. Grate the cheese. Stem, seed, and mince the jalapeño pepper. Whisk eggs lightly in a medium bowl.

COOKING: Heat butter in a large heavy skillet. Add bread and milk and simmer, mashing constantly with a fork, until mixture is smooth and velvety, 3 to 5 minutes. Reduce heat to very low. Gradually add cheese and peppers and continue mashing until cheese has melted and the mixture is very smooth. Gradually stir in eggs and cook until set but not lumpy, about 10 minutes. Mixture will be creamy. Stir in 1/2 teaspoon salt and 1/2 teaspoon pepper and serve immediately.

James Villas
Cookbook author and food editor
Town & Country
New York, NY

LIME MARMALADE

Makes four 1-pint jars

The final marmalade mixture should be sufficiently cooked after 15 minutes; taste for sugar by placing a bit of marmalade on a cold plate at 12 or 13 minutes and add a tablespoon or two if the mixture is too tart. A cold plate is also useful for checking consistency if a candy thermometer is not available.

8 limes (1^1/$_2$ pounds)
6 cups sugar

PREPARATION: Rinse the limes and remove zest with a sharp paring knife or a vegetable peeler. Cut the zest into ^{1}/$_8$-inch strips. Remove and discard the white pith. Coarsely chop the limes.

COOKING: Put the zest and 1 quart of water in a large, nonreactive saucepan. Bring to a boil, cover, and simmer for 2 hours. Put the chopped lime and 1 quart of water in another large, nonreactive saucepan. Bring to a boil, cover, and simmer for 1^1/$_2$ hours. Strain the liquid from the simmered lime pulp through cheesecloth into the pan with the zest, discarding the lime pulp. Add the sugar to the pan and stir until it has dissolved. Bring the lime mixture to a boil over high heat and continue boiling until a candy thermometer registers 220°F, or until mixture gels when cooled. Stir to distribute the rind evenly and then pour the hot marmalade into hot, sterilized jars; seal the jars according to manufacturer's instructions. (Can store in a cool area up to 1 year.)

James Villas
Cookbook author and food editor
Town & Country
New York, NY

MERINGUE MUSHROOMS

Makes 30 small mushrooms

If the finished mushrooms become humid and soggy, crisp them for 30 minutes in a 200°F oven.

2 large egg whites
$^1/_8$ teaspoon salt
$^1/_8$ teaspoon cream of tartar
8 tablespoons sugar
1 teaspoon corn syrup
$^1/_2$ teaspoon vanilla extract

PREPARATION: Line a jelly-roll pan with parchment paper. Put egg whites, salt, and cream of tartar in a heatproof bowl; beat with an electric mixer until soft peaks form, about 45 seconds.

COOKING: Adjust oven racks to middle and low positions and heat oven to 200°F. Put 6 tablespoons of sugar, the corn syrup, and $^1/_4$ cup water in a heavy-bottomed saucepan; boil over medium heat, stirring to dissolve sugar. Wash down sugar crystals from side with a clean, damp pastry brush. Cook to soft ball stage (240°F), about 5 minutes. While syrup cooks, beat remaining sugar with egg white mixture until firm, about 45 seconds. With mixer at medium speed, immediately add hot syrup to meringue, pouring very slowly down the side of the bowl. Add vanilla and continue beating until meringue is cool and stiff, about 7 minutes. Fit a pastry bag with a $^1/_4$-inch pastry tip and fill with meringue. Secure the paper to the jelly-roll pan with a dot of meringue at the corners. Holding the bag about $^1/_4$ inch from paper, pipe 30 rounds (from $^3/_4$ to $^1/_4$ inch) to form mushroom caps. To shape stems, hold the pastry bag close to the paper and, forcing the meringue through the tip, pull the pastry bag up to form thirty 1-inch tall pointed stems. Cover and refrigerate remaining meringue. Bake meringues for $1^1/_2$ hours, then turn oven off and let rest in warm oven until they become dry and very crisp, about 30 minutes longer. Cool on the jelly-roll pan.

ASSEMBLY: Heat oven to 200°F. Make an indentation in the underside of each cap with a knife. Dot reserved meringue into each hole and press each cap onto the point of a stem. Return to oven and bake 1 hour. Turn off oven and let mushrooms rest 30 minutes in warm oven. Cool. (Can store in airtight container up to 1 week.)

Peter Kump
President
Peter Kump's New York Cooking School
    and James Beard Foundation
New York, NY

POACHED EGGS AND CORNMEAL-CRUSTED TOMATOES WITH HAM AND THYME

Makes 4 servings

At a glance, this versatile breakfast or brunch entreé appears to be one more variation of Eggs Benedict. But with its country ham and fried tomatoes, this dish claims down-home Southern roots.

4 ounces fully cooked country *or* smoked ham
2 large tomatoes
1/2 cup yellow cornmeal
Ground black pepper
4 English muffins
1 1/2 cups whipping cream
1 tablespoon minced fresh thyme
1 medium lemon
4 tablespoons butter
Salt
8 eggs

PREPARATION: Trim excess fat from ham and cut meat into 1/4-inch dice (3/4 cup). Cut the tomatoes into eight 1/2-inch thick slices. (Can wrap and refrigerate ham and tomatoes separately for up to 2 hours.) Mix cornmeal with 1/2 teaspoon pepper. Split and put muffins on a baking sheet.

COOKING: Put ham, cream, and thyme in a small saucepan. Bring to a boil and simmer gently, stirring occasionally, until cream reduces to 1 cup, about 20 minutes. Remove sauce from heat, add 1/2 teaspoon pepper, and squeeze in 2 tablespoons lemon juice; cover and set aside.

Adjust oven rack to high position and heat broiler. Melt the butter in a large skillet. Dredge the tomato slices in cornmeal and fry over medium-high heat until lightly browned on both sides, 6 to 8 minutes; drain on paper towels and keep warm. Toast muffins under the broiler until golden brown, about 2 minutes. Bring 2 inches of water and 1 teaspoon of salt to a simmer in a deep skillet. Carefully break the eggs into the water and poach until set, about 1 1/2 minutes. Remove eggs and completely drain on paper towels.

SERVING: Put 2 muffin halves on each warm plate. Top each half with a tomato slice and an egg. Spoon over eggs and serve immediately.

Michael McLaughlin
Free-lance writer
Brooklyn, NY

ROSEMARY-MARINATED TOMATOES

Makes 5 cups

Since this marinade improves with age, it can be refrigerated one week to use with pasta or in other recipes.

**2 cans peeled plum tomatoes
(one 35-ounce can and one
16-ounce can)**
4 scallions
3 medium garlic cloves
**1 tablespoon minced fresh
rosemary leaves *or* 1
teaspoon dried rosemary**
3 tablespoons red-wine vinegar
$1/2$ cup olive oil
**$1/4$ teaspoon dried red-pepper
flakes**
Salt and ground black pepper

PREPARATION: Drain tomatoes and reserve (or discard) juice. Halve and seed the tomatoes. Slice the scallions ($1/2$ cup) and mince the garlic. In a large bowl, mix tomatoes, scallions, garlic, rosemary, vinegar, oil, red-pepper flakes, 1 teaspoon salt, and $1/4$ teaspoon black pepper. (Can cover and refrigerate marinade up to one week.)

Pam Parseghian
Free-lance writer
New York, NY

DRINKS

BELLINI

Makes 1 drink

The Bellini was a favorite drink of Ernest Hemingway, who made it his daily eye-opener while in Venice. It has caught on in the United States, too, especially at Manhattan's Bellini by Cipriani restaurant, which imports frozen white Italian peach puree.

^{1}/$_2$ **small white peach**
3 ounces chilled dry sparkling
   wine such as Prosecco or
   brut Champagne, well chilled
   (about ^{1}/$_3$ cup)
Grenadine (optional)

PREPARATION AND SERVING: Puree and force the peach through a fine strainer. Put the peach puree in a Champagne flute. Add the Champagne and a dash of grenadine, if desired. Stir once or twice. Serve immediately.

Barbara Ensrud
COOK'S wine writer and book author
New York, NY

BLOODY BULLS

Makes 1 drink

"It's nice to have a pristine liquid like consommé in this drink; stock has too much sediment. Canned consommé is an acceptable substitute," says James Villas. Homemade consommé, of course, makes a better drink.

2 medium limes
2 celery stalks
2 cups tomato juice
2 cups beef consommé *or* canned
   beef consommé
2 cups vodka
2 teaspoons Worcestershire
   sauce
2 teaspoons hot red-pepper
   sauce
Salt and ground black pepper
Ice

PREPARATION: Quarter the limes. Rinse and quarter the celery stalks. In a large pitcher, mix the tomato juice, consommé, vodka, Worcestershire sauce, hot red-pepper sauce, $3/4$ teaspoon salt, and $1/2$ teaspoon pepper. Serve over ice in Old-Fashioned glasses, with a lime quarter squeezed and dropped into each drink. Garnish each drink with a celery stick.

James Villas
Cookbook author and food editor
Town & Country
New York, NY

BRONX COCKTAIL

Makes 1 drink

Not to be outdone by Manhattan, the Bronx had its own cocktail — a mix of gin, sweet and dry vermouth, and orange juice — created in 1906 by bartender Johnny Solon at the old Waldorf Astoria Hotel. As one chronicler wrote of that night, "Until this historic moment, no more than a dozen oranges were used at the bar. With the advent of the Bronx Cocktail, a case had to be delivered every morning."

1 small orange
$^1/_4$ ounce sweet vermouth (1$^1/_2$ teaspoons)
$^1/_4$ ounce dry vermouth (1$^1/_2$ teaspoons)
2 ounces gin ($^1/_4$ cup)
Crushed ice

PREPARATION AND SERVING: Remove a $^1/_4$- by 2-inch strip of orange zest for garnish. Squeeze 1$^1/_2$ teaspoons of orange juice into a shaker. Add vermouths, gin, and crushed ice. Shake well, then strain into a Martini glass. Garnish with orange twist and serve immediately.

John Mariani
Free-lance writer and book author
Tuckahoe, NY

CHAMPAGNE COCKTAIL

Makes 1 drink

The exhilarating nature of this drink comes from the tense counterpoint of the crisp, taut wine and sugar-laced bitters. The combination is brilliant.

1 lemon
1 sugar cube
$1/2$ teaspoon bitters
4 ounces brut Champagne, well chilled ($1/2$ cup)
1 ice cube (optional)

PREPARATION AND SERVING: Remove a 1- by $1/2$-inch strip of zest from the lemon. In a small bowl, infuse the sugar cube with the bitters and transfer the sugar to a Champagne flute. Add the Champagne. Twist the lemon strip over the glass to release the oils, then toss it in as a garnish. Add an ice cube, if desired.

Barbara Ensrud
COOK'S wine writer and book author
New York, NY

CHAMPAGNE TROPICALE

Makes 1 drink

This exotic combination of mango puree, mango liqueur, and Champagne was invented in the Rainbow Room, in New York City.

1 fresh mango, peeled
3 ounces brut Champagne, well
    chilled (about ¹/₃ cup)
Mango liqueur

PREPARATION AND SERVING: Puree and press ¹/₄ cup mango through a fine strainer. Put the mango puree in a Champagne flute, then add the Champagne and a dash of liqueur. Stir once or twice and serve.

Barbara Ensrud
COOK'S wine writer and book author
New York, NY

CHARTREUSE CHAMPAGNE

Makes 1 drink

Chartreuse, the liqueur concocted by the Carthusian Fathers of Grenoble, is said to contain 130 herbs and spices, but its formula remains a closely guarded secret. This drink is made with green Chartreuse, a bit stronger and less sweet than its yellow counterpart.

1 lemon
¹/₂ teaspoon green Chartreuse
¹/₂ teaspoon Cognac
4 ounces brut Champagne or other sparkling wine, well chilled (¹/₂ cup)

PREPARATION AND SERVING: Chill a Champagne flute. Remove a 1- by 1¹/₂-inch strip of zest from the lemon. Measure the Chartreuse and Cognac into the chilled glass. Add the Champagne of sparkling wine, and stir once or twice.

Twist the lemon strip over the glass to release the oils, and toss it in as a garnish. Serve immediately.

Barbara Ensrud
COOK'S wine writer and book author
New York, NY

FRENCH 75

Makes 1 drink

World War I gave us at least one famous cocktail — the French 75. Some say that this drink was the bright idea of Harry MacElhone's, but others claim it was made for Count Leon Bertrand Arnaud Casenave, owner of Arnaud's restaurant in New Orleans. The French 75, made from orange liqueur, lemon juice, and Champagne, was named after a World War I French howitzer with a 75 millimeter muzzle whose kaboom was comparable to that derived from the cocktail.

1 small lemon
1 teaspoon sugar
1 ounce gin
$^1\!/_2$ ounce orange liqueur
Crushed ice
2 ounces Champagne ($^1\!/_4$ cup)

PREPARATION AND SERVING: Remove a $^1\!/_4$- by 2-inch strip of lemon zest for garnish. Squeeze 1 tablespoon lemon juice into a 6-ounce stemmed cocktail glass. Add the sugar, gin, and orange liqueur; stir until sugar dissolves. Add crushed ice and Champagne. Garnish with lemon twist and serve immediately.

John Mariani
Free-lance writer and book author
Tuckahoe, NY

GIBSON

Makes 1 drink

Bartenders, like chefs, have often named their creations after famous people. The Gibson (a Martini garnished with a small white onion) was supposedly created when American illustrator Charles Dana Gibson, whose wife inspired the Gibson Girl, ordered his usual Martini at the bar of the Players (the famous club whose founding members included Edwin Booth and Mark Twain). Bartender Charlie Connolly reached for the olives, found the cupboard bare, and substituted a cocktail onion. Gibson loved the drink, which immediately became fashionable, and was dubbed the Gibson.

2 ounces gin (¹/₄ cup)
¹/₂ teaspoon dry vermouth
Ice
1 white cocktail onion

PREPARATION AND SERVING: Mix the gin, vermouth, and ice in a shaker. Strain into a Martini glass, garnish with a cocktail onion, and serve immediately.

John Mariani
Free-lance writer and book author
Tuckahoe, NY

KIR ROYALE

Makes 1 drink

"New Yorkers like Champagne by the glass, or Kir Royale," says Henry Mielke of The Four Seasons restaurant. The thick, dark red *crème de cassis* (black currant liqueur) mixes charmingly with dry, biting Champagne or sparkling wine. To make a Kir Imperiale, substitute raspberry liqueur for *cassis*. (Do not confuse raspberry liqueur with *framboise*, the raspberry *eau-de-vie*, a colorless brandy.)

¹/₂ teaspoon *crème de cassis*
4 ounces Champagne or
sparkling wine, well chilled
(¹/₂ cup)

PREPARATION AND SERVING: Measure *crème de cassis* into a Champagne flute. Add Champagne and serve immediately.

Barbara Ensrud
COOK'S wine writer and book author
New York, NY

LONG ISLAND ICED TEA

Makes 1 drink

As with the Mai Tai, Long Island Iced Tea was created by a bartender killing time. In this case, the mixologist was one Robert "Rosebud" Butt of the Oak Beach Inn in Hampton Bays, Long Island, back in 1967. "I was fooling around with some drinks," he recalls. "I'm a tequila drinker, so I put together one shot each of tequila, light rum, vodka, and gin, a dash of Triple Sec, and a splash of sour mix, and topped it off with Coca-Cola and a slice of lemon, served on the rocks in a Collins glass, and the thing just tasted like iced tea. I started serving it to the public about a year later."

$1/2$ ounce **Triple Sec**
   (1 tablespoon)
1 ounce light rum
   (2 tablespoons)
1 ounce gin (2 tablespoons)
1 ounce vodka (2 tablespoons)
1 ounce tequila (2 tablespoons)
$1/2$ **ounce liquid sour mix**
   (1 tablespoon)
Ice cubes
2 ounces cola ($1/4$ cup)
Sprig of fresh mint *or* slice of
   lemon

PREPARATION AND SERVING: Stir the Triple Sec, rum, gin, vodka, and tequila in a 12-ounce tumbler. Stir in the sour mix. Add ice cubes and cola. Garnish with mint or lemon, and serve immediately.

John Mariani
Free-lance writer and book author
Tuckahoe, NY

MAI TAI

Makes 1 drink

As Trader Vic Bergeron told the story, he was fiddling at the bar and came up with a synthesis of dark and light rums, Curaçao, sugar syrup, and orgeat (an almond-flavored sugar syrup available in Italian grocery stores). He then asked Ham and Carrie Guild — friends who were just in from Tahiti — to give it a try. "Carrie took one sip," recalled Bergeron, "and said 'Mai Tai — Roa Ae.' In Tahitian this means 'Out of this world — the best.' Well, that was that. I named the drink Mai Tai [and] anybody who says I didn't create this drink is a dirty stinker."

1 small pineapple
1 small lime
2¹/₂ ounces light rum
 (5 tablespoons)
¹/₂ ounce orange Curaçao
 (1 tablespoon)
¹/₂ teaspoon superfine sugar
¹/₂ ounce grenadine syrup
 (1 tablespoon)
¹/₂ ounce orgeat (1 tablespoon)
Crushed ice and ice cubes

PREPARATION AND SERVING: Cut a pineapple round in quarters for garnish. Squeeze 1 tablespoon lime juice into a shaker. Add the rum, orange Curaçao, sugar, grenadine, orgeat, and crushed ice. Shake well and strain into an Old-Fashioned glass over ice. Garnish with 1 fresh pineapple quarter and serve immediately.

John Mariani
Free-lance writer and book author
Tuckahoe, NY

MOSCOW MULE

Makes 1 drink

After World War II, a whole flood of new spirits hit the market, including vodka, which was a very tough sell at first for distributors Jack Martin and Rudy Kunett. One day in 1947, they tried to make a sale to Jack Morgan, owner of the Cock 'n Bull restaurant in Los Angeles. Martin also had been trying to sell off an oversupply of ginger beer, so the three of them came up with a drink called the Moscow Mule. The drink became a hit, and sales of vodka took off.

$^1/_2$ **small lime**
Ice cubes
2 ounces vodka ($^1/_4$ cup)
4 ounces ginger beer ($^1/_2$ cup)

PREPARATION AND SERVING: Squeeze lime juice into an 8-ounce copper mug. Add ice cubes, vodka, and ginger beer and serve immediately.

John Mariani
Free-lance writer and book author
Tuckahoe, NY

RAMOS GIN FIZZ

Makes 1 drink

The Ramos Gin Fizz, a frothy concoction of gin, lemon juice, orange flour water, egg whites, and a little cream (sometimes a drop or two of vanilla is added) was the handiwork of Henry C. Ramos, owner of the Imperial Cabernet Saloon, on the corner of Carondelet and Gravier Streets, in New Orleans. The first drink was made in about 1888. Ramos later bought the Stag Bar where, during the 1915 Mardi Gras, 35 bartenders were kept busy shaking the fizzes while celebrants waited up to an hour for the drinks to be poured.

¹/₂ lemon
1 egg white
¹/₄ teaspoon orange flower water
2 ounces heavy cream (¹/₄ cup)
1 teaspoon sugar
2 ounces gin (¹/₄ cup)
Crushed ice
2 ounces carbonated water (¹/₄ cup)

PREPARATION AND SERVING: Remove a ¹/₄- by 2-inch strip of lemon zest for garnish. Squeeze 1 tablespoon lemon juice into a shaker. Add the egg white, orange flower water, cream, sugar, gin, and crushed ice. Shake the mixture until foamy and smooth, about 5 minutes. Or, mix in a blender set on high speed for 1¹/₂ minutes. Strain into an 8-ounce highball glass. Add carbonated water, garnish with a lemon twist, and serve immediately.

John Mariani
Free-lance writer and book author
Tuckahoe, NY

ROB ROY

Makes 1 drink

Soon after the creation of the Manhattan, a variation using Scotch instead of blended whiskey came along. It was called the Rob Roy, after the legendary hero in Sir Walter Scott's novel.

1 small lemon
2 ounces Scotch ($^1/_4$ cup)
$^3/_4$ **ounce sweet vermouth**
   ($1^1/_2$ tablespoons)
Ice

PREPARATION AND SERVING: Remove a $^1/_4$- by 2-inch strip of lemon zest for garnish. Mix the Scotch, vermouth, and ice in a shaker. Strain into a Martini glass and garnish with lemon twist.

John Mariani
Free-lance writer and book author
Tuckahoe, NY

SIDECAR

Makes 1 drink

The Sidecar, originated by Harry MacElhone, owner of Harry's New York Bar in Paris, was named after a customer who always arrived in such a vehicle outside 5 Rue Daunou ("Sank Roo Doe Noo," the most famous address in Paris for visiting Americans). This drink of brandy, orange liqueur, and lemon juice is again becoming popular, and is a capital way to end an evening.

1 small lemon
³/₄ ounce orange liqueur
  (1¹/₂ tablespoons)
³/₄ ounces brandy
  (3¹/₂ tablespoons)
Crushed ice

PREPARATION AND SERVING: Remove a ¹/₄- by 2-inch strip of lemon zest for garnish. Squeeze 1 tablespoon of lemon juice into a shaker. Add the orange liqueur, brandy, and cracked ice. Shake and strain into a Martini glass. Garnish with lemon twist and serve immediately.

John Mariani
Free-lance writer and book author
Tuckahoe, NY

INDEX